FOCUSING ON LANGUAGE

FOCUSING ON LANGUAGE
A Reader

Edited by

HAROLD B. ALLEN
Professor Emeritus
University of Minnesota

ENOLA BORGH
University of Wisconsin—Milwaukee

VERNA L. NEWSOME
Professor Emeritus
University of Wisconsin—Milwaukee

Thomas Y. Crowell Company
New York   Established 1834

Copyright © 1975 by
Thomas Y. Crowell Company, Inc.
All Rights Reserved

Except for use in a review, the reproduction or utilization of this work in any form or by any electronic, mechanical, or other means, now known or hereafter invented, including photocopying and recording, and in any information storage and retrieval system is forbidden without the written permission of the publisher. Published simultaneously in Canada by Fitzhenry & Whiteside, Ltd., Toronto.

Library of Congress Cataloging in Publication Data
Allen, Harold Byron, comp.
    Focusing on language.

    Includes bibliographical references.
    1. College readers. 2. English language.
I. Borgh, Enola, joint comp. II. Newsome, Verna Louise, joint comp. III. Title.
PE1122.A36   808'.04275   75-32462
ISBN 0-690-68052-X

Thomas Y. Crowell Company
666 Fifth Avenue
New York, New York 10019

Designed by Elliot Epstein
Manufactured in the United States of America

CONTENTS

Introduction   *Harold B. Allen*   ix

One: THE NATURE OF LANGUAGE

1. The Story of My Life   *Helen Keller*   3

2. The Nature of Language   *Wallace L. Chafe*   7

3. Linguistics   *William G. Moulton*   20

4. The Principles of Newspeak   *George Orwell*   32

Two: THE HISTORICAL BACKGROUND OF THE ENGLISH LANGUAGE

5. Development of the Language   *L. M. Myers*   45

6. Change in Language   *Harold R. Hungerford*   56

Three: THE ALPHABET AND ENGLISH SPELLING

7. The Invention of Writing   *Charles L. Barber*   71

8. Regularity in English Spelling   *Paul R. Hanna and Jean S. Hanna*   82

9. Obstacles to Spelling Reform   *William J. Stevens*   97

Four: GRAMMAR AND GRAMMARS

10. Grammar down the Ages   *Janet Rankin Aiken*   111

11. English Grammar and the Grammars of English
    Kenneth G. Wilson   119

12. The Structural Revolution   *Miriam Goldstein Sargon*   124

13. How Little Sentences Grow into Big Ones   *Kellogg W. Hunt*   136

Five: USAGE

14. Usage Is Something Else Again   *Harold B. Allen*   157

15. The Study of Nonstandard English   *William Labov*   174

16. The Dream World of English Grammar   *James C. Bostain*   185

17. Trials of a Word-watcher   *Charlton Ogburn, Jr.*   193

18. Now Everyone Is Hip about Slang   *Bergen Evans*   203

Six: REGIONAL DIALECTS

19. American Dialects   *Jean Malmstrom*   215

20. The English Language in the South   *Cleanth Brooks, Jr.*   227

Seven: WORDS AND DICTIONARIES

21. The Dictionary's Function   *Philip B. Gove*   239

22. Etymology and Meaning *Simeon Potter* 245

23. Sexism in English: A Feminist View *Alleen Pace Nilsen* 257

Eight: ENGLISH IN THE WORLD

24. English Spoken: Here, There, Everywhere *William Benton* 271

25. The Hooter's the Horn *Robert L. Coard* 278

INTRODUCTION
Harold B. Allen

Until about a quarter of a century ago most students and, indeed, the general public were rather effectively shut off from lively and accurate information about their own language—their linguistic heritage.

A principal barrier both in the classroom and in the public prints was the simplistic notion that the study of the English language was the study of its grammar. This barrier was made more formidable by the traditional restriction of "grammar" to the "do" and "don't" rules prescribing what was "correct English." One result was the exclusion of the rich new knowledge about language that appeared in the historical grammars of the late nineteenth and early twentieth centuries.

A second barrier was the attitude of those persons in colleges and universities who were concerned with the preparation of English teachers. This attitude limited the field of English to the study of literature, with some reluctant admission of a necessary concern with composition. A natural result was that teachers without language preparation in content and classroom practice felt uneasy in dealing with whatever language content did appear in available textbooks.

Happily, this situation is rapidly changing. Demands of special committees and organizations in recent years have steadily expanded English language offerings in institutions that prepare teachers and have insisted upon their inclusion in the preparation of English teachers. State and national conventions of English teachers and their professional publications have increasingly given time and space to the English language as content in the teaching of English. Each year more and more teachers are ready to introduce their students to wider and deeper knowledge of the significance of language in their lives. And for the general public, national publications have increasingly found space for articles reflecting interest in language attitudes, language variety, language learning, and the place of language in school and college English programs.

One danger has not quite disappeared. Sounder principles of English usage have widely replaced the rigid and often unrealistic rules of old-fashioned textbooks, but both in teacher preparation and in some textbook series there persists the notion that the study of language is essentially the study of grammar. True, contemporary linguists now provide a much more revealing and powerful grammar than the schools had available two decades ago. But there is much more to the study of language than can be derived from the involved and sometimes controversial linguistic theories that attempt to account for the underlying relationships of our language system and for their overt realization in speech and writing. If grammar, even transformational grammar, provides the only classroom concern with the English language, then this narrow range of content effectively deprives students of much of what is rightfully theirs to acquire and achieve in any comprehensive English program: the opportunity to become aware of the extraordinary social and regional variety in their language inheritance and of their own intricate role as language users in various communicative situations.

But even if students have access to a basic textbook with some language content, they are likely to find that content affected by sharp limitation of space as well as by the author's own interests. This present anthology is intended by the editors to offer more information than a single basic text and to provide that information from the points of view and varied backgrounds of many different persons—linguists, professional writers, and teachers. It thus can supplement a basic textbook, as well as be used independently by students and general readers without an accompanying text. For in itself this book offers a sound and comprehensive body of knowledge about our language, as it has been and as it is.

The editors strongly suggest reading the articles in this book in the given sequence. The articles have been carefully selected and ordered, with the accompanying *Questions for Study and Discussion* and *Suggested Activities* being both cumulative and interlocking.

Awareness of the rich variety and power of language can come from many sources. Probably nowhere can be found a more moving account of the arousal of this awareness than that of the late Helen Keller in the first selection in this anthology, a passage from her autobiography. Then, a different and more precise dimension is added in the description of language by two linguists, Wallace L. Chafe and William G. Moulton. Next, a terrifying misuse of the power of language is revealed in the grim explanation of George Orwell's Newspeak, a misuse held by some to be prophetic of some of the terms and expressions made public in the Watergate trials of 1974–75.

The second section of this book adds the fundamental concept of language change. Even the alphabet used in the overt appearance of language is seen in the third section to have undergone an amazing series of changes, although the likelihood of further change is reduced because of the retarding influence of printing. How the alphabet is related to problems of modern spelling is then taken up in turn by Paul R. and Jean S. Hanna and by William J. Stevens.

What people usually have identified as language study, the study of grammar, is looked at historically by four writers in part four of the anthology. The late Janet Rankin Aiken follows the long trail of grammatical thought and study since the ancient Greeks, and finally Kellogg W. Hunt offers an encapsulated discussion of recent transformational generative grammar.

During the 1930s American schools and colleges participated in what has sometimes been called "the battle of usage," the outcome of which was greater acceptance of a realistic view of how people actually speak and write their native tongue. Among the several articles in the section on usage, that by Charlton Ogburn, Jr., particularly reflects the tribulations of those who consider grammar to consist of concern for artificial correctness.

The consideration of usage is itself an indication of differences in how people use their language. These differences are often treated in terms of regional and social variation under the heading "dialects." Jean Malmstrom defines the major regional dialects of the United States, and Cleanth Brooks, Jr., attempts to trace the origin of one of them, the Southern Negro dialect.

Single words, regardless of where they occur, hold their own fascination—not only in their origin but also in their various related meanings. The late Philip B. Gove, editor of one of the most influential dictionaries in the world, explains the principles of lexicography. Simeon Potter explains why and how the meanings of words change. Alleen Pace Nilsen explains how these meanings often reflect cultural bias in her essay on sexism in English.

Finally, this anthology carries our interest to English outside the United States—to its place of origin. "The Hooter's the Horn" contrasts the British and American lexicons. William Benton explains why English is now a world language.

Although specific acknowledgment appears with each article, the editors wish to add here their deep appreciation to publishers and editors and especially to individual authors for permission to reprint these essays. The work of an anthologist is minor in comparison with that of the original writer. It is to each writer that a special debt is owed for the insight and competence and particular knowledge he has drawn upon in preparing the article here included.

Part One

THE NATURE OF LANGUAGE

1
THE STORY OF MY LIFE
Helen Keller

Helen Keller (1880–1968), blind and deaf from the age of eighteen months, could not learn the language of her culture as most children do, by hearing sounds structured in certain ways over and over again; to her language was a marvelous thing. In this widely known passage from her autobiography, she describes the kind of person she was until the age of seven, when Anne Sullivan (1866–1936) came to her parents' home to try to teach her in her soundless and sightless world. Miss Sullivan, whose own eyes were seriously weakened, had learned a manual alphabet which she hoped to use to break through the terrifying isolation of the handicapped child. She was dramatically successful. Helen Keller was graduated from Radcliffe College in 1904 and became internationally famous as an author and a lecturer.

This short, triumphant account describes some very important characteristics about the nature of language. First, language is a social phenomenon; no one person can make it, and no one can be truly human without it. Sharing a language is simply a necessary condition of human society. Second, language is an important instrument of thought, for it enables us to systematize experience. Notice how Miss Keller's responses to the experience of water changed once she was able to give the sensation a name. Psychologists would tell us that she was able to "conceptualize" the experience—in short, think about it.

The most important day I remember in all my life is the one on which my teacher, Anne Mansfield Sullivan, came to me. I am filled with wonder when I consider the immeasurable contrasts between the two lives which it connects. It was the third of March, 1887, three months before I was seven years old.

On the afternoon of that eventful day, I stood on the porch, dumb,

---

Source: *The Story of My Life* (New York: Doubleday, 1905), pp. 34–37. Copyright 1902, 1903, 1905 by Helen Keller. Reprinted by permission of the publisher.

expectant. I guessed vaguely from my mother's signs and from the hurrying to and fro in the house that something unusual was about to happen, so I went to the door and waited on the steps. The afternoon sun penetrated the mass of honeysuckle that covered the porch, and fell on my upturned face. My fingers lingered almost unconsciously on the familiar leaves and blossoms which had just come forth to greet the sweet southern spring. I did not know what the future held of marvel or surprise for me. Anger and bitterness had preyed upon me continually for weeks and a deep languor had succeeded this passionate struggle.

Have you ever been at sea in a dense fog, when it seemed as if a tangible white darkness shut you in, and the great ship, tense and anxious, groped her way toward the shore with plummet and sounding-line, and you waited with beating heart for something to happen? I was like that ship before my education began, only I was without compass or sounding-line, and had no way of knowing how near the harbour was. "Light! give me light!" was the wordless cry of my soul, and the light of love shone on me in that very hour.

I felt approaching footsteps. I stretched out my hand as I supposed to my mother. Some one took it, and I was caught up and held close in the arms of her who had come to reveal all things to me, and, more than all things else, to love me.

The morning after my teacher came she led me into her room and gave me a doll. The little blind children at the Perkins Institution had sent it and Laura Bridgman had dressed it; but I did not know this until afterward. When I had played with it a little while, Miss Sullivan slowly spelled into my hand the word "d-o-l-l." I was at once interested in this finger play and tried to imitate it. When I finally succeeded in making the letters correctly I was flushed with childish pleasure and pride. Running downstairs to my mother I held up my hand and made the letters for doll. I did not know that I was spelling a word or even that words existed; I was simply making my fingers go in monkey-like imitation. In the days that followed I learned to spell in this uncomprehending way a great many words, among them *pin*, *hat*, *cup* and a few verbs like *sit*, *stand* and *walk*. But my teacher had been with me several weeks before I understood that everything has a name.

One day, while I was playing with my new doll, Miss Sullivan put my big rag doll into my lap also, spelled "d-o-l-l" and tried to make me understand that "d-o-l-l" applied to both. Earlier in the day we had had a tussle over the words "m-u-g" and "w-a-t-e-r." Miss Sullivan had tried to impress it upon me that "m-u-g" is *mug* and that "w-a-t-e-r" is *water*, but I persisted in confounding the two. In despair she had dropped the subject for the time, only to renew it at the first opportunity. I became impatient at her repeated attempts and, seizing the new doll, I dashed it upon the floor. I was keenly delighted when I felt the fragments of the broken doll at my feet. Neither sorrow nor regret followed my passionate outburst. I had not loved the doll. In the still, dark world in which I lived there was no strong sentiment or tenderness. I felt my teacher sweep the fragments to one side of the hearth, and I had a sense of satisfaction that the cause of my discomfort was removed. She brought me my hat, and I knew I was going out into the warm sunshine. This thought, if a wordless sensation may be called a thought, made me hop and skip with pleasure.

We walked down the path to the well-house, attracted by the fragrance of the honeysuckle with which it was covered. Some one was drawing water and my teacher placed my hand under the spout. As the cool stream gushed over one hand she spelled into the other the word *water*, first slowly, then rapidly. I stood still, my whole attention fixed upon the motions of her fingers. Suddenly I felt a misty consciousness as of something forgotten—a thrill of returning thought; and somehow the mystery of language was revealed to me. I knew then that "w-a-t-e-r" meant the wonderful cool something that was flowing over my hand. That living word awakened my soul, gave it light, hope, joy, set it free! There were barriers still, it is true, but barriers that could in time be swept away.

I left the well-house eager to learn. Everything had a name, and each name gave birth to a new thought. As we returned to the house every object which I touched seemed to quiver with life. That was because I saw everything with the strange, new sight that had come to me. On entering the door I remembered the doll I had broken. I felt my way to the hearth and picked up the pieces. I tried vainly to put them together. Then my eyes filled with tears; for I realized what I had done, and for the first time I felt repentance and sorrow.

I learned a great many new words that day. I do not remember what they all were; but I do know that *mother, father, sister, teacher* were among them—words that were to make the world blossom for me, "like Aaron's rod, with flowers." It would have been difficult to find a happier child than I was as I lay in my crib at the close of that eventful day and lived over the joys it had brought me, and for the first time longed for a new day to come.

QUESTIONS FOR STUDY AND DISCUSSION

1. Miss Keller compares her existence before Miss Sullivan became her teacher to a ship in a fog. Does this metaphor help you to feel and understand that existence? What other metaphor can you think of that might have been used? Would it have been more effective for you than Miss Keller's? Why?
2. What was Miss Sullivan trying to do when she tapped out on Helen's hand the series that represented the word *doll*? Why do you think she failed?
3. What is the difference between Helen's experience with the doll and her experience with water in the well-house? What important step occurred because of the second experience?

4. Miss Keller wrote that she came to realize that everything has a name. Can you think of anything that does not have a name? Does it seem to you that there is one right name for a thing? Would *dog* or *canine* be the right name? The French call a dog *chien*, the Germans *Hund*, the Spanish *perro*, and the Arabs *kalb*. Which is the right name?
5. When a child learns language, its outward shape—word choice, pronunciation, grammatical forms—is determined by the child's social contacts. Because Helen Keller did not have such contacts and was physically handicapped as well, she had to be almost superhuman in order to learn language as well as she did. But even a normal person may be somewhat handicapped if his social contacts are limited to those in one speech community. A teacher from Montana, for example, may feel handicapped if he is teaching in South Carolina, for he may not understand everything his students say. A white teacher from Iowa will be handicapped in trying to understand the speech of black students in a Philadelphia classroom. The black students, too, will have difficulty in understanding the Iowan. Do you think these difficulties in understanding are more likely to be due to geographical differences or social differences related to the degree of education, kind of occupation, economic status? Do you know, or can you find out, whether anything is being done about language differences?
6. Probably most tasks which a child learns are taught him with the help of language. What things did you learn to do without that help, without anyone talking to you about them? Could Helen Keller have learned to do the same things?
7. Until about the eighteenth century it was generally believed that deaf persons could not be taught language, and often they were treated like idiots. The difficulty for the teacher lies in finding a substitute for hearing speech. For a deaf person with sight, what methods have been devised? How would you describe the method Miss Sullivan used?

SUGGESTED ACTIVITIES

1. An individual's facility in calling up several ideas about a given topic is called "ideational fluency." Compare what *water* now means to you with what it probably meant to Miss Keller when she made her great discovery.
2. Concepts clustering around a word can be enlarged through experience. Compare your concepts of *moon* before and after the lunar landing. Develop the comparisons into a short paper.
3. If you are interested in the education of a deaf and blind person, read *The Story of My Life* in its entirety and write a summary of Miss Keller's progress in acquiring language.

2
THE NATURE OF LANGUAGE
Wallace L. Chafe

No one knows just how language originated. Although several theories have been advanced, they all have been widely discredited. There is reason to believe, Chafe states, that language and man gradually emerged together hundreds of thousands of years ago; and language still belongs exclusively to human beings.

Language is a way of relating human experience to vocal sound. It should not be confused with writing, which was developed only about five thousand years ago. Like man, other animals communicate through sound; but their systems are very simple in contrast to the complex, flexible system of language, which permits the speaker to create new sentences and to combine several messages in a single sentence by means of recurring use of a relatively few sound symbols. Even animals that learn to utter words and sentences do not have control over language. The parakeet that reiterates "Billy is a pretty bird" cannot vary the vocabulary or the sentence structure to say, "Billy is handsome," "I am a beautiful parakeet," or "Billy is pretty, isn't he?"

There are approximately five thousand languages in the world, each reflecting a culture and the needs of that culture. Each language selects its own vocal sound symbols and combines them into certain patterns. The result is a distinctive lexicon (vocabulary and word-forming elements) and a distinctive grammatical structure of words and of sentences.

No one language is more difficult than another. All over the world children with normal hearing learn to talk at approximately the same age and are using most of the basic structures of their language by age five or six. Acquiring language is not the problem for the hearing child that it was for Helen Keller. The ease with which children learn to manipulate a complex language system—any language system to which they are exposed—has led to the formulation of two closely related language theories: that the child has an inborn capacity for learning

---

Source: *The National Elementary Principal* 45 (September 1965): pp. 10–15. Copyright © 1965 by the National Association of Elementary School Principals. Reprinted by permission of the publisher and the author.

language and that all languages have certain characteristics in common, called language universals. Chafe mentions nouns and verbs as possible language universals. Other linguists have listed questions, commands, negatives, pronouns, all present in the many languages that have been studied, as probable universals.

Wallace L. Chafe is professor of linguistics at the University of California at Berkeley.

Language is so much a part of our day to day existence that we seldom if ever take any notice of it. Every normal human being uses language constantly, not only for the purpose of communicating with others but also during a great part of what we call thinking. But the use of language is so automatic that the average person neither knows nor cares what it involves.

INACCURATE VIEWS OF LANGUAGE

To the extent that there is popular awareness of language, it is often misguided. For example, in our society there is a prevalent confusion of language with writing. Sequoyah, the American Indian who invented a writing system for the Cherokee in the early nineteenth century, is sometimes said to have "given his people a language." Linguists like myself who have worked extensively on "unwritten languages" have frequently heard people speak of these languages as if they were basically inferior, or not "real" languages. As a matter of fact, man has had language ever since he has been man. That is, there is reason to consider the gradual emergence of *Homo sapiens* hundreds of thousands of years ago as coincident with the gradual emergence of language. Writing systems have been in existence for only about five thousand years, and until very recently knowledge of their use was restricted to a minute proportion of the world's population. Nowadays, we may think of illiterates as disadvantaged, but it is not because they are without language; it is because they are without writing.

Recognition of the difference between language and writing led to another distortion which was especially widespread among American linguists during the decades immediately preceding and following World War II: the idea that language could be approached only through the observation of sounds. The most obvious thing a person does when he uses language is to make sounds, and it was easy to conclude that making sounds *was* language. This approach left out of consideration some of the most basic aspects of language, but it did enable linguists to learn a great deal about how a language handles sounds. Ultimately it showed that there was much in language which could not be explained on that basis alone.

LANGUAGE IN PERSPECTIVE

When people have tried to look at language in perspective, one of the ways it has appeared is as a particular kind of animal communication system. Every animal has ways of influencing and being influenced by other animals. Those who, like man, possess a nervous system of great complexity have developed a variety of means by which they are able to link one nervous system with another. The result is that information can be transmitted across the gap between individuals, where actual nerve fiber connections are lacking.

Communication necessarily takes place through a channel of some kind. There must be some physical medium into which one animal inserts a message and from which another receives it. This channel must be some medium perceptible to the senses; something that can be seen, for example, or heard or smelled or touched. Animals do, in fact, make use of all these channels. Dogs make particularly good use of smell. The antennae of insects are adapted to communication by touch. Man himself makes use of all the channels in communication of various kinds. The channel of language, however, is sound.

Sound, we can say, serves in language as the symbol for a message. A message originates within the central nervous system of an individual and is linked within his brain to impulses which activate muscles of his mouth and respiratory tract in such a way as to produce sound. The sound travels through the air and strikes the ear of the intended recipient, who transforms it back into something approximating the message that was sent. There are various ways in which the message may be distorted en route, but, on the whole, language performs its function with remarkable effectiveness.

Other animals communicate through sound, too. Dogs bark and whine, cats meow and hiss, while apes and dolphins produce a large array of different noises. In nonhuman communication, however, and in most human communication outside of language, the system is a very simple one. The available messages are few, and each is linked to a particular noise in an essentially one-to-one correspondence. The experience of a chimpanzee can be focused on one of a relatively small number of different messages. Each is associated with a particular sound. When the animal is motivated to transmit a certain message, he makes the sound which is appropriate. Another animal perceives it and relates the sound to his own experience in accordance with the system which the two animals share.

SPECIAL CHARACTERISTICS OF LANGUAGE

Language is not nearly so simple. It has two characteristics in particular which distinguish it from other systems and which enormously increase its effectiveness. One is easy to appreciate: it is that language permits the communication of more than one simple message at a time. A chimpanzee has his small repertoire of individual messages—excitement, the presence of food, or whatever they may be—only one of which he can transmit in any one utterance. A man, even in a short sentence, may communicate a number of individual units all combined to form one complex message. This ability to put together many simple units of experience to form a larger complex unit provides a unique flexibility in communication. The system is patterned in such a way that there is actually no finite limit to the number of different messages which can be transmitted. A person can and constantly does say things he has never said before, and his listener, who has never heard them before, has no trouble understanding. The underlying units and patterns are ones that the speaker has often used, but he is able to combine familiar elements in an infinite variety of ways.

The other noteworthy characteristic of language is not as obvious, but it serves as an underlying condition for the ability to produce and receive an unlimited number of different messages. In simpler communication systems, each distinct message is symbolized by a totally distinct sound. If this kind of symbolization were maintained as the number of different messages increased to infinity, the number of distinct sounds would have to increase in the same manner and the system would become unworkable. An analogy from our system for writing numbers is instructive. Suppose that for each number from zero to infinity we had to use a totally different written symbol, not made up of repeatable smaller parts. Long before we reached any very high numbers we would probably reach the limits of our ability to discriminate different symbols of any practical size, and we would have a staggering problem in learning which symbols went with which numbers. The solution which has developed with numbers, of course, is the use of a small number of digits—only ten—from which we are able to form an infinity of systematic arrangements.

Language solves the problem in the same way. It makes use of a small number of distinct sound symbols, something on the order of a couple of dozen, within a system which allows these symbols to be arranged in an unlimited number of different combinations. Such a symbol, for example, is manifested in the closing of the lips at the beginning of words such as *pit* and *bit*. This symbol, called "bilabiality," does not in itself convey any message at all. Only in combination with other sound symbols, as in the words cited, does it perform its function as a basic unity of the sound system of English.

The advantages of the human ability to communicate an unlimited range of different messages are incalculable. People are able to exchange their experiences of the moment in extensive and subtle detail. But they are also able to communicate regarding the past and future and regarding phenomena that may be far removed in space. They are even able to express notions that have no objective existence at all, but are entirely imaginary. Nearly all of the institutions which go to make up human culture—all the things which particularly distinguish men from other animals—would be inconceivable without language at their core. Language makes possible the organized sharing and dissemination of human experience in a unique richness and complexity.

Sound, as a communication channel, has certain drawbacks. It is ephemeral. It fades away as soon as it is produced, and until the invention of modern recording devices, it was necessarily gone for good. Without such devices, too, sound has the disadvantage of being limited to use between people who are within hearing range of each other. Before the advent of modern technology, however, and even necessary as a background for that technology, the development of writing served to extend the effectiveness of language beyond the narrow temporal and spatial boundaries of sound. Writing was a new communication system which added to language the advantages of permanence and range provided by the visual communication channel. It made use of visible symbols to carry a message which was language itself. Writing, as we know it, would have been impossible without the prior existence of language, for language was actually the message which writing communicated. But writing made it possible to preserve and transmit language in revolutionary ways. Its own effect on human institutions has also been incalculable.

THE COMPONENTS OF LANGUAGE

Suppose we look more closely at the major components of language. We have seen that language is a way of relating human experience to sound. On this basis, it is possible to see within it three interrelated parts: a system for organizing experience, a system for organizing sound, and a system by which items of experience are related to items of sound.

The sounds of language are made with certain organs of the body, the "vocal organs." For the most part, the sounds begin with a stream of air which is sent upward from the lungs and then modified in various ways by the larynx, the mouth, and sometimes the nose and other parts of the respiratory tract. In theory, there is a limitless number of different sounds which can be produced in this way, although there are limits to the differences in sounds which the human ear can discriminate.

This universe of vocal sound provides a storehouse from which each language selects a relatively small number of minimal elements like the "bilabiality" mentioned above. It then allows these elements to combine in accordance with its own conventional patterns to form complex symbols. No two languages make the same selections or have the same patterns of arrangement. Bilabial sounds might seem one of the most natural kinds for a language to use, but there are some American Indian languages in which the lips are never closed during speech. Many languages—French, for example—make a distinction between vowels pronounced with the nose partially open and those in which the nose is shut off. In English, such a difference is not significant. We may usually pronounce *man* with a nasalized vowel, but it makes no difference whether we do or not. Sometimes we utter a gesture of commiseration which is spelled *tsk tsk* in the comics. Such a sound, called a "click," is not integrated into our language, for it does not combine with other sounds to form complex symbols. In some African languages, on the other hand, clicks of various kinds are a regular part of the sound system.

A language handles experience in much the same way that it handles sounds. We can think of the entire range of communicable human experience as another infinite universe, incomparably more extensive than the universe of vocal sounds. But a language selects from this universe in much the same way. It chooses a number (this time a very large, but still manageable number) of experiential units which it then allows to combine in specific patterns to form an infinite number of complex arrangements. The spectrum of colors, for example, which in raw experience may be a continuous gradation, is crystallized by our language into a few focal areas: *red*, *orange*, and so on. Other languages divide up this part of experience quite differently, lumping together part of our *green* with part of our *blue*, for example, or making distinctions between colors which the English language treats as one. Experience is multidimensional, and it is often the case that properties like texture, moistness, or something else enter into the delineation of so-called "color terms." In English, for example, the colors *gold* and *silver* involve (for obvious reasons) a metallic texture. I once bought a bath towel that was labelled "gold," but I was impressed by the fact that this use of the word did not coincide with the way I had learned to use it.

A theory that received considerable attention a decade or so ago asserted that all of experience is filtered through language, so that we experience only what our language treats as significant. If this theory were wholly valid, it would mean that I could not tell the difference between instances of *red* unless I had different names for them like *scarlet* or *crimson*. But, in fact, I seem to have no trouble at all distinguishing between things that my language treats as the same. I constantly see colors around me that I would be hard put to give names to, but they are no less a part of my experience for that reason. What my language does do, however, is to make it much easier for me to communicate some things than others. It is easier for me to tell you about the color of my red pencil than to communicate the "nondescript" color of the wall of the room I am sitting in.

The experiences which a language makes it easiest to communicate are, on the whole, the experiences which we most often need to communicate. In consequence, the way a language organizes experience tends strongly to reflect the way a culture as a whole is organized. If, as is often the case, a language makes a distinction between one's older brother and one's younger brother, it is usually true that the distinction between older and younger brothers is an important one within the culture, one that often needs to be communicated. Studies of "language and culture" are of great interest in anthropology, for language very often provides a key to what is important in a society.

LINGUISTIC DIFFERENCES

If language is common to all mankind, it is also true that its individual manifestations are widely different. The differences range from total lack of communicability such as is found between speakers of English and Japanese, for example, to the kinds of differences one finds within a single classroom or even within a single family.

Earlier investigators thought that language was undergoing continuous evolution analogous to the evolution of plants and animals. It was thought further that the gamut of evolutionary stages could still be observed in the world at the present time; that primitive tribes were in the early stages of language development, if they had anything that could be truly called language at all, while advanced civilizations like our own had achieved something of a wholly different order. Another view, following the reverence for antiquity which had begun with the Renaissance, held that classical Latin, Greek, or Sanskrit represented the zenith of linguistic perfection and that more modern languages showed a gradual deterioration from them.

In reaction against such views and in line with a general trend in anthropology, there developed subsequently a belief in linguistic relativity. No valid standard for measuring the worth of languages had been found to exist, and it was concluded that one language was just as good as another. Relativism holds that all languages show a similar degree of complexity in grammatical structure and that there are no languages in existence now, and probably have not been any for hundreds of thousands of years, which can be called primitive in the sense that they represent a more rudimentary stage of linguistic development.

Furthermore, it is held that every language serves the communicative needs of its users, given a stable cultural environment, with equal effectiveness. It may be true that peoples remote from Western culture have a deficient vocabulary when it comes to listing the parts of an automobile. But it is also true that we fall behind the Eskimo in being able to refer to different kinds and conditions of snow, and behind the Arab in being able to list the parts of a camel. Every language shows itself to be remarkably flexible, moreover, and new cultural environments quickly bring linguistic adjustments. Utilizing their own resources, American Indian languages provide ways of talking easily not only about lions, tigers, and elephants, which were not present on the American continent before Columbus, but also about baseball and television.

Linguistic relativism brought emphasis on the infinite variety possible among languages, and for a while there was little interest in what languages had in common beyond the gross ways in which they all structured experience and sound. The most recent trend, however, is to look for more specific language "universals." It is thought that there are complex biological and environmental limitations on the extent of linguistic variation and that these limitations are as worthy of study as are the differences among languages. At one time, for example, it was emphasized that the distinction which most languages seem to make between "nouns" and "verbs" is not a necessary distinction, that what is a noun in one language may be a verb in another, and that some languages may not have categories of this kind at all. The tendency now is to interpret this pervasive if not universal linguistic phenomenon as a symptom of something that is common to all human experience.

Linguistic differences, however, continue to be of great theoretical interest and practical concern. There are something like five thousand mutually unintelligible languages in the world and a countless number of dialects. On a still finer level of difference, it can be observed that there are no two individuals who speak exactly alike and, furthermore, that almost everyone has varying ways of speaking that he uses as appropriate in varying situations.

The causes of linguistic differences are numerous, but lying behind all of them is the fact that change is a constant and inevitable feature of human institutions, language included. The English of King Alfred was different from the English of Chaucer, which was different from that of Shakespeare, which was clearly different from the English of today. English tomorrow will be a different language again. Such change—and it is simply change, not progress and not retrogression—will proceed inexorably in spite of efforts to impede it.

Among peoples with a tradition of written literature, however, the language of earlier times is preserved in writing and usually taught as something that should be highly valued and imitated. As the normal language of a people continues to change, the gulf between it and the literary language continues to widen, to the extent that the latter must sometimes be learned as if it were a foreign language. The literary language always enjoys prestige, partly because conservatism is a universal human trait, partly because the earlier language is preserved chiefly in works of artistic merit, works that were valuable enough to be preserved. In some cultures, people will go so far as to deny knowing any other language, even though they may constantly use a vernacular that is very different.

THE DISTRIBUTION OF DIFFERENCES

The more people are in constant communication with each other, the more likely are their language habits to undergo changes in common. Conversely, the greater the barriers to communication, the more likely it is that significant linguistic differences will develop. Both political and geographic barriers have produced a marked difference between British and American English over the last couple of centuries. People also tend to imitate the language of those with whom they would, for whatever reason, identify. It is common for "centers of prestige," whether important cities or other social nuclei, to radiate linguistic influence over the people they dominate. Linguistic homogeneity thus tends to be proportional to the degree of both communicative interaction and common allegiance to prestigeful models.

These factors explain the characteristic pattern of linguistic differences which we find in all parts of the world. In brief, linguistic differences are distributed both geographically and socially. It is obvious, even within the United States, that people speak differently according to their geographic origins. It should be equally obvious that within a single region there are linguistic differences associated with differences between social groups. Business executives generally do not speak in the same fashion as taxi drivers; there are noticeable differences between the speech of women and that of men. But the differences exhibited even by one person in varying situations are equally real. Children speak one kind of language in the classroom, another on the playground; politicians speak differently to voters than they do to their wives.

Linguists are at present much interested in looking deeper into the relations between social differences and differences of language. In the end, linguists can point to the kinds of relations which exist and can develop theories to explain why they exist. On the basis of such knowledge, it should be possible for others to decide rationally whether there is one variety of a language like English which teachers ought to emphasize because of its social correlations, what that variety consists of, the problems and results of teaching it to children whose vernacular is very different, and the best ways to maintain flexibility so that regional differences and normal linguistic change can be accommodated and total uniformity avoided.

QUESTIONS FOR STUDY AND DISCUSSION

1. Did you hold any notions about language that were changed by reading this essay? If so, how were they different and why did you give them up?
2. Among the several theories of language origin is the onomatopoeic theory, that language originated through the imitation of sounds of nature: *buzz, meow, quack* . . .
   a. How many words can you name that you think are onomatopoeic? Do you think onomatopoeic words form a large part of our vocabulary?
   b. Compare the following onomatopoeic words in different languages. Use them as evidence to show that onomatopoeic words do or do not closely represent sounds in nature.

English	German	French	Italian	Spanish
hum	summen	bourdonner	cantarellare, borbottare	zumbar, ronronear
hiss	zischen	siffler	fischiare, sibilare	sisear, silbar
cackle	gackern	caquet	gracidare	cacareo
buzz	summen	bourdonner	ronzare	zumbido
whiz	schwirren, zischen	siffler	fischiare, sibilare	zumbar, silbar

3. "Eve named the dodo the *dodo* because the bird looked so like a dodo," Mark Twain supposedly said. Use this humorous comment as a springboard for a discussion of the theory advanced by the Greek philosopher Plato and others that words belong to things by nature—that there is an inherent connection between the word and the thing—as opposed to the modern linguistic theory that the use of vocal sound in language is symbolic. The word is not the thing. (A symbol is anything which has the power to summon from our consciousness an image, an emotion, a belief, an idea.) In your discussion try to answer these questions by presenting evidence. Which theory does the evidence seem to support?
    a. Does the same word always designate the same thing or experience?
    b. Do different words sometimes designate the same thing or experience?
    c. Do different languages use the same words or different words to designate the same thing or experience?
4. Language permits the communication of more than one simple message at a time, Chafe states. How many messages are included in this twenty-one-word sentence from his essay?

A man, even in a short sentence, may communicate a number of individual units all combined to form one complex message.

5. Chafe draws an analogy between digits and sound symbols in speech. Explain the analogy and its significance. Test the validity of the analogy.
6. How many of these kinds of communication is man alone capable of?
    a. Signaling danger.
    b. Describing an unfamiliar object.
    c. Communicating the quality of food recently eaten.
    d. Enumerating the sequence of past events.
    e. Exchanging plans for a hunting expedition.
    f. Communicating experiences about an imaginary trip to the land of the trolls.

7. Articles in popular magazines have described dolphins as so intelligent that they have a language. What criteria would Chafe use to take issue with this argument? How would you define language to include what dolphins do? In what ways does language differ from the communication system of any nonhuman species?
8. The sounds in different languages are not identical.
   a. If you have some acquaintance with a foreign language, are there any sounds in that language not present in English? Have you had any difficulty producing those sounds? Are there any sounds in English not present in the foreign language?
   b. If you are studying French, prepare yourself to tell the class what in speech signals the difference in meaning between *ban* and *bât*.
9. Individual languages combine sounds in different sequences. Which of these invented words fit into the sound patterns of English so that you can pronounce them readily?

tlap   peng   ngep   slpo   gambow   sprittling

10. Does your experience coincide with the author's in your ability to differentiate colors that you cannot name? Illustrate. Does your experience seem to indicate that all experience is or is not filtered through language?
11. What information does each of these terms designating a family relationship fail to provide: *grandmother, grandfather, cousin, aunt, uncle, brother, sister*?
12. What comment would you make if someone said that the French language is superior to that of the Bushmen of Australia?
13. On the surface, languages differ greatly both in lexicon (vocabulary and word-making elements) and in grammar, or structure. But there is now a search for underlying universals in all languages, Chafe indicates, and he mentions the distinction which most languages seem to make between nouns and verbs. Among the other characteristics common to the languages that have been studied are these: vowels and consonants; sentences (statements, questions, commands, negatives); a system of joining two or more sentences; pronouns; words for true and false. Though obviously it is impossible to discover language universals by comparing two or three closely related languages, it is interesting and rewarding to look for those characteristics common to the languages and to note their differences.
    a. What common characteristics do you find in one or two foreign languages and in English? Consider the characteristics listed above as well as others.
    b. What are the chief differences between a specific foreign language and English? Give particular consideration to sounds, word forms, word order, and grammatical structures.

SUGGESTED ACTIVITIES

1. Chafe uses the bilabials /p/ and /b/ to illustrate the importance of recurring vocal sound symbols in a language system. Another set of recurring sound symbols in English, /t/ and /d/, is made with the tip of the tongue against the alveolar ridge behind the upper front teeth. Form as many words as you can beginning with these sound symbols: *tan, Dan* . . .
2. The number of possible sentences in a language is infinite; few sentences are repeated identically. Moreover, we can deliberately create new sentences. For example, here is an unlikely sentence that you probably have never heard before.

   Five young donkeys dangle perilously from the upper branch of a young birch tree.

   Construct a sentence that you have never heard or uttered. What is the significance of the fact that human beings can constantly create new sentences?
3. a. The possible length of any sentence is infinite. Nursery rhymes and some simple songs illustrate this principle. Try lengthening "Old Macdonald had a farm" or a rhyme or song of your own choosing.
   b. Show that the following sentences can be lengthened indefinitely.

      (1) The Smiths travel widely in Arizona, New Mexico. . . .

      (2) We saw Jim, Joe, Sue. . . .

      (3) We made camp in the clearing that. . . .

4. Unlike animals, which use certain sounds for specific messages, people can transmit the same message through different sounds or through the rearrangement of certain sequences of sounds. Illustrate this fact by conveying these messages in different ways. Vary the structure and the vocabulary.

   a. **Close the door.**

   b. **Gerald sent Sue the gift yesterday.**

   c. **It's 10:45.**

   d. **A stranger is at the door.**

   e. **I had my watch repaired last week. It still doesn't run.**

5. Read Poe's "The Bells." Select those words that you think are onomatopoeic and then check them in a dictionary to find out whether they originated as imitative of sounds. In addition, write a paragraph in

which you show how these words contribute to the sound effects that Poe is trying to create.
6. You have read that "the way a language organizes experience tends strongly to reflect the way a culture as a whole is organized." Thus the Eskimos have many different words for snow as have the Arabs for parts of camels. As a highly industrialized society, we have many words to designate kinds of automobiles, airplanes, roads, houses, and so on; and as a society concerned with beauty aids, we have a vocabulary that might baffle an Eskimo or a Laplander. Write a paper in which you introduce someone from a different civilization to the elaborate vocabulary of one aspect of our society and discuss the characteristics of our culture which this vocabulary seems to reflect.

3
LINGUISTICS
William G. Moulton

Helen Keller, in describing her personal experience with language learning, dramatically demonstrates the symbolic nature of language. Chafe contrasts animal signals with language, which is a distinctly human achievement. William G. Moulton is concerned in this article with the way language works, the process which makes it possible for two people to understand each other. Like all linguists, he looks at language as a scientist would, analyzing the communication process as a scientist would approach any other complex natural phenomenon.

Here Moulton discusses language as a code, a special kind of system used for communication. Every code is composed of symbolic units that have arbitrary meanings assigned to them. These units then operate according to some kind of system. There is an encoder, who channels the units into the system, and a decoder, who receives and interprets the message. Codes that are used for brevity or secrecy, like shorthand or the Morse code, are really based on the more elaborate code of natural language. But there are other codes, like traffic signals, that do not employ language at all.

William G. Moulton is professor of linguistics at Princeton University.

How language changes through time, how it varies through space, how it differs from one social group to another, and most of all how it *works*—these things are studied in linguistics. Because modern linguistics has roots which go back to the early nineteenth century and beyond, many people are familiar with some of the things which interested linguists then and still interest them today.

They find it understandable that a linguist should try to find the line which separates those areas in New England where *barn* is "*barrn*" (with *r*) from those areas where it is "*bahn*" (without *r*); and they may even envy him a bit when he goes to an Indian reservation or South America or Africa to investigate some hitherto undescribed tongue and thus add his little bit to our meager knowledge of the world's 2,000 to 4,000 languages. (No one knows how many there are.)

But when a linguist says that he is doing some research which he hopes will help us understand a little better how it is that "two people are able to talk together," most people shake their heads in puzzlement.

Yet how two people are able to talk together is, of course, the central problem. During the 1930's and 1940's, most American linguists attacked it by trying to work out better techniques of discovering the structure of language—any language—and of analyzing and classifying what they found. Then, in the late 1950's there came a rather dramatic swing in another direction: away from mere classification of data toward a search for universals and a broad, inclusive "theory of language."

In a sense this has been merely a return to some of the prime interests of our nineteenth century predecessors—Wilhelm von Humboldt, for example. It has also brought American linguistics out of the scholarly isolation from which it suffered for a time, and into closer contact with such related disciplines as psychology and philosophy. (The contact with anthropology has always been close.)

How *are* two people able to talk together? Since most of us never ask this question, but take the matter for granted, it is useful to consider just what goes on. Let us assume that we have a speaker A and a hearer B, that A says something to B, and that B understands him without difficulty. Here an act of communication via language has taken place. But *how* did it take place? What went on inside of A? How did the communication move from A to B? And what went on inside of B? The process seems to consist of at least eleven different steps. [See the diagram on page 25.]

1. SEMANTIC ENCODING

We assume that A has some sort of "meaning" (or whatever we want to call it) which he wishes to convey to B. His first step is to get this meaning into proper shape for transmission in the language he is using (English, we shall say). Since this is like putting a message in shape to fit the code in which it is to be sent, we can call the process *semantic encoding*.

If A wants to talk to B about some sort of timepiece, his encoding will depend on whether he means the kind that hangs on the wall or stands on a table (a *clock*), or the kind that is carried in the pocket or worn on the wrist (a *watch*). In German the single semantic unit *Uhr* includes both types. If he wants to ask whether B "knows" something, he can use the single semantic unit *know*. Spanish would force him to choose between *conocer* (for a person, place, or thing) and *saber* (for a fact).

As these examples show, each language "slices the pie of reality" in its own capricious way. In English, we group a host of different objects, of many types, colors, sizes, and shapes, into the semantic unit *stool*. If to a stool we add a back, however, it suddenly becomes the semantic unit *chair*. If we widen it so that two or more people can sit on it, it is a *bench*. If to a chair we add upholstery, it is still a *chair*. But if to a bench we add upholstery, it suddenly becomes a *sofa*.

Using a bold and imprecise metaphor, we can think of every language as a vast sieve with thousands of semantic slots in it. Any idea which we want to express in that language first has to be put through this sieve. And every language has a special sieve of its own. The discipline which studies such metaphorical sieves is semantics. (A semanticist would describe his valuable and difficult work more elegantly, but this is a reasonable approximation to part of what he does.)

2. GRAMMATICAL ENCODING

Once speaker A has found the proper semantic units for his message, he must next arrange them in the particular way the grammar of his language requires. If in English he wants to get across the idea of "dog," "man," and "bite"—with the dog and not the man doing the biting—he has to encode it in the order *dog bites man*; the order *man bites dog* gives quite a different message.

The grammatical code of Latin employs totally different devices. For the meaning "dog bites man" it marks the unit "dog" as nominative (*canis*), the unit "man" as accusative (*virum*), and it can then combine these words with *mordet* "bites" in any order whatever. For the opposite message it would mark "dog" as accusative (*canem*), "man" as nominative (*vir*), and it could then again combine these with *mordet* in any order at all.

English grammar signals the difference between subject and object by means of word order; Latin grammar signals it by means of inflectional endings; other languages use still other devices.

The basic units used in grammatical encoding are called morphemes (from Greek *morphē* "form"). Morphemes may be either words: *dog, bite, man*, or parts of words: the *-s* of *bites*, the *-ing* of *biting*, etc. Some clearly correspond to semantic units: *dog, bite, man*; with others, however, the semantic connection is less clear, e.g. *-s, -ing*. Still others seem to have no semantic connection at all, the *to* of *try to come*, for example, or the *-ly* of *quickly*.

Morphemes are then arranged grammatically into such higher level units as words: *bites, biting, quickly* (some morphemes are of course already words: *dog, bite, man, quick*); then phrases of various sorts, e.g. *the dog* (which can function, among other ways, as a "subject"); then clauses of various sorts (in English, such constructions contain a subject and predicate); and finally sentences, which are marked in some way as not being parts of still larger constructions.

Recent interest in grammar has focused on the following familiar and yet astonishing (and somehow disturbing) fact—any speaker can say, and any hearer can understand, an infinite number of sentences; and, indeed, many of the sentences we say and hear have never been said before.

How does our grammar provide for this enormous variety and flexibility? If we merely want to reach infinity quickly, we need only allow ourselves to use the word *and* over and over again. There are, however, two far more elegant devices. One is that of *embedding*: putting a construction inside a construction inside a construction, etc., like a Chinese puzzle. A classic example is the old nursery tale: "This is the cat that killed the rat that ate the malt (and so on and on and on) . . . that lay in the house that Jack built."

Still more elegant is *transformation*, whereby a basic sentence type may be transformed into a large variety of derived constructions. Thus *the dog bites the man* can be transformed into: *the dog bit (has bitten, had bitten, is biting, was biting, has been biting, can bite,* etc.) *the man; the man is bitten (was bitten, has been bitten,* etc.) *by the dog; (the dog) that bites* (etc.) *the man; (the man) that the dog bites; (the man) that is bitten by the dog; (the dog) that the man is bitten by;* etc.

3. PHONOLOGICAL ENCODING

When grammatical encoding has been completed, the message enters the phonological component of the code as a string of morphemes, and these must now be encoded for sound. This is accomplished by encoding each morpheme into one or more basic phonological units or phonemes (from Greek *phōnḗ* "sound").* The morpheme *-s* of *bites* is converted to the phoneme /s/, *check* to /ček/, *stone* to /stōn/, *thrift* to /θrift/, etc.

(Written symbols for phonemes are customarily placed between slant lines to distinguish them from the letters of regular spelling and from the symbols used in phonetic transcription. Just what symbols are used for phonemes is unimportant; one must merely have a different symbol for each phoneme in the language.)

This device of encoding morphemes into *one or more* phonemes each is an extraordinarily powerful one, and in terms of sheer economy it is hard to overestimate its importance. If a language used only one phoneme per morpheme, it could have only as many morphemes as it has phonemes. But if a language uses from one to five phonemes per morpheme (as in the above English examples), the number of possible morpheme shapes soon becomes astronomical.

For a stock of twenty phonemes the figure is 3,368,420; for thirty phonemes

---

* Every language contains a large number of speech sounds, or phones, which are classified into a smaller number of significant classes of sound called phonemes.—Eds.

it is 25,137,930; and for forty phonemes (English has between thirty and forty, depending on just how you figure them) it reaches the fantastic total of 105,025,640 possible morpheme shapes.

We have given these figures to show what an enormous economy is achieved by having in human language this "duality principle," as it has been called: first an encoding into morphemes, and then a separate encoding of morphemes into *one or more* phonemes each.

There is, however, a very bad flaw in our figures: We have assumed that it is possible for phonemes to occur in any mathematically possible sequence, such as (for English) /ppppp/, /fstgk/, etc. But English of course does not do this: like every language, it places very strict limitations on possible sequences of phonemes. Nevertheless, even with the strictest sorts of limits, the duality principle permits every language to form far more morpheme shapes than it will ever use.

If we take English to be a thirty-phoneme language (it has more than thirty, no matter how you figure them), permit no morpheme shape of more than five phonemes (*glimpse*/glimps/ actually has six), and assume that only one out of every 1,000 possible sequences can be used, we still end up with a total of 25,137 possible morpheme shapes (the above 25,137,930 divided by 1,000)—enough to take care of any language.

If we remind ourselves that English words can easily consist of three or more morphemes (e.g. *un-friend-li-ness*), it is clear that we are also provided with an overabundance of possible word shapes—more than enough for Lewis Carroll to invent "slithy toves did gyre and gimble in the wabe," using a few of the thousands of available word shapes which had not previously been claimed.

In the preceding paragraphs we have assumed, for purposes of presentation, that a message is neatly encoded first semantically, then grammatically, and then phonologically. But since normal speech is full of false starts, hesitations, grammatical slips, and the like, it seems clear that we behave a good deal more like the young lady who, when told that she should "think before she spoke," replied with rare honesty: "But I can't do that! How do I know what I'm going to say until I start talking?"

If we do *not* normally plan out our entire message before we start sending it, then we must possess some sort of feedback device which permits us to "monitor" the message as it is sent and to make necessary adjustments as we proceed—adjusting a present tense verb to agree with its singular subject, for example.

4. FROM BRAIN TO SPEECH ORGANS

When phonological encoding has been completed, the message has been changed from a string of morphemes to a string of phonemes. Speaker A must now somehow program and send on down to his speech organs a set

Encoding the message

1. Semantic encoding
2. Grammatical encoding
3. Phonological encoding

The speaker and his "code"

Transmission

4. From the brain
5. Speech organs
6. Sound waves
7. The ear
8. To the brain

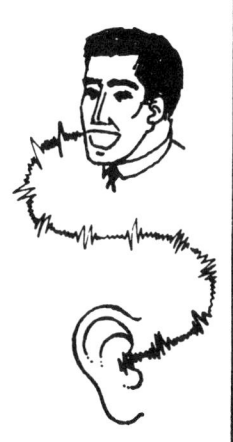

Decoding the message

9. Phonological decoding
10. Grammatical decoding
11. Semantic decoding

The hearer and his "code"

of instructions telling them what movements to make so as to turn each phoneme into sound. We can compare this with the way paper tapes are punched to provide instructions to automatic typewriters, telegraph transmitters, computers, and the like. Programmed in this way, the message is sent sequentially from the brain to the speech organs.

5. MOVEMENTS OF THE SPEECH ORGANS

Triggered by successive innervations, the speech organs (vocal cords, tongue, lips, etc.) now perform the proper series of movements. As they do so, an interesting and rather disturbing thing happens. We have assumed that, when the message is sent to the speech organs, it is transmitted in the form of a string of separate instructions, one for each phoneme.

If the message is the word *pin* /pin/, for example, there are first instructions for producing a /p/, then for producing an /i/, and then for producing an /n/. This seems, at least, to be the most reasonable assumption. If the speech organs responded ideally to these instructions, they would first assume the position for /p/, then move jerkily and instantaneously to the position for /i/, then jerkily and instantaneously to the position for /n/.

Common sense tells us that they cannot do this, and X-ray moving pictures of the speech organs in action prove it beyond a doubt. Instead of moving instantaneously from one position to the next, the speech organs bobble back and forth in a constant flow of motion which does not seem to consist of any specific number of segments at all.

A remarkable transformation has taken place. Where the message previously consisted of a string of discrete segments—three, we assume, in the case of /pin/—it has now been "smeared" into a continuum. As the speech organs move into position to produce the /p/, they already anticipate part of the position for the following /i/. (The reader can test this by whispering the *p*'s of *peer, par, poor*; the sound of each *p* shows clearly which vowel would follow if he went on with the rest of the word.)

As the speech organs then move into the /i/ they carry over part of the position of the /p/ and anticipate part of the position for the following /n/. (We normally "nasalize" such a vowel slightly.) And when the speech organs get to the /n/, they still have part of the position of the proceeding /i/. This drastic change in the shape of the message may seem quite harmless now, but it means that later on this "smeared continuum" of sound will have to be turned back into a string of discrete segments if the message is to be recovered. This is what must take place at stage 9, "phonological decoding."

When the speech organs interact so as to produce a speech sound, they are said to articulate the sound. The study of this aspect of the speech event, *articulatory phonetics*, has long been a highly developed research field.

6. VIBRATIONS OF THE AIR MOLECULES

As the speech organs articulate, they set the air molecules into vibration and produce audible sound. The study of this aspect of the speech event is *acoustic phonetics*. Here again a great deal of research has been done, and some remarkable advances have been achieved, especially since World War II.

7. VIBRATIONS OF THE EAR

When the vibrations of the air molecules reach hearer B's eardrum, they produce corresponding vibrations which are then transmitted via the three bones of the middle ear to the cochlear fluid of the inner ear. The study of this aspect of the speech event is *auditory phonetics*. It is usually combined with study of the ear in general, and with the study of auditory perception (which of course involves also the activity of the brain farther up the line).

8. FROM EAR TO BRAIN

Though this stage is in a sense the mirror image of stage 4, "From brain to speech organs," there are two important differences.

First, when the message went from A's brain to his speech organs, it was transmitted as a string of discrete segments: but since it was then turned into a "smeared continuum" by A's speech organs, this is the shape in which it now reaches B's brain.

Second, speaker A was able to send the message only because, somewhere inside his head, he possessed the proper code; hearer B, however, can receive all the energy in the message whether he knows the code or not—though of course he can do nothing further with it unless he *does* know the same code. We can "hear" all there is to hear in a foreign language message: we can "understand" the message only if we also know the foreign language code.

9, 10, 11. PHONOLOGICAL, GRAMMATICAL, AND SEMANTIC DECODING

Though we surely use these three different types of decoding when we hear and understand a message, the evidence suggests that we do not use them in a step-by-step procedure but rather race back and forth from one to the other, picking up all the information we can get.

Suppose, for example, that we receive a message which we tentatively decode phonologically as, "I hope this'll suture plans." A quick check with the grammatical component of the code reveals that there is indeed a morpheme *suture* marked "transitive verb" (that is to say, we know that one can "suture something"), so all is well for the moment. But a check farther up the line in the semantic component tells us that one just does not "suture plans," so something must be wrong.

Back we race to the phonological component. Again the message (held in the meantime by some sort of storage device) is decoded as having the phonemic structure "I hope this'll suture plans." But a second check in the grammatical component now reveals that the phoneme sequence "suture plans" can be grammatically either one of two different things: *suture plans* or *suit your plans*. So we check this *second* possibility in the semantic component of the code. This now "makes sense"—and we accept it.

Our brain can function so swiftly that all of this happens in a flash. Only rarely does this "searching process" take so long that it interferes with our understanding of the speaker's next sentence.

In addition to the message itself, our decoding brings us information of three other types. First, there is information about the identity of the speaker (the quality of his voice tells us that it is Jones and not Smith who is speaking), his state of health (hoarse voice, stuffed up nose), and the like. Such things are presumably the same in all languages and hence not part of any code.

Second, there is the kind of information we often refer to as "it wasn't what he said but how he said it"—things indicating that the speaker is angry, excited, sarcastic, unctuous, etc. Since such matters are different in English from what they are in French or Vietnamese, they are clearly part of the English language in the wider sense of the term. (They also make a fascinating subject for linguistic study.)

Third, there is information as to where the speaker comes from and what social and educational class he belongs to. If he uses the phonological encoding "thoity-thoid," this will suggest that he comes from Brooklyn or thereabouts; if he says "thihty-thihd" we may suspect that he comes from the vicinity of Boston.

If he uses the grammatical encoding "I seen him when he done it," we will place him at a relatively low social and educational level—even though (and this is an interesting point) the message comes through just as clearly as if he had said "I saw him when he did it." Matters of this third sort are also part of the English language in the wider sense of the term.

In the above description of a speech event, the part which is of most fundamental interest to the linguist is of course the code itself: its phonological component (here great progress was made in the 1930's and 1940's), its grammatical component (again great progress at that time, and a whole new approach opening up since the late 1950's), and its semantic component (long neglected by American linguists, though there has been a recent revival of interest).

When one looks back upon it all, one is perhaps inclined to say: What is it good for? Is it just a game? To the linguist it is more than a game: It is a thing of beauty and wonder, and it needs no more justification than this. At the same time, with a bit of a sigh, he will say that (like such long "useless" fields as astronomy) it *can* be of practical value. It has obvious applications to foreign language teaching and—with great help from the teachers themselves—these applications are now being exploited.

If presented clearly and simply (and this has in general not been the case —nor is it easy) it seems likely that it could also be applied usefully to the teaching of reading and writing, and to the teaching of the English language at all levels. Tentative applications of this sort have already been made; with cooperation on all sides, perhaps they can lead to truly useful results.

QUESTIONS FOR STUDY AND DISCUSSION

1. Moulton links linguistics with psychology, philosophy, and anthropology. How is the study of language related to these three disciplines?
2. Moulton says that every language is "a vast sieve with thousands of semantic slots." When we talk, we fill these slots with words. Translation from one language to another is fairly easy if the languages have the same semantic slots. All we have to do is find the correct word. Take the idea of "father." In German it is *Vater*; in French, *pere*; in Spanish, *padre*. Contrast the ways different languages say "farewell." Would the language of a primitive African tribe have a semantic slot for "airplane," "subway," or "lunar landing"?
3. See whether you understand the process of *embedding* by putting the second sentence inside the first in each group.

    a. The President made a tour of the Far East.
    b. The tour included India, Pakistan, and Korea.

    a. American rivers are becoming polluted.
    b. The rivers are the repositories of industrial wastes.

4. *Transformation* gives us an opportunity to make selections within the grammatical code. Transform each of these sentences at least twice.

    a. The Communists attack the Senator's speech.
    b. The reporter describes the fire.

5. Moulton says that the phonemes of English and the mathematical possibilities of their combinations provide us with an overabundance of realizable word shapes. But some phoneme combinations are not possible in English. Wherever possible, arrange each of the following groups of letters, which represent phonemes, into other English sequences. Are there sequences that won't work or won't work in particular positions in a word? (*Ng* represents one phoneme.)

    a-n-t   l-o-o-t   a-p-t   s-i-ng   r-i-ng-i-ng

    What do you discover about the possible position of *ng* in a word?

6. Show how morphemes function as the building blocks of our vocabulary by forming as many words as you can, using the following morphemes in various combinations.

breath	-ed	-ly
box	-es	-ship
child	-ful	-y
faith	-less	be-
friend	-ish	un-
sleep		
thank		

7. The name of Mrs. Malaprop, a character in Sheridan's *The Rivals*, explains the meaning of *malapropism*. How would Moulton explain Mrs. Malaprop's language difficulty?

   "I would by no means wish a daughter of mine to be a progeny of learning."

   "... I hope you will represent her to the Captain as an object not altogether illegible."

   "He is the very Pine-apple of politeness."

8. A favorite device of both poets and comedians is the pun, a play on words in which there is the possibility of a double meaning because of similarity in sounds. Read these lines aloud to discover the punning.

   the bigness of cannon is skilful   E. E. Cummings

   Ask for me tomorrow, and you shall find me a grave man.
   (The dying Mercutio in *Romeo and Juliet*)

   A little more than kin, and less than kind.
   (Hamlet in an aside about King Claudius)

9. In addition to the message itself, our decoding can tell us something about the identity of the speaker. Printed language cannot transmit the quality of a speaker's voice, but it can provide other clues. What can you tell about these three characters from Eugene O'Neill's play, *The Hairy Ape*? What clues did you use?

   Listen 'ere, Comrades! Yank 'ere is right. 'E says this 'ere stinkin' ship is our 'ome.

—and I'm thinking 'tis only slaves do be giving heed to the day that's gone or the day to come—

Everyting else dat makes de woild move, somep'n makes it move. It can't move witout somep'n else, see?

SUGGESTED ACTIVITIES

1. The concept of a code can be clarified by considering specific codes. Investigate the development of the Morse code, explaining its separate and discrete parts and how they work together. What code do sailors use when they signal with flags? What meaning do train whistles have?
2. Review the steps in the decoding process and note that they reverse the order of the encoding process. Ordinarily we seem to decode the phonology, grammar, and meaning of a message almost simultaneously. But when a listener obtains a different message from the one transmitted, it becomes more apparent that phonology comes first and meaning last. What were the probable messages transmitted for these messages received?

    Bells on cocktail ring.

    And a cartridge in a bare tree (from *The Family Circus* by Bill Keane).

    One naked individual and just for all.

    Listen for other examples of faulty decoding and share them with your classmates.
3. Poets are especially aware of the complicated processes of encoding and decoding a message and often experiment with established features of the code. What adaptations in the code does E. E. Cummings make to convey his message in a poem such as "In Just—"?
4. The semantic slots in a language represent the way a culture divides the world of perception. For example, what are the basic colors we see? Do all cultures see the world in the same colors as we do? Anthropology books will give you some interesting data, which you can summarize in a paper or speech.
5. Moulton says that *how* a person delivers a message also reveals something. Gestures, facial expressions, and tone of voice help us to decode a message. Write a paragraph of description in which you begin with a statement made by a character you have invented for a story. Then describe the way the statement was made so that your reader understands what kind of person is talking.

4
THE PRINCIPLES OF NEWSPEAK
George Orwell

In Miss Keller's autobiographical account we sense how language freed her to function as a human being and as an individual. George Orwell in *1984* also acknowledges the power of language when he describes Newspeak, the controlled language which inhibits personal freedom by making possible only one mode of thought. Orwell (1903–50), a British satirist who hated all forms of totalitarianism, expressed his contempt with some humor in *Animal Farm* (1946) and with bitterness in *1984* (1949).

In the appendix to *1984*, Orwell describes the principles of Newspeak, which was especially devised to meet the ideological needs of English Socialism, the government of Big Brother. Orwell is concerned here not with the role of language in organizing the sensory world of experience but with its capacity to establish values and loyalties.

Other writers have made attempts to develop artificial languages, some seriously, others in fun. All have utilized their knowledge of the way natural languages structure and have simply patterned variations of a known language. Here Orwell suggests changes in the vocabulary and grammar of English to diminish the range of thought.

Orwell also raises some very interesting questions. Do different language codes have different influences on the thinking processes and so on human behavior? Or do different "life styles" or "world views" dictate the vocabulary and the grammar? Can anyone really decide to change a language?

Newspeak was the official language of Oceania and had been devised to meet the ideological needs of Ingsoc, or English Socialism. In the year 1984 there was not as yet anyone who used Newspeak as his sole means of

Source: *1984* (New York: Harcourt, Brace & World, Inc., 1949), pp. 131–37. Copyright 1949 by Harcourt, Brace & World, Inc. Reprinted by permission of Brandt & Brandt.

communication, either in speech or writing. The leading articles in the *Times* were written in it, but this was a tour de force which could only be carried out by a specialist. It was expected that Newspeak would have finally superseded Oldspeak (or Standard English, as we should call it) by about the year 2050. Meanwhile it gained ground steadily, all Party members tending to use Newspeak words and grammatical constructions more and more in their everyday speech. The version in use in 1984, and embodied in the Ninth and Tenth Editions of the Newspeak dictionary, was a provisional one, and contained many superfluous words and archaic formations which were due to be suppressed later. It is with the final, perfected version, as embodied in the Eleventh Edition of the dictionary, that we are concerned here.

The purpose of Newspeak was not only to provide a medium of expression for the world-view and mental habits proper to the devotees of Ingsoc, but to make all other modes of thought impossible. It was intended that when Newspeak had been adopted once and for all and Oldspeak forgotten, a heretical thought—that is, a thought diverging from the principles of Ingsoc—should be literally unthinkable, at least so far as thought is dependent on words. Its vocabulary was so constructed as to give exact and often very subtle expression to every meaning that a Party member could properly wish to express, while excluding all other meanings and also the possibility of arriving at them by indirect methods. This was done partly by the invention of new words, but chiefly by eliminating undesirable words and by stripping such words as remained of unorthodox meanings, and so far as possible of all secondary meanings whatever. To give a simple example. The word *free* still existed in Newspeak, but it could only be used in such statements as "This dog is free from lice" or "This field is free from weeds." It could not be used in its old sense of "politically free" or "intellectually free," since political and intellectual freedom no longer existed even as concepts, and were therefore of necessity nameless. Quite apart from the suppression of definitely heretical words, reduction of vocabulary was regarded as an end in itself, and no word that could be dispensed with was allowed to survive. Newspeak was designated not to extend but to *diminish* the range of thought, and this purpose was indirectly assisted by cutting the choice of words down to a minimum.

Newspeak was founded on the English language as we now know it, though many Newspeak sentences, even when not containing newly created words, would be barely intelligible to an English-speaker of our own day. Newspeak words were divided into three distinct classes, known as the A vocabulary, the B vocabulary (also called compound words), and the C vocabulary. It will be simpler to discuss each class separately, but the grammatical peculiarities of the language can be dealt with in the section devoted to the A vocabulary, since the same rules held good for all three categories.

THE A VOCABULARY

The A vocabulary consisted of the words needed for the business of everyday life—for such things as eating, drinking, working, putting on one's clothes, going up and down stairs, riding in vehicles, gardening, cooking, and the like. It was composed almost entirely of words that we already possess—words like *hit, run, dog, tree, sugar, house, field*—but in comparison with the present-day English vocabulary, their number was extremely small, while their meanings were far more rigidly defined. All ambiguities and shades of meaning had been purged out of them. So far as it could be achieved, a Newspeak word of this class was simply a staccato sound expressing *one* clearly understood concept. It would have been quite impossible to use the A vocabulary for literary purposes or for political or philosophical discussion. It was intended only to express simple, purposive thoughts, usually involving concrete objects or physical actions.

The grammar of Newspeak had two outstanding peculiarities. The first of these was an almost complete interchangeability between different parts of speech. Any word in the language (in principle this applied even to very abstract words such as *if* or *when*) could be used either as verb, noun, adjective, or adverb. Between the verb and the noun form, when they were of the same root, there was never any variation, this rule of itself involving the destruction of many archaic forms. The word *thought*, for example, did not exist in Newspeak. Its place was taken by *think*, which did duty for both noun and verb. No etymological principle was followed here; in some cases it was the original noun that was chosen for retention, in other cases the verb. Even where a noun and verb of kindred meaning were not etymologically connected, one or other of them was frequently suppressed. There was, for example, no such word as *cut*, its meaning being sufficiently covered by the noun-verb *knife*. Adjectives were formed by adding the suffix *-ful* to the noun-verb, and adverbs by adding *-wise*. Thus, for example, *speedful* meant "rapid" and *speedwise* meant "quickly." Certain of our present-day adjectives, such as *good, strong, big, black, soft*, were retained, but their total number was very small. There was little need for them, since almost any adjectival meaning could be arrived at by adding *-ful* to a noun-verb. None of the now-existing adverbs was retained, except for a very few already ending in *-wise*; the *-wise* termination was invariable. The word *well*, for example, was replaced by *goodwise*.

In addition, any word—this again applied in principle to every word in the language—could be negatived by adding the affix *un-*, or could be strengthened by the affix *plus-*, or, for still greater emphasis, *doubleplus-*. Thus, for example, *uncold* meant "warm," while *pluscold* and *doublepluscold* meant, respectively, "very cold" and "superlatively cold." It was also possible, as in present-day English, to modify the meaning of almost any word by prepositional affixes such as *ante-, post-, up-, down-*, etc. By such methods it was found possible to bring about an enormous diminution of vocabulary. Given, for instance, the word *good*, there was no need for such a word as *bad*, since the required meaning was equally well—indeed, better— expressed by *ungood*. All that was necessary, in any case where two words formed a natural pair of opposites, was to decide which of them to suppress. *Dark*, for example, could be replaced by *unlight*, or *light* by *undark*, according to preference.

The second distinguishing mark of Newspeak grammar was its regularity. Subject to a few exceptions which are mentioned below, all inflections followed the same rules. Thus, in all verbs the preterite and the past participle were the same and ended in *-ed*. The preterite of *steal* was *stealed*, the preterite of *think* was *thinked*, and so on throughout the language, all such forms as *swam, gave, brought, spoke, taken*, etc., being abolished. All plurals were made by adding *-s* or *-es* as the case might be. The plurals of *man, ox, life* were *mans, oxes, lifes*. Comparison of adjectives was invariably made by adding *-er, -est* (*good, gooder, goodest*), irregular forms and the *more, most* formation being suppressed.

The only classes of words that were still allowed to inflect irregularly were the pronouns, the relatives, the demonstrative adjectives, and the auxiliary verbs. All of these followed their ancient usage, except that *whom* had been scrapped as unnecessary, and the *shall, should* tenses had been dropped, all their uses being covered by *will* and *would*. There were also certain irregularities in word-forming arising out of the need for rapid and easy speech. A word which was difficult to utter, or was liable to be incorrectly heard, was held to be ipso facto a bad word; occasionally therefore, for the sake of euphony, extra letters were inserted into a word or an archaic formation was retained. But this need made itself felt chiefly in connection with the B vocabulary. *Why* so great an importance was attached to ease of pronunciation will be made clear later in this essay.

THE B VOCABULARY

The B vocabulary consisted of words which had been deliberately constructed for political purposes: words, that is to say, which not only had in every case a political implication, but were intended to impose a desirable mental attitude upon the person using them. Without a full understanding of the principles of Ingsoc it was difficult to use these words correctly. In some cases they could be translated into Oldspeak, or even into words taken from the A vocabulary, but this usually demanded a long paraphrase and always involved the loss of certain overtones. The B words were a sort of verbal shorthand, often packing whole ranges of ideas into a few syllables, and at the same time more accurate and forcible than ordinary language.

The B words were in all cases compound words.* They consisted of two

---

* Compound words, such as *speakwrite*, were of course to be found in the A vocabulary, but these were merely convenient abbreviations and had no special ideological color.

or more words, or portions of words, welded together in an easily pronounceable form. The resulting amalgam was always a noun-verb, and inflected according to the ordinary rules. To take a single example: the word *goodthink*, meaning, very roughly, "orthodoxy," or, if one chose to regard it as a verb, "to think in an orthodox manner." This inflected as follows: noun-verb, *goodthink*; past tense and past participle, *goodthinked*; present participle, *goodthinking*; adjective, *goodthinkful*; adverb, *goodthinkwise*; verbal noun, *goodthinker*.

The B words were not constructed on any etymological plan. The words of which they were made up could be any parts of speech, and could be placed in any order and mutilated in any way which made them easy to pronounce while indicating their derivation. In the word *crimethink* (thoughtcrime), for instance, the *think* came second, whereas in *thinkpol* (Thought Police) it came first, and in the latter word *police* had lost its second syllable. Because of the greater difficulty in securing euphony, irregular formations were commoner in the B vocabulary than in the A vocabulary. For example, the adjectival forms of *Minitrue, Minipax,* and *Miniluv* were, respectively, *Minitruthful, Minipeaceful,* and *Minilovely,* simply because *-trueful, -paxful,* and *-loveful* were slightly awkward to pronounce. In principle, however, all B words could inflect, and all inflected in exactly the same way.

Some of the B words had highly subtilized meanings, barely intelligible to anyone who had not mastered the language as a whole. Consider, for example, such a typical sentence from a *Times* leading article as *Oldthinkers unbellyfeel Ingsoc*. The shortest rendering that one could make of this in Oldspeak would be: "Those whose ideas were formed before the Revolution cannot have a full emotional understanding of the principles of English Socialism." But this is not an adequate translation. To begin with, in order to grasp the full meaning of the Newspeak sentence quoted above, one would have to have a clear idea of what is meant by *Ingsoc*. And, in addition, only a person thoroughly grounded in Ingsoc could appreciate the full force of the word *bellyfeel*, which implied a blind, enthusiastic acceptance difficult to imagine today; or of the word *oldthink*, which was inextricably mixed up with the idea of wickedness and decadence. But the special function of certain Newspeak words, of which *oldthink* was one, was not so much to express meanings as to destroy them. These words, necessarily few in number, had had their meanings extended until they contained within themselves whole batteries of words which, as they were sufficiently covered by a single comprehensive term, could now be scrapped and forgotten. The greatest difficulty facing the compilers of the Newspeak dictionary was not to invent new words, but, having invented them, to make sure what they meant: to make sure, that is to say, what ranges of words they canceled by their existence.

As we have already seen in the case of the word *free*, words which had once borne a heretical meaning were sometimes retained for the sake of convenience, but only with the undesirable meanings purged out of them.

Countless other words such as *honor, justice, morality, internationalism, democracy, science,* and *religion* had simply ceased to exist. A few blanket words covered them, and, in covering them, abolished them. All words grouping themselves round the concepts of liberty and equality, for instance, were contained in the single word *crimethink*, while all words grouping themselves round the concepts of objectivity and rationalism were contained in the single word *oldthink*. Greater precision would have been dangerous. What was required in a Party member was an outlook similar to that of the ancient Hebrew who knew, without knowing much else, that all nations other than his own worshiped "false gods." He did not need to know that these gods were called Baal, Osiris, Moloch, Ashtaroth, and the like; probably the less he knew about them the better for his orthodoxy. He knew Jehovah and the commandments of Jehovah; he knew, therefore, that all gods with other names or other attributes were false gods. In somewhat the same way, the Party member knew what constituted right conduct, and in exceedingly vague, generalized terms he knew what kinds of departure from it were possible. His sexual life, for example, was entirely regulated by the two Newspeak words *sexcrime* (sexual immorality) and *goodsex* (chastity). *Sexcrime* covered all sexual misdeeds whatever. It covered fornication, adultery, homosexuality, and other perversions, and, in addition, normal intercourse practiced for its own sake. There was no need to enumerate them separately, since they were all equally culpable, and, in principle, all punishable by death. In the C vocabulary, which consisted of scientific and technical words, it might be necessary to give specialized names to certain sexual aberrations, but the ordinary citizen had no need of them. He knew what was meant by *goodsex*—that is to say, normal intercourse between man and wife, for the sole purpose of begetting children, and without physical pleasure on the part of the woman; all else was *sexcrime*. In Newspeak it was seldom possible to follow a heretical thought further than the perception that it *was* heretical; beyond that point the necessary words were nonexistent.

No word in the B vocabulary was ideologically neutral. A great many were euphemisms. Such words, for instance, as *joycamp* (forced-labor camp) or *Minipax* (Ministry of Peace, i.e., Ministry of War) meant almost the exact opposite of what they appeared to mean. Some words, on the other hand, displayed a frank and contemptuous understanding of the real nature of Oceanic society. An example was *prolefeed*, meaning the rubbishy entertainment and spurious news which the Party handed out to the masses. Other words, again, were ambivalent, having the connotation "good" when applied to the Party and "bad" when applied to its enemies. But in addition there were great numbers of words which at first sight appeared to be mere abbreviations and which derived their ideological color not from their meaning but from their structure.

So far as it could be contrived, everything that had or might have political significance of any kind was fitted into the B vocabulary. The name of every organization, or body of people, or doctrine, or country, or institution, or public building, was invariably cut down into the familiar shape; that is, a single easily pronounced word with the smallest number of syllables that would preserve the original derivation. In the Ministry of Truth, for example, the Records Department, in which Winston Smith worked, was called *Recdep*, the Fiction Department was called *Ficdep*, the Teleprograms Department was called *Teledep*, and so on. This was not done solely with the object of saving time. Even in the early decades of the twentieth century, telescoped words and phrases had been one of the characteristic features of political language; and it had been noticed that the tendency to use abbreviations of this kind was most marked in totalitarian countries and totalitarian organizations. Examples were such words as *Nazi, Gestapo, Comintern, Inprecorr, Agitprop*. In the beginning the practice had been adopted as it were instinctively, but in Newspeak it was used with a conscious purpose. It was perceived that in thus abbreviating a name one narrowed and subtly altered its meaning, by cutting out most of the associations that would otherwise cling to it. The words *Communist International*, for instance, call up a composite picture of universal human brotherhood, red flags, barricades, Karl Marx, and the Paris Commune. The word Comintern, on the other hand, suggests merely a tightly knit organization and a well-defined body of doctrine. It refers to something almost as easily recognized, and as limited in purpose, as a chair or a table. *Comintern* is a word that can be uttered almost without taking thought, whereas *Communist International* is a phrase over which one is obliged to linger at least momentarily. In the same way, the associations called up by a word like *Minitrue* are fewer and more controllable than those called up by *Ministry of Truth*. This accounted not only for the habit of abbreviating whenever possible, but also for the almost exaggerated care that was taken to make every word easily pronounceable.

In Newspeak, euphony outweighed every consideration other than exactitude of meaning. Regularity of grammar was always sacrificed to it when it seemed necessary. And rightly so, since what was required, above all for political purposes, were short clipped words of unmistakable meaning which could be uttered rapidly and which roused the minimum of echoes in the speaker's mind. The words of the B vocabulary even gained in force from the fact that nearly all of them were very much alike. Almost invariably these words—*goodthink, Minipax, prolefeed, sexcrime, joycamp, Ingsoc, bellyfeel, thinkpol*, and countless others—were words of two or three syllables, with the stress distributed equally between the first syllable and the last. The use of them encouraged a gabbling style of speech, at once staccato and monotonous. And this was exactly what was aimed at. The intention was to make speech, and especially speech on any subject not ideologically neutral, as nearly as possible independent of consciousness. For the purposes of everyday life it was no doubt necessary, or sometimes necessary, to reflect before speaking, but a Party member called upon to make a political or ethical judgment should be able to spray forth the correct opinions as automatically as a machine gun spraying forth bullets. His training fitted him to do this, the language gave him an almost foolproof instrument, and the texture of the words, with their harsh sound and a certain willful ugliness which was in accord with the spirit of Ingsoc, assisted the process still further.

So did the fact of having very few words to choose from. Relative to our own, the Newspeak vocabulary was tiny, and new ways of reducing it were constantly being devised. Newspeak, indeed, differed from almost all other languages in that its vocabulary grew smaller instead of larger every year. Each reduction was a gain, since the smaller the area of choice, the smaller the temptation to take thought. Ultimately it was hoped to make articulate speech issue from the larynx without involving the higher brain centers at all. This aim was frankly admitted in the Newspeak word *duckspeak,* meaning "to quack like a duck." Like various other words in the B vocabulary, *duckspeak* was ambivalent in meaning. Provided that the opinions which were quacked out were orthodox ones, it implied nothing but praise, and when the *Times* referred to one of the orators of the Party as a *doubleplusgood duckspeaker* it was paying a warm and valued compliment.

THE C VOCABULARY

The C vocabulary was supplementary to the others and consisted entirely of scientific and technical terms. These resembled the scientific terms in use today, and were constructed from the same roots, but the usual care was taken to define them rigidly and strip them of undesirable meanings. They followed the same grammatical rules as the words in the other two vocabularies. Very few of the C words had any currency either in everyday speech or in political speech. Any scientific worker or technician could find all the words he needed in the list devoted to his own specialty, but he seldom had more than a smattering of the words occurring in the other lists. Only a very few words were common to all lists, and there was no vocabulary expressing the function of Science as a habit of mind, or a method of thought, irrespective of its particular branches. There was, indeed, no word for "Science," any meaning that it could possibly bear being already sufficiently covered by the word *Ingsoc.*

QUESTIONS FOR STUDY AND DISCUSSION

1. In describing the A vocabulary, Orwell says that all ambiguities and shades of meaning have been eliminated. Does Modern English admit any ambiguity or "double" meaning for these words: *hit, run, can*?
2. Do you see any advantage to having the parts of speech interchangeable? What grammatical signals does Modern English have to indicate the part of speech, or form class, of the following words: *walk, stand, talk, feature*?

3. Students of English have complained for a long time about irregularities in the inflectional system. (An inflection is a change in the formation of a word to indicate a change in grammatical meaning, like singular to plural number for nouns and present to past tense for verbs.) Do you approve of the second distinguishing mark of Newspeak grammar, the regularity of its inflectional system?
4. Words in the B vocabulary are all amalgams, or blends. Do we use this kind of word formation in Modern English? Examine these words: *radar, noncom, astronaut, spacecraft, phys. ed.*
5. Why did such words as *honor, truth, love, beauty* cease to exist in Newspeak?
6. Would we consider Newspeak a euphonious language if compared, for example, with the language of Edgar Allan Poe's "The Raven"? What criteria do we use for judging language harsh or euphonious?

SUGGESTED ACTIVITIES

1. Translate the following sentences into Newspeak, following the principles of the vocabulary and grammar outlined on page 34 and page 35.

   a. The men ran quickly.

   b. The children swam very well.

   c. The government was thought to be better than before.

2. The method of forming adverbs in Newspeak has recently been widely used in English to form new adverbs. Name some of them and form others of your own.
3. The ambiguity in language which Orwell describes may be considered lexical; that is, a word may refer to any of several things or ideas. Another kind of ambiguity may be called structural, resulting from the arrangement of the words into structural units. Analyze the ambiguity in these sentences:

   a. Norwegian teachers visited Little Norway in Wisconsin.

   b. Give us more specific details.

   c. I am planning to take courses in Greek mythology, literature, and history.

   d. I was describing the paintings I had seen in the gallery.

   e. The flight attendant welcomed the man with a smile.

   Would any of the principles of Newspeak eliminate any of these ambiguities?

4. Modern English, like Newspeak, telescopes long titles. A more common practice than blending seems to be the shortening into acronyms, abbreviations that form pronounceable words. What do these acronyms stand for: COPE, CARE, CORE, UNICEF, WAVE, WAC? Add to this list.
5. In his three-volume work, *The Lord of the Rings*, J. R. R. Tolkien creates a language called Westron, or Common Speech, for his characters, the Hobbits, the inhabitants of Middle-earth. If you study this language, you will discover that Tolkien begins with sounds. Those who enjoy adult fairy stories will find the world and the language of the Hobbits fascinating. A summary of the principles of Westron occurs in the Appendix of the volume entitled *The Return of the King*. Some of you may want to investigate Westron and report on its features.
6. In an essay, "Politics and the English Language," Orwell characterizes the language of politics with its dying metaphors ("no axe to grind"), its padded phrases ("exhibit a tendency to"), its pretentious diction ("epoch-making"), and its meaningless words (generalizations like "socialism"). Although Orwell made his observations over twenty years ago, this tendency toward "over-writing" seems to be increasing. Analyze a political statement, looking for some of the characteristics listed above. Summarize what you find.
7. American history is studded with slogans containing words canceled by Newspeak: "Give me liberty or give me death!"; "First in war, first in peace, and first in the hearts of his countrymen"; "With malice toward none, with charity for all . . . "; "Make the world safe for democracy." How are these and other slogans used by modern politicians? Why would such slogans be impossible in Newspeak?
8. The four selections you have read in this section should have enlarged your understanding of the nature of language. Record the letter of each of the following statements that you accept:

   a. All languages are systems of human conventions, not systems of natural laws.
   b. Imitation of animal cries accounts for a large part of language.
   c. Language is primarily a system of writing.
   d. Each language has unique features of sounds, grammar, and vocabulary.
   e. Some languages are more difficult for children as native speakers to learn than other languages.
   f. It is possible for a word to refer to more than one thing.
   g. The normal child of five, who speaks his native language intuitively, necessarily uses the grammar of that language.

- h. Certain animals, such as dolphins, and certain birds, such as parakeets, have a language.
- i. Communication through language represents complex processes of encoding and decoding messages involving patterns of sounds, grammatical structures, and meanings.
- j. The ears, the so-called speech organs, and the brain are all vitally involved in the learning and production of language.
- k. It is possible for language to exert influences upon the culture which initially produced it.

After you have compared your responses with those of your teacher and classmates, try out these statements on several people who have not thought objectively about the nature of language. Then write a paper entitled "The Notions Some People Have about Language."

Part Two

THE HISTORICAL BACKGROUND OF THE ENGLISH LANGUAGE

5
DEVELOPMENT OF THE LANGUAGE
L. M. Myers

Languages have been identified as members of a particular family by certain relationships in sounds and in grammatical structures and by a common stock of native words. As a member of the Indo-European family of languages, English is related to most of the languages of Europe and to Persian and Sanskrit, an ancient language of India. As a member of the Germanic subgroup of the Indo-European family, English is even more closely related to the modern Scandinavian languages. But its closest relatives are the still smaller group of West Germanic languages—German, especially Low German, spoken in northern Germany; Frisian, spoken in northern Holland; and Dutch.

The English language did not originate in Britain. It was carried to the island in the fifth century by the Anglo-Saxon invaders, who spoke several West Germanic dialects. There it underwent the influence of more invaders, and later was brought to America by the colonists.

It is this historical background of the language that L. M. Myers, emeritus professor of English at Arizona State University, presents.

If you looked at the French and Italian words for *hundred*—*cent* and *cento* respectively—you would easily guess that they are related, and they are. They both developed from the Latin word *centum*. And if you looked at the German word *hundert* you could recognize it as a close relative of the English word. You would be right again, but you could not prove it quite so easily, because we do not have any written records of the early form of Germanic from which modern English and German developed. We have to prove the relationship by other methods which are too complicated to go into here.

You would probably not guess that *hundred* and *centum* are also related; but

---

Source: *Guide to American English*, 3d ed. (Englewood Cliffs, N.J.: Prentice-Hall, 1963), pp. 11–17, 20–21. Copyright © 1963 by Prentice-Hall. Reprinted by permission of Prentice-Hall, Inc., Englewood Cliffs, New Jersey, and the author.

if you happened to think of these two words along with *horn* and *corno, house* and *casa*, and various other pairs that begin with *h* in English and *c* in Italian, you might suspect that these resemblances were systematic, and that English is also related to Italian, although not nearly as closely as French is. Your suspicions would be justified. Experts can trace the relations among all four of these languages and a good many others. We can say roughly that French and Italian are sister languages, both born of Latin; that English and modern German are approximately second cousins; and that English and Italian are something like third cousins twice removed.

Nobody knows for sure how language began, or even whether it began just once or at a number of different times and places. What we do know is that some languages, as we have just seen, show evidence of a common origin, while others do not. If our written records went back a few thousand years further it is possible that we might find signs of resemblance between the languages that we have just mentioned and Chinese or Arabic or Navajo. But if such resemblances ever existed, they disappeared a long time ago, and it seems most unlikely that we will ever find any evidence to prove them. We must therefore study them as separate families, though they may have had a common ancestor about which we now know nothing.

ORIGIN OF ENGLISH

English belongs, in a rather complicated way, to the Indo-European family, which includes most of the European languages and a few Asiatic ones. We do not know where the original speakers of the parent Indo-European language lived. Guesses about their homeland range all the way from northwestern Europe to central Asia. According to all the early records they were a tall, blond, and warlike people, with a good deal of energy and intelligence. In their native land they had developed neither writing nor cities, so there is not much evidence about how they lived when they were at home. But when they left home and went out in search of new lands—which they did in various waves from about 2500 B.C. to about 1000 B.C.—the Indo-Europeans seem to have been generally successful in conquering the countries they came to.

When a wave of them settled in a territory already crowded, they mixed with the original population. In time they lost their distinctive appearance by intermarrying with the earlier inhabitants, and sometimes they also gave up most of the features of their language. When a wave went to a more thinly settled territory, they naturally preserved their physical characteristics comparatively unchanged for a much longer time; and they were likely to preserve the distinctive features of their language also, though the two things did not always go together.

The Slavic and Celtic languages, as well as Indian, Persian, and some others, are of Indo-European origin, but the three branches with which English is most concerned are the Greek, Latin, and Germanic, particularly the last. All languages are changing to some extent all the time; and before the invention of writing they seem to have changed faster. Since the various waves left at different times, they were speaking noticeably different varieties of Indo-European at the times of their departures; and the further changes that took place after they left made their languages more and more unlike. As they split up and settled (more or less) in different regions, the differences became so great that the Greeks, for instance, could not possibly understand the Germans; and a little later some of the Germans could not understand the others.

Old Germanic split into North, East, and West Germanic. West Germanic split into High and Low German. And Low German split into further dialects, including those of the Angles, Saxons, and Jutes. There were differences in pronunciation, and even in word endings, among these last three; but most of the root words were enough alike to be recognizable, and the three tribes seem to have had no great difficulty in understanding each other. About 450 A.D. members of all three tribes moved into what is now called England (from Angle-land), and began to take it over. It is at this time that we usually say the English language, as such, began.

It is worth noticing that even at the very beginning of English as a separate language there was no one simple standard. The Jutes undoubtedly thought that the Angles "talked funny," and vice versa. Efforts have been made for centuries to develop a set of standard practices, and there is much to be said in their favor; but they have never been quite successful, and they never will be. There is just no way to make millions of people talk exactly alike.

These early English settlers do not seem to have made much of an effort to understand the language of the Britons who lived in England (then called Britain) before they came. The Britons also spoke an Indo-European language, but it belonged to the Celtic rather than the Germanic branch, and was by now completely unrecognizable to the newcomers. The English added only a handful of Celtic words to their language—not nearly as many as the Americans later picked up from the Indians.

We can only guess about how the language would have developed if the descendants of these three tribes had been left to themselves. The fact is that two great invasions and a missionary movement changed the language enormously. The total result of these and other influences was that the English vocabulary became the largest and most complex in the world, and the grammar changed its emphasis from inflections (changes in the forms of words) to word order.

THE SCANDINAVIAN INFLUENCE

Some three hundred years after the West Germanic tribes had settled in England, there was another wave of invasions, this time by Scandinavians. In the history books these people are usually referred to as "Danes," but there were Swedes and Norwegians among them, and their speech was probably no more uniform than that of the first wave. The dialects they spoke belonged to the Northern rather than the Western division of Germanic. They differed rather more from the dialects of the Angles, Saxons, and Jutes than these differed from each other—roughly, about as much as Spanish differs from Italian. In spite of different habits of pronunciation, most of the root words were enough alike to be recognizable. The difficulty caused by differences in inflection was partly solved by dropping some of the inflections altogether and being broad-minded about the others. Spelling was not much of a problem, because most people could not read or write, and those who could, spelled as they pleased. There were no dictionaries to prove them wrong.

Although these Danes moved in on the English, and for a time dominated them politically, their conquest was nothing like as thorough as that of the English over the Britons. After the early fighting the two peoples settled down together without much attention to their separate origins, and the languages mingled. On the whole, English rather than Danish characteristics won out; but many of the words were so much alike that it is impossible to say whether we owe our present forms to English or Danish origins, and occasionally the Danish forms drove out the English ones. Sometimes both forms remained, usually with a somewhat different meaning. Thus we have *shirt* and *skirt*, both of which originally meant a long, smock-like garment, although the English form has come to mean the upper part, and the Danish form the lower. Old English *rear* and Danish *raise* are another pair—sometimes interchangeable, sometimes not.

THE NORMAN CONQUEST

In 1066 the Normans conquered England. They, like the Danes, had originally come from Scandinavia. But they had settled in northern France, and for some undiscoverable reason had given up their own language and learned to speak a dialect of French. For several centuries Normans, and other Frenchmen that they invited in later, held most of the important positions in England, and it seemed quite possible that French would become the standard language of the country. But the bulk of the population were still English, and they were stubborner than their rulers. Most of them never learned French, and eventually—though only after several centuries—all the nobles and officials were using English.

It was not, however, the English of the days before the conquest. A good many French words had gotten into the language; and most of the inflections that had survived the Danish pressure had dropped out, with a standard word-order making up for their loss. We need not go into the argument about whether the new word-order had to develop because the endings dropped out, or the endings disappeared because the new word-order made them unnecessary. The two changes took place together, and by the time of Chaucer (died 1400) the language had become enough like modern English to be recognizable. The pronunciation was quite different and the spelling was still catch-as-catch-can; but a modern student can get at least a general idea of Chaucer's meaning without special training, while he can no more read Old English than he can German or Latin, unless he has made a special study of it. Compare the two following passages:

1. *Hwaet! We gardena   in geardagum*
   Theodcyningas   thrym gefrunon

2. *Whan that Aprille with his shoures soote*
   The droghte of March hath perced to the roote

In the first two lines from *Beowulf* (about 700 A.D.), only *we* and *in* are readily recognizable; while in the first two from Chaucer's *Canterbury Tales*, only *soote* (sweet) offers much of a problem.

From Chaucer's time to our own the language has developed with no outside pressure comparable to that of the Danish and Norman invasions. Still more endings have disappeared, and there have been other changes; but the greatest development has been in the vocabulary. A considerable number of Chaucer's words have dropped out of use, and a much greater number of new words have been added. Some of these new words have been made by compounding or otherwise modifying old ones, but most of them have been borrowed from other languages, particularly Latin.

THE LATIN INFLUENCE

Even before they came to England our ancestors had picked up a few Latin words; and they learned others from the Christian missionaries who began to convert them in the sixth century. These early borrowings were taken directly into the spoken language, and most of them have now changed so that their Latin origins are not easy to recognize. *Street, wine, bishop, priest,* and *church* (the last three originally borrowed from Greek by the Romans) are examples.

After the Norman Conquest borrowings from Latin were enormously increased. French itself is directly descended from Latin, and we cannot always tell whether an English word came directly from Latin or through French. *Suspicion,* for instance, could have come into English by either route. But we do know that many words must have come straight from Latin, either because they don't occur in French or because their French forms are different. Scholars often could not find an English word for an idea they wished to express; and even if they could, they might think that a Latin word was more exact or more impressive.

English has also borrowed words from many other languages, particularly Greek, and is continuing to do so at present; but ever since the late Middle English period it has been a matter of helping ourselves, rather than yielding to pressure.

DEVELOPMENT OF A LITERARY STANDARD

The changes that took place in the language throughout the Old and Middle English periods were a natural development, unguided by any theory. Men talked more or less as their neighbors did, and anybody who wrote tried to indicate the sound of his speech on paper. There were no dictionaries, no grammars, and no printed books of any kind. As far as we know, very few people thought about the language at all; and most of those who did think about it seem to have considered it a crude and rather hopeless affair, unworthy of serious study. There were exceptions, of course, but they did not have much influence. Local differences were so great that a man trained in northern England would have serious difficulty reading a manuscript written in the southern part. However, the dialect of London had a certain prestige throughout the country; and although this dialect itself was by no means uniform, and changed with shifts in city population, it gradually came to be accepted as the standard. By the latter half of the fifteenth century it was quite generally used in writing throughout the country except in the extreme north. The introduction of printing in 1476, with London as the publishing center, greatly strengthened the influence of the London dialect. Strong local differences in spoken English remain to this day, especially among the less educated classes. But throughout the modern period written (or at least published) English has been surprisingly uniform.

. . . . .

AMERICAN ENGLISH

In the early part of the seventeenth century English settlers began to bring their language to America, and another series of changes began to take place. The settlers borrowed words from Indian languages for such strange trees as the hickory and persimmon, such unfamiliar animals as raccoons and woodchucks. Later they borrowed other words from settlers from other countries—for instance, *chowder* and *prairie* from the French, *scow* and *sleigh* from the Dutch. They made new combinations of English words, such as *backwoods* and *bullfrog*, or gave old English words entirely new meanings, such as *lumber* (which in British English means approximately *junk*) and *corn* (which in British means any grain, especially wheat). Some of the new terms were needed, because there were new and un-English things to talk about. Others can be explained only on the general theory that languages are always changing, and American English is no exception.

Aside from the new vocabulary, differences in pronunciation, in grammatical construction, and especially in intonation developed. If the colonization had taken place a few centuries earlier, American might have become as different from English as French is from Italian. But the settlement occurred after the invention of printing, and continued through a period when the idea of educating everybody was making rapid progress. For a long time most of the books read in America came from England, and a surprising number of Americans read those books, in or out of school. Moreover, most of the colonists seem to have felt strong ties with England. In this they were unlike their Anglo-Saxon ancestors, who apparently made a clean break with their continental homes.

A good many Englishmen and some Americans used to condemn every difference that did develop, and as recently as a generation ago it was not unusual to hear all "Americanisms" condemned, even in America. It is now generally recognized in this country that we are not bound to the Queen's English, but have a full right to work out our own habits. Even a good many of the English now concede this, though some of them object strongly to the fact that Americanisms are now having an influence on British usage.

There are thousands of differences in detail between British and American English, and occasionally they crowd together enough to make some difficulty. If you read that a man, having trouble with his *lorry*, got out his *spanner* and lifted the *bonnet* to see what was the matter, you might not realize that the driver of the *truck* had taken out his *wrench* and lifted the *hood*. It is amusing to play with such differences, but the theory that the American language is now essentially different from English does not hold up. It is often very difficult to decide whether a book was written by an American or an Englishman. Even in speech it would be hard to prove that national differences are greater than some local differences in either country. On the whole, it now seems probable that the language habits of the two countries will grow more, rather than less, alike, although some differences will undoubtedly remain and others may develop.

It also seems probable that there will be narrow-minded and snobbish people in both countries for some time to come. But generally speaking, anybody who learns to speak and write the standard English of his own country, and to regard that of the other country as a legitimate variety with certain interesting differences, will have little trouble wherever he goes.

QUESTIONS FOR STUDY AND DISCUSSION

1. Do the events of English history suggest that English may have undergone greater changes than some other languages? If so, why? Confer with a foreign language teacher for further information.
2. If the Anglo-Saxons had not invaded England, what presumably would be the language of England today? If you want to hear this language spoken, where will you go? Will you find it in wide use?
3. a. Why did the dialect of London become Standard English? Was it intrinsically superior to other dialects? Myers lists two or three reasons for the ascendancy of the London dialect. From your knowledge of history and geography, can you think of others?

b. How does Myers's use of the term "dialect" differ from popular notions of the meaning of the word?
c. What is the source of standard French? of classical Latin? of classical Greek? What is the similarity between these sources and the source of Standard English?
4. Can the argument for a single standard of language correctness be justified on historical grounds?
5. How do you account for the fact that it is difficult to determine whether certain words in English are of Danish or English origin and not so difficult to determine whether words are of French or English origin?

SUGGESTED ACTIVITIES

1. One identification for members of the Indo-European family of languages is a common word stock—words that are similar in form and in meaning, although there is no evidence of borrowing. Such words are called *cognates*, meaning literally "born together." Study the similarities in the following cognates* and then write the corresponding English words.

Persian	*Sanskrit*	*Greek*	*Latin*	*Celtic*
thri	tri	treis	tres	tri
me	me	me	me	me
matar	matar	meter	mater	mathair
———	bhratar	phrater	frater	brathair

French	*Italian*	*Spanish*	*German*	*Dutch*
trois	tre	tres	drei	drie
me	mi	me	mich	mij
mere	madre	madre	mutter	moeder
frere	fratello	hermano	bruder	broeder

2. Certain place names reflect the language of the invader. For example, the Latin word *castra* (camp) appears in variant forms in many place names: *Winchester, Lancaster, Worcester*, etc. The suffix *-by* identifies more than 600 Scandinavian place names: *Rugby, Derby, Whitby*, etc. The *-by* suffix

---

* Many of these illustrations are from W. D. Whitney, *Language and the Study of Language* (New York: Charles Scribner's Sons, Inc., 1867), p. 196.

(from ON *byr*, town) contrasts with the English suffix *-ton* (from OE *tun*, town). Consult an atlas and add to the list of place names in the three groups. In what part of England do you find most Scandinavian place names? Why?
3. Check the derivation of the word *by-law*. Explain its relationship to the suffix on place names.

Note: In using a dictionary for the following activities, you will come upon these abbreviations: ON (Old Norse, ancient Scandinavian); Scand (Scandinavian); OF (Old French); MF (Middle French); Fr (French); L (Latin); OE (Old English); ME (Middle English). The symbol < means "derived from."

Old English represents a period from about 450 A.D., when the first Germanic tribes began to settle in England, until about 1100, following the Norman invasion; Middle English from about 1100 to about 1500; and Modern English from about 1500 to the present.
4. Divide the words in the following alphabetical list into two groups on the basis of differentiating sounds. What do you think is the national origin of the words in each group? Myers gives you a clue. Verify your hypothesis by checking the origin of a few words in a dictionary.

bush	score	sharp	ship	shut
dish	scot	shave	shoe	skate
fish	scrap	shear	shoot	skeet
hush	scrape	shed	shop	ski
mash	shade	sheep	short	skill
rush	shadow	sheet	shoulder	skin
scale	shaft	shell	shove	skoal
scalp	shag	shield	show	skulk
scant	shake	shift	shred	skull
scare	shale	shin	shriek	sky
scarf	share	shine	shrink	wish

5. Myers mentions *shirt* and *skirt* as a pair of words that entered the English language through different routes, although they had a common Germanic origin. Thus such word pairs, called *doublets*, at least at one time had the same meaning. Consult a standard dictionary to find out how five of the following doublets entered the language. (You will discover that some doublets resulted from a Norman French word borrowed during the Middle English period and a Parisian French word borrowed later.)

Example: shirt   ME *shirte*, from OE *scyrte*; akin to ON *skyrta*, shirt
            skirt   ME, from ON *skyrta*, shirt, kirtle

a. cattle	chattel
b. corpse	corps
c. blame	blaspheme
d. feast	fete
e. feeble	foible
f. frail	fragile
g. from	fro
h. faith	fidelity
i. no	nay
j. royal	regal
k. rear	raise
l. warden	guardian

6. Some of the following words are native English words, some came into English directly from Latin, others from French during the Old English or the Middle English periods. Classify the words according to the cultural areas which they represent. For example, *dinner* is a term pertaining to eating; *anthem* is a term pertaining to religion. Check a few words in each category in a standard dictionary to discover which words were borrowed from Latin, which from French, which are native.

    What can you conclude about the kinds of words each language contributed to English during these periods? What areas of life do the native words represent? Do you think there is any significance to the fact that these words were not replaced by borrowed words?

abbot	cloak	garment	napkin	soldier
alms	coat	general	navy	son
altar	council	government	parliament	sovereign
angel	court	gown	plate	supper
anthem	cousin	hymn	pope	swine
apparel	cow	judge	pork	table
armor	daughter	jury	priest	troops
army	dinner	king	psalm	uncle
aunt	disciple	lance	queen	veal
beef	dress	lieutenant	robe	veil
brother	enemy	minister	sergeant	
candle	father	mother	sister	
chancellor	fork	mutton	sheep	

Development of the Language **55**

7. Write a paragraph in which you summarize the areas of influence which the Norman French apparently had upon England as suggested by the French origins which you found for words listed in 6.
8. Chaucer describes the knight in *The Canterbury Tales* as one who loved

> ... chivalrye,
> Trouthe and honour, fredom and curteisye.

Which of these qualities of the knight do you think were basically English, which basically French? What is the reason for your opinion? Make an intelligent guess and then consult a standard dictionary for the origin of *chivalry, truth, honor, freedom,* and *courtesy.*
9. Ten of the following words are listed in *A Dictionary of Americanisms on Historical Principles.* On the basis of your general background, select the ten words which you think most likely to be Americanisms. As defined in this dictionary, *Americanisms* include (1) words or expressions that originated in the United States; (2) borrowed words which first became English in the United States; and (3) words used in senses first given them in the United States. Check your judgment by consulting a standard dictionary. Record the origin of each word.

barbecue	cafeteria	cavalry	law	rule
bayou	canyon	city	maverick	squash
blue law	caucus	fief	moccasin	toboggan

6
CHANGE IN LANGUAGE
Harold R. Hungerford

Myers discusses the external events that have affected the English language. Hungerford examines the language itself to reveal some of the important changes that have occurred since the Old English period. Though events may hasten language change, such change is not dependent upon happenings outside of the language; for all living languages change—not in a haphazard fashion, but in a systematic way. In the following essay the changes in the English language have a threefold classification: changes in sound, changes produced by analogy, and changes in vocabulary.

Harold R. Hungerford is professor of English at Illinois Wesleyan University.

Ye knowe ek that in forme of speche is chaunge
Withinne a thousand yeer, and wordes tho
That hadden pris, now wonder nyce and straunge
Us thinketh hem, and yet thei spake hem so
And spedde as wel in love as men now do;
Ek for to wynnen love in sondry ages,
In sondry londes, sondry ben usages.

This stanza from Chaucer's *Troilus and Criseyde*, written close to six hundred years ago, can help remind us of three facts about change in language. First, though modern sensibilities may sometimes find Chaucer's spellings, and the pronunciations they represent, "wonder nyce and straunge"—that is, remarkably foolish and odd—nevertheless men got through all their business of living talking so, and found nothing either foolish or odd about their speech. Their language was quite adequate to all the needs they felt,

---

Source: *The High School Journal* 49 (January 1966): pp. 173–78. Copyright © 1966 by the University of North Carolina Press. Reprinted by permission of the publisher and the author.

and contained all the necessary resources for adaptation to new needs. It had changed much already, and was to change much more, but no change in language is ever crippling. Second, wise men in all times have been aware that language changed, and most of them have also been aware that they themselves could do little or nothing about these changes. The wisest have also realized that there was nothing wrong with change itself. Third, a language is a good deal more than its written representation: Chaucer says "forme of *speche*" and probably would not have made the common error of assuming that written forms of language, because of the greater effort made to preserve them, are somehow more important than spoken forms. Actually, the reverse is true: men spoke long before they wrote, and change in language is change in speech which comes gradually to be reflected in written documents.

We are often less aware of changes in our language than, perhaps, we should be—mainly because the conventions of our spelling system were largely frozen when printing began in England five hundred years ago. As most of us have learned by bitter experience, modern English spelling is a far better guide to medieval than to modern English pronunciation. Thus the changes from Chaucer's spelling system to ours are on the whole trivial ones which hardly impede our ability to read the passage even without special training in Middle English. The similarity in spelling almost completely hides the drastic changes in pronunciation since Chaucer's day— and for that matter since Shakespeare's day, and Milton's and Pope's and even Wordsworth's. Sometimes we are reminded of these changes: a couplet of Pope's may fail to rhyme perfectly for us, or a Shakespearian pun may require a solemn footnote. And because the spelling of Shakespeare and Pope are almost invariably modernized for the busy modern reader, we forget easily that Shakespeare talked more like Chaucer than like us, and that he did not talk at all like a modern Shakespearian actor; we also forget that Pope spoke what would now resemble a comic Irish dialect.

So, both to understand the literature of the past aright and to understand something of the nature of the language which we help to shape and which in turn helps shape us, we should know something of the patterns and processes of linguistic change, and we may use Chaucer's stanza for evidence. What sorts of changes have there been in pronunciation? We can speak with any kind of certainty only about the vowels and consonants; on matters of intonation we are almost ignorant. But we can say, for instance, that Chaucer pronounced the *k* in *knowe*; that his pronunciation of the *th* in *that* was the kind we use in "thin"; and that the *e* of *speche* and the *au* of *chaunge* were pronounced like Modern English *a* in "spate" and *ou* in "house." And there are still other changes in this one line: the *f* of *of* and the *s* of *is* were pronounced as they were spelled—not with the *v* and *z* of Modern English.

These changes, so stated, may appear to be freakish—as though English had merely changed randomly, without direction. But for a century and a half now grammarians—or, to use the newer term, linguists—have sought for the principles of changes like these, and many of their efforts have been greeted with success. At least we can explain some of the hows of linguistic change, even if we are not sure of the whys. Changes in language are usually grouped under three main headings: sound-change, analogical change, and borrowing. Any change starts with one speaker—who is ordinarily quite unconscious that he is making a change—and gradually spreads to others until it is the dominant usage, at least in some given area. Because a natural language like English is a system, a change at one point is likely to bring about changes at other points as well, either to fill a gap in the sound-system or the vocabulary or to bring the language back, unconsciously, to a state of balance (or, to use Martin Joos's term, homeostasis).

What sorts of sound-change has English undergone since Chaucer's day? Three changes are most important: the loss of inflectional *n*, the voicing of voiceless sounds in weakly stressed syllables, and the Great Vowel Shift. In Chaucer, a final -*n* on verbs is regularly the sign of the infinitive (as in *wynnen*) or of a plural (*hadden*); but even in Chaucer's lifetime these *n*'s were being dropped in speech and writing. An infinitive could be recognized by the *to* before it, a plural verb by its plural subject; hence, no loss of meaningful distinctions was involved. The change was accelerated, and perhaps caused, by the fact that these inflectional *n*'s were very weakly stressed and could easily be "swallowed." Weak stress is also responsible for the second change, the voicing of voiceless sounds. Not long after Chaucer's time, *f*, *th*, and *s* were regularly voiced in weakly stressed syllables. The most likely explanation for the change is that all English vowels are voiced, and that in weakly stressed syllables it is much easier to permit the vocal cords to continue to vibrate than to turn them off for the consonant and on for the vowel. (Somewhat the same kind of change is going on in many parts of America today in words like *latter* and *metal*, which are often pronounced just like *ladder* and *medal*.)

For the Great Vowel Shift, we have no such simple explanation. We do know that during the centuries between 1400 and 1700, a gradual series of changes altered the pronunciation of all long stressed vowels so that nearly all of them are pronounced one notch higher in the mouth than they were in Chaucer's day, and so that two of Chaucer's long vowels became diphthongs. (This shift is the reason why many vowels in borrowed words differ so much from the corresponding vowels in the same words in the original language—French or German, for example.)

The following words, all but two drawn from the Chaucerian stanza at the beginning of this article, illustrate the changes brought about by the Great Vowel Shift:

pris in Chaucer's day had the vowel of Modern English *geese*; the original long *i* became a diphthong, *ai* (not "long i" at all!).

speche moved from a long *e*, as in Modern English *sake*, to a long *i*.

spake in Chaucer's day was pronounced almost like the name of the popular physician, Dr. Spock; the long *a* moved to a long *e*.

knowe had the vowel of Modern English *gnaw*; the long open *o* moved to long close *o*.

fode was pronounced like Modern English *rowed*; the long close *o* became long *u*.

mus was pronounced like Modern English *moose*; the long *u* became a diphthong, *au* (not "long u").

Further changes related to the Great Vowel Shift are still going on. For instance, *gode* 'good' and *fode* 'food' rhymed for Chaucer but *good* and *food* do not rhyme for us because the vowel of *good* has undergone a further change. The frequent Midwestern pronunciation of *hoof* and *roof* as "huf" and "ruf" illustrates the same pattern of change, not yet universally adopted as the change in *good* has been.

The important point about all these changes is that they are systematic: they preserve the function of language as, in part, a tool of communication and at the same time they show that the system can change considerably and still be a system. Language is in no danger whatsoever of "collapsing" or of "losing its communicative and expressive functions" as a result of change.

Even more systematic is analogical change—that is, a change in one part of the system of a language to make it conform, by analogy, to other parts of the system. An excellent example in the text from Chaucer is *us thinketh hem*, which illustrates the old impersonal construction (cf. Modern English "it's raining"). Because the *us*, which is really an indirect object, regularly preceded the verb, it came to be thought of as the subject and was therefore regularly put in the subject case instead of the object case. Thus *think* was regularized to the subject-object pattern of the majority of English verbs. Exactly the same principle is responsible for "it's me." *Be* is the only verb which is regularly followed by the subject case of pronouns; the distinction is, for all practical purposes, valueless; hence many speakers regularize the pattern by analogy. In much the same way, the ten different classes of Old English verbs, each of which showed tense distinctions in a different way, were regularized by analogy, so that today only about 65 verbs still preserve the vowel-change which in Old English was the major means of indicating contrasts in tense. Among them are *ring-rang-rung* and *drive-drove-driven*.

The most drastic change in English in the last thousand years has been the alteration of the vocabulary. Some eighty-five per cent of the Old English vocabulary has been lost, although the remaining fifteen per cent is the very heart of our language. Of the 57 words in the passage from Chaucer, eight are borrowed from other languages and 49 come from Old English. Seven of the borrowed words are from Old French, the major contributor to the English vocabulary—*forme, chaunge, pris, nyce, straunge, usage,* and *age*. All begin to appear in written documents during the thirteenth century but were surely in use in speech long before their first appearances in writing. The eighth borrowed word, *thei*, illustrates an extraordinary phenomenon. Languages seldom borrow such important function words as conjunctions, prepositions, or pronouns; but English borrowed from Old Norse the third person plural pronouns *they*, *them*, and *their* for reasons which are not hard to suggest. The Old English pronouns included *he* 'he,' *heo* 'she,' and *hie* 'they.' So long as the vowels were given their full quality in pronunciation, there was no danger of confusion; but in early Middle English the vowels were weakened and *he*, *heo*, and *hie* became virtually indistinguishable. In the middle of the twelfth century *they* begins to show up instead of *hie*, and by the fourteenth century it was the regular form. *Them* and *their* were adopted more slowly—Chaucer never uses them—but by the beginning of the sixteenth century they too had been universally adopted.

Just as "forme of speche" changes, so also the meanings of words change; and the meaning a word once had may have no bearing on its meaning today. Chaucer's *nyce* is a case in point: some speakers try valiantly to maintain its "original" meaning of 'carefully discriminated,' as against the general adolescent and post-adolescent use to mean 'generally pleasing.' But *nyce* for Chaucer had still essentially the meaning of the Latin word from which it ultimately derives, *nescius* 'ignorant, foolish.' All the world would stare, and rightly, if anyone tried to restore that "original" meaning today.

Students of meaning have isolated a number of patterns of semantic change. One is generalization: *to sail* may be used of any ship regardless of its means of propulsion; *to drive*, similarly, can be applied to self-propelled vehicles; and *zest* once meant 'bit of lemon peel.' The opposite pattern is specialization: *to starve* once meant 'to die (in any manner)'; *meat* was food in general, by contrast to drink; *deer* was any wild animal. Elevation and degradation do not usually involve such drastic changes in meaning; but some extreme examples include *villain* 'farm laborer,' *knave* 'boy,' and *lewd* 'ignorant.' On the other hand we have *knight* 'youth,' *marshal* 'horse-servant,' and *steward* 'sty-guardian.' Closely associated with elevation and degradation is euphemism, by which a harsh fact like death, madness, or excretion is, supposedly, made less harsh.

Such changes as these have been going on since men first began to speak, and will continue to go on until the last human voice is silent. Yet they raise problems for the teacher trapped, for instance, between the drastic alteration in function of *like* and *as* in recent years, and the shibboleths of polite literary society. Just as one must accept the universe, one must accept change; and the only choice for the teacher is how much resistance to put up. Pope's dictum helps a little:

Be not the first by whom the new are tried,
Nor yet the last to lay the old aside.

Yet often the "new" is now the solidly accepted; and every teacher must wrestle with his own conscience in choosing what changes to accept and what to reject. For reason is but choosing, and no handbook or guide can, in the last analysis, replace the free choice of the individual.[1]

QUESTIONS FOR STUDY AND DISCUSSION

1. In English there is a group of words written with the initial letters *kn*: *knave, knight, knee, knife, knit, knuckle, knead, kneel*. Does Hungerford shed any light on these spellings? How would you pronounce the Scandinavian family name *Knutson* or *Knutsen*?
2. The loss of the inflectional ending *-n*, usually *-en*, on verbs as a sign of the infinitive or of the plural began to occur long before Chaucer's time (1340–1400), but Chaucer still used the *-n* quite often. In the following lines from *The Canterbury Tales*, determine when the ending denotes the infinitive, when the plural. In instances where the ending is omitted, how can you determine whether the verb is an infinitive or a plural?

   And smale fowles maken melodye
   That slepen al the night with open yë,
   (So priketh hem nature in hir corages):
   Than longen folk to goon on pilgrimages
   (And palmers for to seken straunge strondes)
   To ferne halwes, couthe in sondry londes;
   And specially, from every shires ende
   Of Engelond, to Caunterbury they wende,
   The holy blisful martir for to seke,
   . . . . .
   —Prologue to *The Canterbury Tales*, lines 9–17

3. The loss of final, unstressed *e* is one of the most important features that distinguish the pronunciation of Modern English from that of Middle English. Chaucer's poetry indicates that he usually retained the final *e*, although he quite likely did not use it in ordinary conversation. Read the following description of the "yong Squyer," assuming that the final *e* at the end of the lines represents schwa /ə/, a weak vowel with the sound represented by the *a* in *ago* and *sofas*.

---

[1] Some useful books which bear on change in language are: Otto Jespersen, *Growth and Structure of the English Language* (Anchor); Martin Joos, *The English Verb* (University of Wisconsin, 1964); W. P. Lehmann, *Historical Linguistics: An Introduction* (Holt, Rinehart, and Winston, 1962); Thomas Pyles, *The Origins and Development of the English Language* (Harcourt, Brace, and World, 1964); and Stuart Robinson and Frederic G. Cassidy, *The Development of Modern English* (Prentice-Hall, 1954). I am particularly indebted for examples to the last of these.

Embrouded was he, as it were a mede
Al ful of fresshe floures, whyte and rede,
Singinge he was, or floytinge, al the day;
He was as fresh as is the month of May.
Short was his goune, with sleves longe and wyde.
Wel coude he sitte on hors, and faire ryde.
He coude songes make and wel endyte,
Juste and eek daunce, and wel purtreye and wryte.
—*Ibid.*, lines 89–96

4. How do you think the letter *e* at the end of these Modern English words can be accounted for: *wide, ride, indite, write*?
5. What analogies probably explain these forms sometimes used by young children: *foots, tooths, mans; commed, hitted, runned, drinked; Higher the window*?
6. The nonstandard pronoun forms *hisn, hern, ourn, yourn* are occasionally found in fictional dialog representing the speech of the uneducated. What analogy might account for these forms?
7. What analogies might explain these misspellings: *pronounciation, greatful, picniced, disasterous, explaination, curiousity, hinderance, playwrite*?
8. After the noun *practice teacher* came into use, the verb *practice teach* was developed by back-formation. Would you form the past tense of this verb by analogy with *preach* or with *catch*?
9. Hungerford explains the development of "It's me" on the basis of analogical change. What analogy do you think might account for the frequent use of *who* rather than *whom* in these sentences?

Who did you see?

Who did you give it to?

10. a. In Old English these verbs had four principal parts with internal vowel change:

Infinitive	Past Singular	Past Plural	Past Participle
helpan (help)	healp	hulpon	holpen
sāwan (sow)	sēow	sēowon	sāwen
slǣpan (sleep)	slēp	slēpon	slǣpen
steppan (step)	stōp	stōpen	stapen
wascan (wash)	wōsc	wōscon	wascen

What are the present-day forms for the past tense and the past participle (the form used after *have*)?

b. In Old English there were different patterns for forming the plurals of nouns. One group added the inflectional ending -*as*, another -*an*, another -*u*, another -*a* or -*e*, etc.

Singular	Plural
stān (stone)	stānas
hunta (hunter)	huntan
lim (limb)	limu
wund (wound)	wunda, -e

What are the plural forms of these nouns in present-day English? Which pattern do most nouns follow today? Is there a noun that follows the plural pattern of *hunta*?

c. State the linguistic principle that brought about the changes in verb forms and plurals of nouns illustrated above.

11. What is the probable explanation of the italicized forms below?

   a. Softly, silently now the moon
      Walks the night in her silver *shoon*.
      —Walter de la Mare, "Silver"

   b. The lead has melted—but *molten* lead.

   c. The farmer has mowed the hay—but new-*mown* hay.

   d. He has just shaved—but a clean-*shaven* face.

   e. He *clomb* a tree. (This form alternated with *climbed* as the past tense of *climb* as late as the seventeenth century and still occurs occasionally in Appalachian speech.)

SUGGESTED ACTIVITIES

1. During the Old and Middle English periods there was little change in English vowels. If you have read Chaucer, you know that his vowels sound like those of French, German, or Spanish. But since the fourteenth century, English vowels have undergone the Great Vowel Shift. All "long stressed vowels" (prolonged and pronounced with relatively tense muscles) are "pronounced one notch higher in the mouth than they were in Chaucer's day," Hungerford explains. A vowel that could not go any higher broke into a diphthong, a combination of two vowels in one syllable. This shift in vowels is so systematic that it is easy to figure out what many Old English words have become in Modern English.

The following exercise shows the systematic nature of some important parts of the Great Vowel Shift.

List each Old English word and after it the Modern English word which resulted from the Great Vowel Shift. Follow the pattern at the top of each group. The pronunciation symbols are those used in *Webster's New Collegiate Dictionary*. The symbol > means *became*.

OE ā = ä as in *father*		>	Mn E ō as in *go*	
Example:	bān	>	bone	
1. hām	3. stān		5. bāt	7. lār
2. rād	4. nā		6. sār	8. lād

OE ō = ō as in *toe*		>	Mn E ü as in *tool*	
Example:	dōm	>	doom	
1. tō	4. nōn		6. bōt	8. mōt
2. tōth	5. rōt		7. mōr	9. sōth
3. mōd				

OE ū = ü as in *too*		>	Mn E au̇ as in *towel*	
Example:	nū	>	now	
1. ūt	3. tūn		5. hūs	7. cū
2. clūd	4. hū		6. mūth	8. brūn

OE ē = ā as in *say*		>	Mn E ē as in *see*	
Example:	hē	>	he	
1. cwēn	3. tēth		5. spēd	
2. mē	4. mēd		6. wē	

OE ī = ē as in *beat*		>	Mn E diphthong ī (ai) as in *bite*	
Example:	līf	>	life	
1. mīl	3. tīd		5. wīf	7. hwīl
2. mīn	4. īs		6. līn	8. hwīt

Note that what is usually referred to as "final silent *e*" performs a function in Modern English spelling—it shows that the preceding vowel is to be diphthongized as illustrated in the last three groups of words above.

In Modern English there is a group of words written with the initial letters *wh-* (*when, where, what, while,* etc.). What Old English spelling is used in words of this type in the last two words above? Does one of these spellings more accurately represent your pronunciation? If not, what spelling would be more representative?

According to the Great Vowel Shift, how would you expect the following words to be pronounced in Modern English: *hook* (OE *hōc*); *root* (OE *rōt*); *book* (OE *bōc*); *roof* (OE *hrōf*)? What is your pronunciation of these words? Why do some of these words seem not to illustrate the Great Vowel Shift?

2. Rhymes used by poets of an earlier period offer clues to pronunciations of that period. Some of Pope's rhymes show that the vowel shift was still incomplete during the first half of the eighteenth century, as indeed it is today.

   a. By reading the following groups of lines, preferably aloud, determine Pope's pronunciation of the rhyme words.

   The spider's touch, how exquisitely fine!
   Feels at each thread, and lives along the line:
   —Essay on Man, lines 217–18

   Good nature and good sense must ever join;
   To err is human, to forgive divine.
   —Essay on Criticism, lines 524–25

   In women, two almost divide the kind;
   Those, only fixed, they first or last obey,
   The love of pleasure, and the love of sway.
   —Epistle II. To a Lady, lines 208–10

   Hear thou, great Anna! whom three realms obey,
   Dost sometimes counsel take—and sometimes tea.
   —The Rape of the Lock, III, lines 7–8

   Why did I write? What sin to me unknown
   Dipt me in ink, my parents', or my own?
   —Epistle to Dr. Arbuthnot, lines 124–25

   Unblemish'd let me live or die unknown;
   Oh, grant an honest fame or grant me none!
   —The Temple of Fame, lines 523–24

   Now Jove suspends his golden scales in air,
   Weighs the men's wits against the lady's hair;
   —The Rape of the Lock, V, lines 71–72

   Some, orb in orb, around the nymph extend;
   Some thread the mazy ringlets of her hair;
   Some hang upon the pendants of her ear:
   —Ibid., II, lines 139–40

b. Read the following couplets, using the nonitalicized words to determine the rhyme.

> *Thus critics of less judgment than* caprice,
> *Curious, not knowing, not exact, but* nice.
> —*Essay on Criticism*, lines 1185–86

> *Dreading even fools, by flatterers* besieg'd,
> *And so obliging that he ne'er* oblig'd;
> —*Epistle to Dr. Arbuthnot*, lines 207–8

> *But still the* Great *have kindness in* reserve,
> *He helped to bury whom he helped to* starve.
> —*Ibid.*, lines 247–48

3. Read the account of the return of the prodigal son (Luke 15: 20–21) in Old English and then in Modern English. Compare the word order in Old English with that in Modern English and the similarities in vocabulary.

```
And   hē    ārās      thā    and    cōm     to    his    fæder.
      he    arose     then          came    to    his    father.

And   thā   gīet      thā    hē     wæs     feorr        his    fæder,
      then  yet       when          was     far from

hē    hine  geseah    and    wearth mid     mildheortnesse
      him   saw              became with    pity

āstyred,    and   ongēan    hine   arn,   and   hine
stirred           toward    him    ran

beclypte    and   cyste     hine.  Thā    cwæth    his    sunu,
embraced          kissed           Then   spoke           son,

Fæder,      ic    syngode   on     heofon,   and   beforan   thē;
            I     sinned    against heaven          before    thee:

nū    ic    ne    eom   wierthe   thæt   ic    thīn   sunu
now   I     not   am    worthy    that   I     thy    son

bēo   genemned.
be    named.
```

4. Hungerford states that the fifteen percent of the Old English vocabulary that remains in our language today is at "the very heart of our language." These two sentences, chosen at random, help to illustrate this point.

> The days passed. During my second year my stipend was raised to $70 a month, allowing me to save a little money and also to have a larger social life.—John Kenneth Galbraith, "Berkeley in the Age of Innocence," *The Atlantic*, June 1969, p. 67.

Check the origin of each word in both sentences. Then count each OE word every time it occurs and figure out the percentage of OE words to the total number of words in the sentences. (Consider $ as *dollars*.) Would you classify the OE words as learned words or as everyday words?

5. Some of the following words have become generalized in meaning; others have become specialized. Record the original meaning of each word and label the change either *Generalization* or *Specialization*.

   Example: deer————beast   Specialization

cannon	curfew	girl	miniature	picture
corn	fowl	hazard	pen	stool

6. Some of the following words represent elevations in meaning; others, degradations. Record the original meaning of each word and label the change either *Elevation* or *Degradation*.

angel	awful	counterfeit	cunning	gossip
asylum	charity	crafty	fond	

7. Though word meanings change, new meanings usually bear some relationship to original meanings. Explain that relationship for a few of the words in the preceding exercises.

8. It is important for anyone reading literature of an earlier period to be aware that meanings of words change. Consult a standard dictionary to find the most appropriate meaning of the italicized word in each quotation. (*The Oxford English Dictionary*—*OED*—is especially useful for determining the meanings of words in literary texts of earlier eras.)

Sebastian.
I am sorry, madam, I have hurt your kinsman;
But had it been the brother of my blood,
I must have done no less with *wit* and safety.
    —*Twelfth Night*, act 5, scene 1, lines 1–3

Polonius [speaking of *Hamlet*].
This is the very *ecstasy* of love,
Whose violent property fordoes itself . . .
    —*Hamlet*, act 2, scene 1, lines 101–2

Hamlet [considering avenging his father's death].
   Now, whether it be
Bestial oblivion, or some craven scruple
Of thinking too precisely on the *event*—
A thought which, quartered, hath but one part wisdom,
And ever three parts coward—I do not know
Why yet I live to say "This thing's to do," . . .
    —*Hamlet*, act 4, scene 4, lines 39–44

Brutus [to *Lucius,* his servant].
Poor *knave,* I blame thee not . . .
 —*Julius Caesar,* act 4, scene 3, line 240

Cassius [to *Brutus*].
Have you not love enough to bear with me,
When that rash *humour* which my mother gave me
Makes me forgetful?
 —*Julius Caesar,* act 4, scene 3, lines 118–20

"Doth God exact day labor, light denied?"
I *fondly* ask.
 —Milton, *On His Blindness,* lines 7–8

9. A word does not necessarily lose one meaning when it takes on a new one. In fact, radiation into multiple meanings is more likely to occur.
   a. What does the term *Victorian* or *Puritan* suggest to you when you hear it in conversation? Does it have the same meaning in both a history and a literature text? Write a short paper in which you discuss and illustrate the various meanings of the word. Which process of change does the word illustrate?
   b. What new meaning does the word *black* have for you? What did it previously mean? Write a short paper in which you contrast and illustrate these meanings. Which process of change does your discussion reveal?
10. Supply euphemisms for the following terms:

false teeth	burying ground	tax loopholes
foot doctor	sweat	the military draft
undertaker	dirty clothes	the anti-ballistic missile
janitor	drunk	the culturally deprived
die	hearse	old people
naked	slum clearance	old age

11. Keep a list of euphemisms which you hear in conversations and on television and radio or which you come upon in your reading. Do you use euphemisms sometimes and not at other times? Why? What purpose do euphemisms serve?

Part Three

THE ALPHABET AND ENGLISH SPELLING

7
THE INVENTION OF WRITING
Charles L. Barber

Although language itself goes back perhaps a million years or more, writing is a much later invention, and even today there are languages without a writing system. Writing is not language but a symbolic representation of speech, which is a symbolic representation of man's experience. The written word is thus a symbol of a symbol, twice removed from reality.

There were two early systems of writing: *cuneiform*, developed by the Sumerians in southern Mesopotamia between 4000 and 3000 B.C., and *hieroglyphic*, developed by the Egyptians about 3000 B.C. The English alphabet, like all the alphabets of western Europe, seems to have its ancestry in hieroglyphic writing.

Charles L. Barber, professor of English at the State University of New York at Buffalo, traces the development of writing from the pre-writing stages of pictures representing things or ideas through pictures representing language elements: first, words, then syllables. Finally, he shows how the alphabet developed out of pictures to represent units of sound, or phonemes.

THE ORIGINS OF WRITING

Writing, in the strict sense of the word, is derived from speech, and is in fact an imperfect visual representation of it, for such purposes as communication at a distance and the keeping of records. Not all visual communications and records are writing in this sense: primitive peoples often use systems of knots tied in ropes, or of notches cut in sticks, as aids to the memory; these are not writing, because the symbols do not correspond to particular words or other linguistic items: they speak their meaning to anybody initiated into the code, whatever his language. The same is true of the most primitive

---

Source: *The Story of Speech and Language* (New York: Crowell, 1964), pp. 41–50. Copyright © 1964 by Charles L. Barber. Reprinted by permission of Thomas Y. Crowell Company, Inc. and the author.

communications by means of pictures, which tell a story independently of language. Such pictures, indeed, are important for the development of writing, for it is very largely out of them that writing has grown.

PICTURE WRITING

We have already noticed the artistic leanings of paleolithic man, which expressed themselves in paintings on rocks, pictures scratched on bone or ivory, and even female figurines made from clay or soft stone. The purpose of such works was probably magical—to enable the hunter to master the beast depicted or acquire its strength, to promote fertility, and so on. Later, pictures were used for keeping records and for sending messages, and both these uses are known among primitive peoples in historical times. Picture writing was used, for example, among the North American Indians until quite recent times; the pictures were scratched or painted on birch bark or animal skins, and could be used for communication between people who spoke different languages. An example of American Indian picture writing, taken from Colonel Garrick Mallery's enormous work on the subject, is given in Figure 1. This was a notice left on a tree by scouts of the Micmac

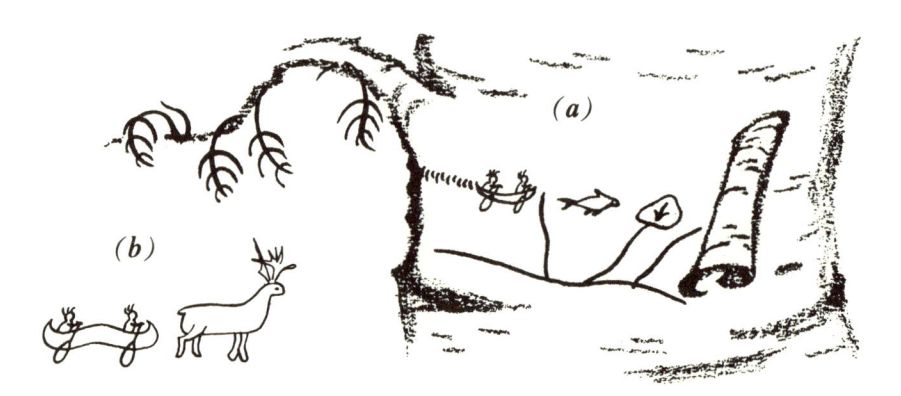

FIGURE 1. AMERICAN INDIANS REPORT ENEMY MOVEMENT
In this pictograph put on a birch tree, (*a*) the warriors are identified as Passamaquoddy by the shape of their canoe and by the fish, their tribal symbol. If the situation is reversed, (*b*) a "humpback" canoe and a deer identify the warriors as Micmac.

tribe, which was at war with the Passamaquoddy tribe, and is a warning that ten Passamaquoddy Indians have been seen in canoes on the lake, going towards its outlet. The ten marks to the left of the canoe indicate the number of enemy seen. The fact that they *are* enemy is shown by the fish which the canoe is following; this is meant to be a pollock, which is the tribal emblem of the Passamaquoddy. The rest of the picture is a map, with an arrow on the lake showing the direction in which the ten Passamaquoddy have been seen moving.

This message depicts a whole situation. It uses conventional signs, such as the tribal emblem and the arrow, but it is not bound to any particular set of words, or even to any one language. We still use pictures in this way, for example a traffic sign showing a boy and a girl stepping into the road . . . or the silhouette figures of a man and a woman used in many airports to mark men's and ladies' lavatories (the use of pictographs rather than writing being desirable in this case because of the mixed nationalities of the passengers). In some cases, the picture has been simplified and conventionalized; for example, like the Micmac Indians, we often use an arrow to show the way to something or the direction in which people must go, but this arrow has taken on a conventional form, and does not much resemble the feathered flights or metal bolts of longbowmen or crossbowmen. In other cases the sign, whatever its origin, is now completely conventional: such are the signs of mathematics, the signs used by astronomers to symbolize the planets, and the signs used by biologists to denote sex, ♂ for male and ♀ for female. These signs are conventional, but they are not tied to any one language; they can be called *ideograms*, because they stand directly for an idea, without the intervention of any specific linguistic form. They are not therefore *writing* in the narrow sense.

In the development of writing out of pictures, two main processes took place: (1) the pictures were simplified and conventionalized, until they were not recognizable as pictures at all; and (2) they were made to stand directly for linguistic items (first words, then syllables, and finally sounds or phonemes) and arranged in the same order as the linguistic items.

THE CONVENTIONALIZATION OF PICTURES

The process of simplification and conventionalization depended to some extent on the materials used for writing. If symbols are scratched on clay, or incised on wood or stone, there is a tendency to avoid curves, and the writing becomes angular. This can be seen in a very famous and very early form of writing (perhaps the earliest true writing) which was developed by the Sumerians in southern Mesopotamia some time between 4000 and 3000 B.C. The Sumerian scribes wrote on clay with a stylus made from a reed. At first they drew little pictures by pulling the tip of the stylus through the clay, but this is not very efficient, for the clay heaps up in front of the stylus and blurs the picture. So later they simply pressed the head of the stylus into the clay as if it were a stamp, thus producing a little wedge-shaped mark about a third of an inch long; each picture was made from a group of wedges of this kind. For this reason the writing is called *cuneiform*, which simply means "wedge shaped." The scribes tended to avoid wedges pointing in some directions, since they were more difficult to make: for example, wedges pointing from right to left were avoided, because they involved

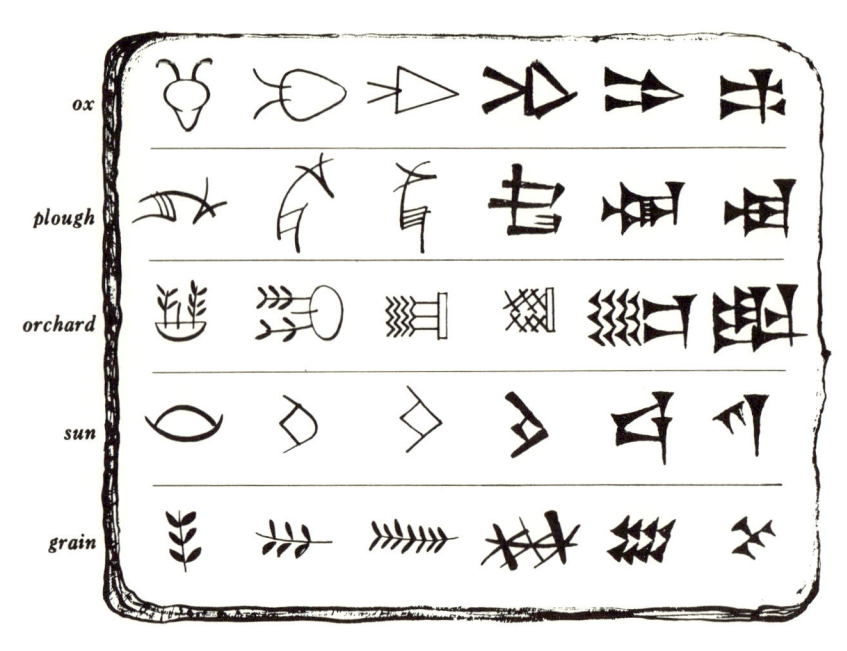

FIGURE 2. HOW TOOLS INFLUENCE WRITING
As these Sumerian picture signs (left) developed into Babylonian and Assyrian symbols (last two columns, right), the symbols were turned over on their side, and curves were changed to angles and then to wedge-shaped marks.

turning the stylus right round. So gradually the marks used became more limited in number, and the signs became increasingly conventionalized and remote from the original pictures. Figure 2 shows how some of the original pictorial signs developed into conventional cuneiform symbols. You will notice that the ultimate signs are at right angles to the original pictures. This is due to the way in which the clay tablet was held: at one period, the tablets were small and were held in the palm of the left hand, with the fingertips gripping the top of the tablet; while the scribe was writing on them with his right hand, the top of the tablet would tend to point to his right rather than upwards, so that the pictures were drawn with their "tops" pointing toward the left-hand edge of the tablet instead of towards its top edge. Later, when tablets became larger and were rested on a table, the scribes continued to draw the symbols facing this way.

The Sumerians were quite early replaced as the great power of the Mesopotamian region by various Semitic peoples, such as the Babylonians and the Assyrians, but the Semites took over the Sumerian writing and improved it, and for many centuries cuneiform was the almost universal script of the Near East. Besides being used by the East Semitic peoples, it was adopted at one time or another by various peoples speaking non-Semitic languages, like the Hittites and the Persians.

But when scribes write with a pen or a brush on leather or papyrus, a different development takes place: curves, far from being difficult, offer the easiest and most rapid forms, and a cursive style of writing may arise. This is seen in ancient Egyptian writing. The original Egyptian script, going back to about 3000 B.C., was pictorial, and is called *hieroglyphic* writing, from a Greek word meaning "holy carved (letters)," because the Greeks believed that the Egyptians used this script mainly for religious inscriptions. In fact it could be painted as well as carved, and it was also used for documents written on papyrus, a paper-like writing material made from a sedge plant. For writing on papyrus, the scribes used a kind of brush pen. The hieroglyphic script was used throughout ancient Egyptian times for religious purposes, but for everyday use a more conventionalized form of writing very soon developed from it, less complicated and much quicker to write, which is known as *hieratic*, or priestly writing; from this, in turn, developed in about 700 B.C. a script called *demotic*, or "popular" writing. Examples of hieroglyphic symbols and their development in hieratic and demotic are given in Figure 3.

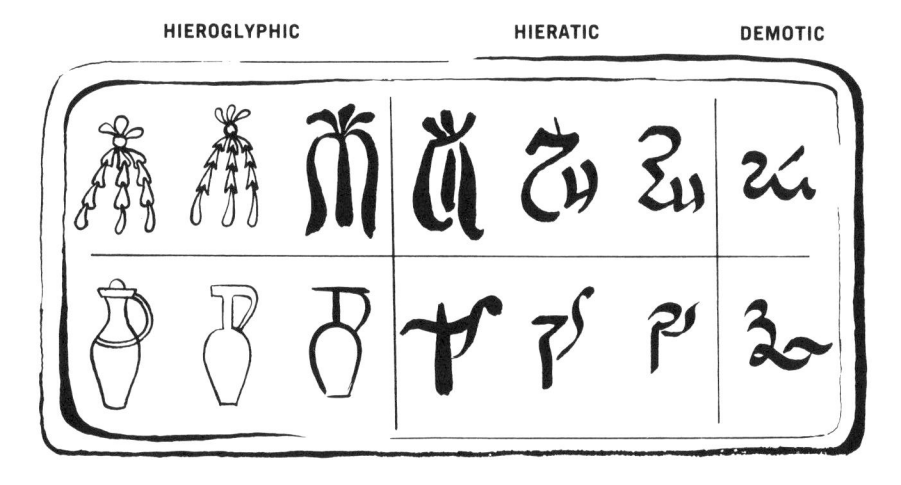

FIGURE 3. HOW COMPLICATED SYMBOLS WERE STREAMLINED

For formal inscriptions and documents, ancient Egyptian priests used a detailed pictorial script (hieroglyphic). But for ordinary communication, they converted picture signs into simplified symbols (hieratic). In popular usage, these were streamlined into a faster, flowing script (demotic).

The conventionalization of a pictorial script seen in Sumerian and Egyptian writing can be paralleled elsewhere, for example in traditional Chinese writing. What about our own alphabet? Where have our letters come from? Our alphabet, like all those of western Europe, is derived from the Latin alphabet. This in turn is derived from the Greek alphabet, which is also the ancestor of the Cyrillic alphabets (used for Russian and some other eastern European languages). The Greeks in turn got their alphabet from a West Semitic people, amost certainly the Phoenicians (who were great sailors and traders), round about 900 B.C. The origin of the West Semitic symbols is not entirely clear, but the most plausible theory is that they are derived from Egyptian hieroglyphic. A link between the Egyptian hieroglyphs and the West Semitic scripts is perhaps provided by some mysterious inscriptions from Sinai, variously dated between 1500 and 1850 B.C., which are not fully understood, but which seem to be in a Semitic language. Figure 4 shows some of the symbols of our alphabet and the way they have probably developed from the Egyptian hieroglyphs of 3000 B.C.

	EGYPTIAN HIEROGLYPHIC	SINAI	WEST SEMITIC	EARLY GREEK	LATE GREEK	LATIN
ox	🐂	🐂	∀	▷	A	A
head	👤	👤	94	4P	P	R
snake	〰	〰	ϟ	ϟ	N	N
mountains	⌒⌒⌒	⌒⌒	W	⟨	Σ	S
courtyard	▯	⊐	99	⊐⊐	B	B

FIGURE 4. HOW PICTURES BECAME LETTERS
We can trace the ancestry of some of our letters—like *A, R, N, S, B*—back to West Semitic symbols. These are probably derived from Egyptian hieroglyphs.

FROM WORD SYMBOL TO PHONEME SYMBOL

The second process, by which pictures cease to be ideograms and come to stand for specific linguistic forms, is even more important. First, pictorial symbols come to represent single words. The earliest Sumerian writings are just lists of objects with symbols for numbers against them: for example, four semicircles and the picture of an ox's head would read "four oxen." It seems that writing arose to meet the needs of the highly centralized city state, and the first writings are records of payments to the temple or city treasury, and similar transactions.

In this way, pictorial symbols come to stand for various words, which are the names of concrete objects like sheep, oxen, the sun, houses, and so on. Next, by a process of extension, the same symbols are made to stand for more abstract words related to the original word. Thus a picture of the sun may come to stand for the words for "bright" or "white," and later for the words "day" and "time," and a picture of a whip for words like "power" or "authority."

Perhaps the really crucial development, however, is "phonetization," the association of a symbol with a particular *sound* (or group of sounds). First, a symbol for a concrete object is transferred to some more abstract object which is denoted by the same or a similar word. For example, the Sumerian word *ti* meant "arrow," and so was represented by an arrow in the script; but there was also a Sumerian word *ti* which meant "life," so the arrow symbol came to be used for this too. The arrow symbol was then felt to stand for the *sound* of the word *ti*, and was used for the syllable *ti* in longer words. In this way, the original word symbols developed into syllable symbols, which could be grouped together to spell out a word.

An analogous process in English can be imagined on these lines. A picture of a tavern is used to represent the word *inn*. Because of the identity of sound, the same symbol then becomes used for the word *in*. At the same time, a picture of an eye is used for the word *eye*, and then by extension is used for the word *sight*. Finally, the tavern symbol and the eye symbol are combined to write the words *incite* and *insight*, and have now become syllabic symbols. If we wanted to distinguish between *insight* and *incite* in our syllabic script, we could add a third symbol to show which of the two was intended: we could draw a picture of an orator to show that we meant *incite*, or add a symbol for some word like "wisdom" to show that we meant *insight*. When we used the eye symbol by itself, we might wish to indicate whether it stood for the word *eye* or the word *sight*; one way of doing this would be to add a symbol after it suggesting one of the sounds used in the word intended: for example, if we had a symbol for the word *sow, sew, so*, we could add this after our eye symbol to indicate that the required word began with *s*. These and similar methods are used in ancient Egyptian and Sumerian writing.

Sumerian writing is very mixed, using ideograms, word symbols, syllable symbols, and various kinds of indicators of the types mentioned. Out of it, however, developed the almost purely syllabic system of cuneiform writing which was used for Akkadian (the language of the ancient Babylonians and Assyrians), and which for centuries dominated the writing of the Near East.

In this system each cuneiform sign stood for a syllable, such as *ba*, or *lu*, or *ir*. This is a great improvement on systems using signs for whole words, since the number of symbols used can be reduced to about a hundred.

Ancient Egyptian writing also developed into a syllabic system, and was particularly important for the development of true alphabetic writing (i.e., a script that has symbols representing *phonemes*). The important thing about the Egyptian system was that the vowels were not indicated. Most of the signs (about eighty) stood for a group of two consonants, plus any vowels whatever. For example, the symbol for a house (*par*) stood for the group *pr*, and this could mean *par, per, apr, epr, epra*, and so on. But there were twenty-four signs which stood for only one consonant plus any vowel; for example, the symbol representing a mouth (*ra*) stood for the consonant *r*, and could mean *ra, ar, re, er*, and so on. When the West Semitic peoples living round the eastern shores of the Mediterranean developed a script, they did so by taking over from the Egyptians just these twenty-four signs. Originally, this must have been a syllable system, in which each of the signs stood for a number of possible syllables, like the Egyptian *ra, ar, re, er*, etc.; but in fact it is formally identical with a purely alphabetic system in which only the consonants are written and the vowels are left out.

The final step, of having fixed and regular symbols for the vowels, was made by the Greeks when they took over this Semitic alphabet. Some of the consonant sounds of Phoenician did not exist in Greek, and the Greeks used the corresponding symbols for vowels. For example, the first letter of the West Semitic alphabet, derived from the picture of an ox, was '*aleph*, and stood for a kind of *h* sound (represented in the spelling by '); the Greeks of that period did not use this sound, and took the letter over as *alpha*, representing an *a* sound. Thus was reached at last a system of writing where symbols stand for phonemes, and all later alphabetic systems are ultimately derived from this Greek achievement. The great advantage of the system is the relatively small number of symbols needed, which makes universal literacy possible. The more unwieldy and difficult the system of writing, the more likely it is to remain the jealously guarded prerogative of an élite, like the priestly caste of the ancient city states or the bureaucracy of classical China: the alphabet is one of the forces making for democracy. It is noticeable, too, that many of the important developments in writing happened when a system was taken over by one people from another: scribes tend to be conservative, and radical changes mostly take place when a system of writing has to be adapted to new conditions.

The importance of the invention of writing hardly needs underlining. Before writing, all cultural traditions had to be memorized. More can be carried in the memory than we tend to think, since we seldom have to exercise ours very hard: pre-literate peoples memorize long genealogical tables, and even whole epic poems. But there is a limit to what the memory can carry, and no very serious expansion of knowledge can take place until permanent records are made in writing.

QUESTIONS FOR STUDY AND DISCUSSION

1. Why, according to Barber, is the early use of pictures and of ideograms for communication, not writing?
2. From various areas of study (mathematics, chemistry, music, biology), add to Barber's list of conventional signs, or ideograms. Try to find signs that are not tied to any one language. Be ready to explain these to your classmates.
3. Compare Figures 2 and 4 and explain how materials influenced the shape of the symbols.
4. If an alphabetic system had not been devised, what would be the chief losses to you as an individual? To modern society? Or do you agree with Marshall McLuhan that television is returning us to pictorial communication?

SUGGESTED ACTIVITIES

1. Draw pictures to represent some of these situations or others of your own choosing: a dog chasing a rabbit, a rabbit chasing a dog, a girl rejecting her suitor, a child stepping into a stream of traffic, a student worn out with study, victory at a football game.
2. Draw pictorial symbols to represent some of the following words or others of your own choosing: scales, clouds, fist, sword, dove, adolescent. By an extension of meaning, what more abstract word might each symbol represent?
3. The possible hazards of communicating by picture are amusingly illustrated in "How the First Letter Was Written" in Rudyard Kipling's *Just So Stories*. The picture message that Taffimai Metallumai entrusted to a stranger from a different tribe to carry to her mother, who was at home in the cave, produced unexpected results. The following story, "How the Alphabet Was Made," tells how Taffy turned pictures into an alphabet. You might be interested in reading these stories if you don't recall them. Is Kipling's fictional account in accord with Barber's historical account?
4. Draw pictures to represent the syllables of ten of the following words:

firefly	earring	foxglove	seesaw	incense
football	treetop	barefoot	betray	inspire
roadbed	sailboat	tulip	belief	offer
manhood	pancake	hairline	invest	occasion
masthead				

Are there any of these words for which you could not draw syllabic representations? What was the difficulty?
5. A limited kind of syllabic writing is the use of letters to represent syllables. Adults sometimes write an IOU; children devise other combinations: ICAB, INVU, and so forth. What others can you think of?
6. Would a writing system such as that of the ancient Egyptians, which represented only consonants, cause difficulty for the reader? Read these sentences in which only consonants are represented:

wrtng s n mprfct vsl rprsnttn f spch

tw strnts lndd n th mn

ths md wmn lvd nr r hs

Write a sentence of your own representing only consonants. Try to make two interpretations possible. Have your classmates read it.
7. *Revelations* 1:7 reads: "I am Alpha and Omega, the beginning and the end, saith the Lord." What is the literal meaning of "Alpha and Omega"? the extended meaning?
8. The article on the alphabet in the *Encyclopaedia Britannica* traces the history of the letters of the alphabet.
   a. Find out where the Greeks got the names for the letters of the alphabet: alpha, beta, gamma, delta, and so forth.
   b. Trace the evolution of one letter, recording its various forms.
9. We write from left to right, but people in the ancient world wrote in various directions: from left to right, right to left, or top to bottom. The Greeks sometimes reversed the direction with each line, going from left to right, right to left, and left to right, as oxen plowed. Since there were no spaces between words, no punctuation, no paragraphs, and no small letters, that system applied to English today would produce the following effect. Read the sentences.

**PEOPLEINTHEANCIENTWORLDWROTEFROMLEFTTORIGHT
SEMITEMOSSKEERGEHTMOTTOBOTPOTROTTFELOTTHGIR
REVERSEDTHEDIRECTIONWITHEACHLINEGOINGFROM
NIAGATHGIRTTOLEFTANDLEFTOTTHGIRTHGIROTTFEL**

10. Hebrew is written from right to left in a consonantal alphabet. If any student in the class knows Hebrew, the class would find it interesting to have him explain the writing system.
11. Students who have studied shorthand might explain how this system has further simplified the writing system.

12. Consult an encyclopedia to find out what the Rosetta and Moabite stones are and what their significance is to the history of writing. Make a report to the class.
13. At the time the Christian missionaries took the Latin alphabet to Britain in the sixth century, an ancient Germanic alphabet known as the runic alphabet was being used by several of the Teutonic tribes of Britain. Consult an encyclopedia to find out what the runic alphabet was, what mysterious connotations it had, and where runic inscriptions were found.
14. Consult a standard dictionary to find out the earliest known meanings of the following words: *alphabet, write, paper, pen*. What information do these word origins supply about the history of writing?
15. In a short paper compare the experiences of a child learning to talk and learning to read and write. Which is more difficult? Why?
16. Write a short paper in which you discuss what you consider would have been the chief losses *either* to you personally *or* to modern society if an alphabetic system of writing had not been developed.
17. The supremacy of the printed word as a medium of communication has been challenged by Marshall McLuhan. Read his *The Medium Is the Massage*. Summarize and evaluate his thesis.

8
REGULARITY IN ENGLISH SPELLING
Paul R. Hanna and Jean S. Hanna

Moulton discusses language as a code, a special kind of communication system. Hanna and Hanna show that writing is a code within the larger language code. The writer encodes a message in a sequence of letters of the alphabet, which represent a sequence of the significant units of speech sounds. The reader decodes the message. Letter classes are called graphemes; the significant classes of speech sounds, phonemes. Phonemes are symbols devised to represent groups of similar speech sounds that we accept as equivalents. For example, the phoneme /l/ represents three variant speech sounds in the words *lap, fill*, and *plain*; yet in English these three sounds are considered the same—they form a single phoneme. (Phonemes are written between slant lines.)

If English had a perfectly phonemic alphabet, it would have one grapheme to represent each phoneme, but since there are only twenty-six letters of the alphabet to represent more than three dozen phonemes, the English spelling system falls far short of this ideal. It is, in fact, less regular than the spelling systems of most languages using the Greco-Roman alphabet. Historical events account for some of the irregularities.

Old English spelling was, for the most part, phonemic, with one grapheme usually representing one phoneme. But changes in spelling did not keep pace with changes in pronunciation. Especially significant in widening the gap between grapheme and phoneme were the loss of final schwa /ə/, represented by the grapheme ⟨e⟩, and the Great Vowel Shift. (See Hungerford, text and exercises.) Though the schwa disappeared, final *e* often remained. Thus such Middle English two-syllable words as *nāme, tāle*, and *rīde* were reduced to one syllable in Modern English. The Middle English words were pronounced

---

Source: *The National Elementary Principal* 45 (November 1965): 20–23. Copyright © 1965 by the National Association of Elementary School Principals. Reprinted by permission of the publisher and the authors.

/nam-ə, tal-ə, riyd-ə/, the long ā representing the phoneme /a/ as in *father*; the long ī, the phoneme /iy/ as in *reed*. The Great Vowel Shift produced the change in the long vowels apparent in the Modern English words.

Certain foreign language influences made English spelling even less representative of speech. Following the Norman invasion, Anglo-French scribes introduced the grapheme ⟨c⟩ before *e* and *i* to represent the phoneme /s/: *cell, city*; and they replaced *cw* with *qu* in such words as *queen* and *quick*. To make matters worse, during the early Modern English period, the spelling of some words borrowed from the French was changed to conform to a more remote Latin word. For example, *dette, doute*, and *parfit* were rewritten *debt, doubt*, and *perfect*. By 1650 the present spelling system was pretty well fixed, but changes in pronunciation went right on.

In spite of many irregularities, just how bad is English spelling? Poking fun at it has long been a favorite pastime of many people, including such notables as George Bernard Shaw. More careful observers of English spelling, however, have recognized frequent recurring patterns that form the "regular" spellings of the language. And now, in the days of the computer, it is possible to determine scientifically the regular spellings of English.

The authors of the following article present some of the regular English spellings as determined by a depth analysis of 17,000 words. Though the article is addressed primarily to teachers, it should be of interest to anyone who finds it necessary to write anything.

Paul R. Hanna is emeritus Lee L. Jacks professor of childhood education and emeritus director of Stanford University International Development Education Center. Jean Hanna is a teacher and author.

WRITTEN LANGUAGE—A CODE

All written language is a kind of code for the transmission of messages over space and time; messages that might be conveyed in a face-to-face encounter through sign language, but ordinarily are transmitted by means of the spoken word. For communication to take place, both sender and receiver must know the code—must know what each symbol stands for and in what order the symbols are arranged. The code for the written form of most present-day languages is an alphabetic code in which letter symbols are used to represent the units of sound that make up the spoken word.

A *phoneme* is the smallest practical unit of speech sound that can serve in a particular language to distinguish one utterance from another. The first sound, represented by the letter *p*, in the word *pan* is a phoneme because substituting for it the sound that the letter *t* usually represents would create a different word with a different meaning.* Similarly, the letter *a* in *pan* represents a middle phoneme which is often called the "short *a* sound." Changing that second sound in *pan* to any other vowel sound would make a crucially different utterance, though not always an accepted and meaningful word. One might, for example, have *pin, pine, pain, pen,* or *pun* as a result of changing the second-position phoneme in *pan*. Likewise, the letter *n* in *pan* stands for a final phoneme that serves to differentiate that word in speech from such words as *pack, pat, patch,* and *pad*.

It is important to note that the word *phoneme* relates only to the sounds of a language. The technical name for a phoneme's representation in written or printed form is *grapheme*.

ENGLISH—AN ALPHABETIC LANGUAGE

English is an alphabetic language in spite of the fact that, unlike such languages as Turkish, Finnish, and Spanish, it can hardly be said to have a one-to-one correspondence between phoneme and grapheme. If there were, spelling as a problem would become unimportant if not actually nonexistent. But written American English is made up of words that are comprised of letters or combinations of letters that stand for the sequential phonemes heard in the spoken form. While this is true in the main, there do exist in American English a number of graphemic options for the spelling of a given phoneme and, conversely, a number of phonemic options for many of the graphemes.

Many of the irregularities in the orthography exist because of borrowings from other languages. There has also been a tendency over the generations to alter the pronunciation of a word without bothering to make a corresponding change in its spelling. However, the phonemic nature of the American-English orthography may be illustrated by the fact that we do not hesitate to pronounce such nonsense syllables as *frip* or *glimp* or to spell them from dictation. A sentence containing words incorrectly though phonetically spelled would cause most readers little difficulty as far as getting the message is concerned. Any good reader would know what is being said in this sentence: *Wee bot sum bate and rented a bote.*

HOW "REGULAR" IS AMERICAN-ENGLISH SPELLING?

Those who insist that the phonemic-graphemic regularity of American English is mythical, or at best highly exaggerated, are fond of citing *ghoti*

---

* Strictly speaking, the first sound in *pan*, represented by the grapheme *p*, is a phone (a speech sound) belonging to a group of sounds, or phone types, that compose the phoneme /*p*/. Three slightly different phone types of this phoneme can be distinguished in *pan, spin,* and *hop*.—Eds.

as a possible spelling of the word *fish*, because (they point out) *gh* represents the sound written *f* in *cough*, *o* represents the short *i* sound in *women*, and the letters *ti* stand for the *sh* sound in *nation*. This absurd spelling (ghoti) ignores completely the extremely important matter of structural pattern. The letters *gh* represent the sound normally spelled *f* only when that sound comes in final position in a root word, and then only when a preceding vowel sound is spelled *ou* as in *cough* and *tough* or *au* as in *laugh*. The letters *ti* represent the *sh* phoneme only when it is an interior one as in *nation* and *partial*, never when it is the initial or final phoneme. The letter *o* as a representation of the short *i* sound is a rare exception (as in *women*) that must be memorized.

So much stress has at times been laid on the irregularity of American-English spelling that we tend to overlook the very high degree of uniformity with which the phonemes of our language are represented in writing, especially when the important matter of the position of the phoneme is taken into consideration. Most consonants and short-vowel phonemes are nearly always represented *in a specific position* by the same grapheme. The majority of variances are found in the representation of vowel phonemes other than the "short" ones, and even these are ordinarily represented in one of only two or three ways. Many of the assumed irregularities are not genuine irregularities but are governed by rather consistent patterns that the good speller follows, often without even being conscious of doing so. For example, the vowel sound of *cow* is almost invariably represented by the letters *ou* except when it is the *last* sound in a word or is followed by a final *l* or *n* sound as in *owl* or in *crown*. In the latter instances, it is usually represented by the letters *ow*, the principal exceptions being *foul* (homonym of *fowl*) and *noun*.

STANFORD RESEARCH PROJECT

A research project sponsored by the United States Office of Education was conducted at Stanford University under the direction of the authors and with the participation of Richard E. Hodges, University of Chicago, and E. Hugh Rudorf, University of Delaware. It made a study of the American-English phonemes and the graphemes used to represent them. It is being published by the U.S. Government Printing Office for the U.S. Office of Education as Project 1991.

A depth analysis of 17,000 words revealed the fact that relatively few words in this sample of our language have no phonological or morphological cues for spelling. With the aid of modern data processing techniques, it was possible to examine the structure of the orthography to a degree never before attempted or even possible by hand analysis. What kinds of insights into the American-English orthography were developed? This statistical analysis ascertained that the correct graphemic option can be predicted for a given occurrence of a phoneme, in these 17,000 words, approximately

90 percent of the time when *the main phonological factors of position in syllables, syllable stress, and internal constraints underlying the orthography* are taken into consideration. In addition, this thorough analysis of the relationship between phoneme and grapheme indicates that other linguistic factors are determinates of the ways in which some parts of some words are spelled.

Further, the evidence obtained from Phase I of this investigation made it possible to design a second computer program, Phase II, which takes the findings of the first study and uses them to *predict* the standard spellings of different words. The results of this second computer run were significant. Of the 17,000 words given only as phonemes to the machine to spell, over 8,000 or 49 percent were spelled correctly on the first computer run. An additional 37.2 percent were spelled with only one error; 11.4 percent with two errors; 2.9 percent with three or more errors. An examination of the error list suggests that many of the misspellings could be obviated with the mastery of simple morphological rules.

Research Project No. 1991 to date suggests that a high degree of regularity does exist in the relationship between phonological elements in the oral language and their graphemic representation in the orthography. A pedagogical method based upon aural-oral cues to spelling (and reinforced with eye and hand-learning) may well prove to be more efficient and powerful than methods that rely primarily upon the visual and/or haptical learning approaches while ignoring the essential alphabetical structure for the encoding or written form of the language.

PHONOLOGICAL FACTORS THAT CONTRIBUTE TO CONSISTENCY

We have said that the American-English language is not based upon a one-to-one relationship between phoneme and grapheme, but that there are patterns of consistency in the orthography which, based upon linguistic factors, may be said to produce correspondences that are surprisingly consistent. The chief phonological factors contributing to this consistency are (1) position of the phoneme in the syllable or word, (2) syllable stress, and (3) internal constraints or surround.

For example: while one can be sure 74 percent of the time that the phoneme heard and articulated at the beginning of such words as *face, find, feet,* and *fact* will be spelled correctly with the letter *f* regardless of the position of this phoneme in a word, it is necessary to remember that this particular phoneme may be spelled differently in a different position in other words. Although this sound is normally written *f*, it is almost never written *f* at the *end* of a word. It may be spelled *ff* as in *off*, *ph* as in *graph*, *gh* as in *cough*, or *lf* as in *half*. Again, when this same phoneme is preceded by a consonant, as in the word *sphere*, the phoneme is spelled *ph*. The initial consonant sound, as in words like *sphere* and *sphinx*, acts as a restraint and dictates the choice of a particular graphemic option (*ph*) for the spelling of this phoneme in the word. One must also note that an exception to the spelling of the beginning sound in such words of Greek origin as *photo* and *phonograph* produces the spelling *ph*, rather than the normal or common spelling, *f*.

When the phoneme typically referred to as the long *a* sound occurs at the *end* of a word, here again *position* determines the choice of grapheme to be used to represent the vowel sound in the word. With the exception of a relatively few words, this long *a* sound, when coming last in a word, is usually spelled with the letters *ay*. Two words that are exceptions and should be used to point up the rule are *they* and *obey*.

When this same vowel sound (long *a*) occurs at the *beginning* or in the *middle* of a one-syllable word, it is almost always spelled one of two ways: *ai* as in *aid* and *rain*; *a-e* as in *ate* and *lake*. A statistically infrequent exception to this rule is found in such words as *eight* and *straight*.

NO "SILENT LETTERS" IN SPELLING

For years, spelling programs have consistently and determinedly identified any grapheme that "doesn't have a sound" (for whatever reason) as a "silent letter," thus confusing encoding (spelling) and decoding (reading). Of course there is no such thing as a "silent letter" in spelling. The so-called silent *e*, a diacritical symbol, becomes part of a set of graphemes in spelling, whether it is used as a helping letter in writing the long vowel sounds in such words as *ate* and *made*, or whether it helps spell the final *s* or *z* sound in words like *fence* and *cheese*.

One should also note the unfortunate tendency to refer to such vestigial letters as the *k* at the beginning of *knee* and the *b* at the end of *lamb* as "silent letters." The beginning sound one hears in *night* and *nine* is spelled *n*; the beginning sound one hears in *knight* and *knee* is spelled *kn*; the last sound one hears in *lamb* and *climb* is spelled *mb*.

Consider the word *straight*. This word has five distinguishable phonemes. The first three (str) constitute a consonant cluster. The last phoneme is regularly represented by the letter *t*. What about the next-to-last sound? It is obviously a long vowel sound which in a certain group of words is written with the set of letters *aigh* as in *straight* and occasionally with the set of letters *eigh* as in *weight*.

There are many correspondences that can be analyzed phonologically by the pupils, and they will soon learn to look for variations in spelling which are governed by position as well as by "surround." They should be helped to discover such patterns as represented by a final *k* sound. This sound, when following a short vowel sound in a one-syllable word (*trick*) is almost always written *ck*. This same *k* sound in initial position, when followed by a short *i* or *e* sound, is written *k* (*kitten*); when followed by any other sound, it is usually written *c* (*cat*).

Building spelling power depends to a large extent (but not exclusively) upon a careful, rational, mature examination of all elements of a phonological analysis of words; on an ability to generalize about the effects that position, stress, and constraint have on the choices one makes among alternative graphemes or sets of graphemes to conform to standard American-English spelling.

MORPHOLOGY AIDS SPELLING ANALYSES

Although the phonological analysis of a word is of primary importance in helping one to develop spelling power, there are other factors that can be of great aid. Morphology, the study of word formation, can be a helpful determinate of a choice of spelling options. In spelling, morphology is primarily concerned with compounding, affixation, and word families.

Compounding is a process whereby independent morphemes* join to form compound words. Once a pupil has learned to spell the independent morphemes in words like *playground* (play and ground), *caretaker*, and *lighthouse*, he should have no trouble in mastering the compounded forms.

Affixation and *assimilation* provide rules which, once understood, can be applied by pupils to the spelling of such words as *acute* and *account*. In both words, the phoneme-grapheme correspondences can be accounted for by applying phonological analyses—except for the *k* sound in each word. In *acute*, the *k* sound is spelled with one *c*; in *account*, with two *c*'s. Simple rules of affixation will readily account for the difference in graphemic representation of the *k* sound in these two words. In *account*, the letters *ac* represent the prefix *ad*, which has been changed to *ac* before being added to the word *count*. This process is called *assimilation* and can be discovered by the pupil with a carefully programed spelling course. And there are reliable rules for adding suffixes to independent morphemes which, when understood, should make the spelling of such groups of words far less burdensome to the average pupil than trying to memorize the spelling of each individual word.

The term *word families*† is a popular bit of nomenclature which has come to be applied to those words that have similar spelling patterns and even partial phoneme similarities (bake, lake, make). Also labeled "families" are groups of words of common etymological origin that have rare graphemic representations for their phonemes. These words are usually spoken of as words of foreign origin, and as the pupil matures in a modern spelling program, he will be able increasingly to recognize the fact that in words like *andante*, *finale*, and *machete*, the final long *a* sound is spelled *e*, a regular representation in words of Romance origin.

---

* A morpheme is a meaningful linguistic unit that may be a free form (child, pray) or a bound form (*hood* in childhood; *un* in unload) that contains no smaller meaningful parts.

† The term is of questionable linguistic respectability and should be replaced by *groups* as soon as practicable.

SYNTACTICAL COMPONENTS

A final group of words whose spelling defies phonological and morphological analysis must be explained by syntax. These words are homonyms and homophones. Their correct spelling can be determined only by the contextual surround. In the case of *steak* and *stake*, one simply must remember that when one refers to a pointed stick used for a fence or to mark a spot, the word is spelled s t a k e (with the vowel sound spelled *a-e*); that when one is speaking of a cut of meat, the word is spelled s t e a k (with the vowel sound *ea*). To master the correct spelling of most homonyms, one ought to use both the visual and haptical approaches in conjunction with the syntactical clues that help to establish the meaning of homonyms. Since consonant phonemes in homonyms are usually written with regular letter representations, phonological clues might be used to establish the way they are written.

QUESTIONS FOR STUDY AND DISCUSSION

1. Mark Twain is supposed to have said that he "wouldn't give a damn for a person who couldn't spell a word in at least three different ways." Twain might have been happy in the sixteenth century, when many words were variously spelled. Shakespeare even spelled his own name in more than one way. Would it be desirable and/or possible to return to this practice today, letting each person spell much as he pleased? Would you like to have that privilege extended to printers?
2. A writer in the *Los Angeles Times* a few years ago stated: "Now the young generation knows everything but can't spell it." How accurate are the two parts of this assertion? Do you spell as well as your parents? Is spelling important? Consider this question from the point of view of the student, the teacher, the employer, the general reader, society.
3. Which of these misspellings violates regular phonemic or morphemic spelling patterns? Explain.

similiar	bild	stoped	denounciation
siezure	occasionaly	ismus	tite
adress	atheletic	cloun	snarade (serenade)

   Should misspellings that violate regular spelling patterns be penalized more heavily than other misspellings? Why or why not?
4. The authors put the term "silent letter" in quotation marks to suggest that this is a popular but inaccurate term. Do any letters have sound? How would the authors explain the function of the so-called "silent letters" in each of the following words: *knee, gnaw, write, bomb, fate, psalm*?

5. Check your dictionary for words beginning with *kn-*. Approximately how many words are listed? From your reading about the history of the English language, do you think the so-called "silent letter" ever represented a phoneme?
6. Consult a dictionary for words beginning with *ph-*. Approximately how many words are included? What is their origin? What phoneme do these graphemes represent? Does this spelling of the phoneme cause you any difficulty? How do you pronounce *diphtheria*?

SUGGESTED ACTIVITIES

1. You have read that changing one sound in a word to a sound belonging to a different phoneme changes the meaning of the word: *pan, pin, pen; pad, pat, pack; tan, tin, ten*. These words fit one of the two major spelling patterns developed in some detail by C. C. Fries.* Fries points out that individual letters do not necessarily represent individual phonemes; rather, spelling patterns represent sequences of phonemes that form the word patterns of speech. The first pattern is for one-syllable words representing the phoneme sequence Consonant (or consonant cluster)-Vowel-Consonant (or consonant cluster). The vowels are so-called "short vowels." "Long vowels" are diphthongs.

    a. Set up the following chart on a large piece of paper.

Initial graphemes	a, as in pat	ă, as in pot	ĕ, as in pet	ĭ, as in pit	ŭ, as in putt
Example b	ban	——	Ben	bin	bun
c	cat	cot	check	shrill	clutch
f					
g					
⋮					

    In a vertical column at the left, insert the following graphemes to represent consonant phonemes: c, f, g, h, j, l, m, n, p, r, s, t, v, bl, br, ch, fl, fr, sh, sp, spl, spr, th. Using any fifteen of the graphemes, insert one-syllable words of the Consonant-Vowel-Consonant pattern in as many of the five columns as possible, as illustrated above.

    b. Set up a similar chart, using the following graphemes to represent consonants or consonant clusters at the ends of words: b, d, g, m, n, p, t, sk, sp, st.

---

* *Linguistics and Reading* (New York: Holt, Rinehart, and Winston, 1963), pp. 169–80.

Regularity in English Spelling 91

	ă	ä	ĕ	ĭ	ŭ	Final graphemes
Example:	sash	bosh	mesh	fish	rush	sh
						b
						d
						⋮

c. Is the phoneme-grapheme relationship consistent in the words you have written? What seems to be the usual spelling for each vowel?
d. The spelling patterns represented in one-syllable words of this type frequently occur in the syllables of longer words and are particularly useful in suggesting the most frequent grapheme-phoneme correspondence for vowels. This correspondence occurs with greater regularity in stressed than in unstressed syllables. Write the full words incompletely represented here, using regular spellings for the vowels.

ant-gon-st-c	tr-gon-metry	s-sp-nd	spr-nkl-ng
br-nd-sh	v-lc-n-c	-ntertain	pol-tical
f-nt-st-c	b-tany	s-parate	acc-mplish
-m-gine	c-ttage	r-min-scent	k-dn-p
s-bst-ntial	c-pyright	f-ndam-ntal	gr-mble
-mateur	l-ngitude	pr-dicate	h-ndred
b-mb-st-c	v-l-ntary	tw-nty	-mbr-lla
f-br-c	d-cum-ntation	h-ndrance	pron-nciati-n
-stron-m-c	rem-nstrate	perm-t	tr-mpet
h-ph-zard	b-nef-t	or-ginal	c-stom
tr-nsm-t	d-finite	d-scipline	p-zzle
gramm-tical	-nd-sp-nsable	pers-stent	r-stle
pr-bable	trem-ndous	m-schief	s-bj-ct-ve
bl-ckade	geom-tr-c	p-ssib-lity	t-mble

e. You have read that the position of a phoneme in a word may determine the grapheme most likely to represent that phoneme. Try to determine the usual spelling for the phonemes /f, s, l, k, j/ at the end of a word of the Consonant-Vowel-Consonant pattern. Set up the following chart on a large piece of paper, and in each column write the words suggested, using the appropriate graphemes to represent the phoneme at the top of the column.

/f/	/s/	/l/	/k/	/j/
sta—	cla—	be—	cra—	ju—
sti—	che—	spe—	sa—	bu—
blu—	me—	te—	de—	smu—
cu—	mi—	ski—	ne—	fu—
mu—	stre—	gri—	tri—	le—
sco—	ki—	sti—	wi—	we—
scu—	le—	do—	lo—	ri—
stu—	gla—	du—	clo—	bri—
cli—	mu—	nu—	du—	lo—

What seems to be the prevailing spelling pattern for representing the above consonant phonemes at the end of a word of the Consonant-Vowel-Consonant pattern? How are the same phonemes represented at the beginning of a word?

If a suffix is added to one of these words, is the spelling of the final consonant phoneme of the original word changed? Find out by selecting suffixes from this group to add to various words on the chart: *-ing, -ed, -s,* or *-es.*

2. The second set of spelling patterns is differentiated from the first by the final grapheme ⟨e⟩. This *e* is not a "silent letter"; it signals that the preceding vowel is a so-called "long vowel." More accurately, the "long vowel" is a diphthong composed of two vowels.

   a. Add *e* to each of the following Pattern 1 words to form Pattern 2 words. Pronounce the words in pairs and note the difference in sound between the vowel and the diphthong.

man	hop	hid	cub
pan	rob	sit	cut
cap	not	dim	tub

   b. These two spelling patterns continue to contrast when a suffix beginning with a vowel is added to a word.

   (1) Write each word, adding the suffixes *-ing* and *-ed*.

can	cane	pin	pine
tap	tape	mop	mope
plan	plane	hop	hope
din	dine	tub	tube

Regularity in English Spelling 93

(2) Add the suffixes indicated to each word.

slim + -er   slime + -y
cut + -er   cute + -er
hug + -er   huge + -er
bit + -en   bite + -ing
rip + -ed   ripe + -en

(3) Make a generalization about what happens to the spelling of words of each pattern when a suffix beginning with a vowel is added.

3. Though the spelling of diphthongs (long vowels) is more irregular than that of vowels (short vowels), recurring patterns are apparent and form useful spelling guides.

a. Write the following words, supplying graphemes to represent the diphthong commonly referred to as long *ā*.

excl—m   refr—n   portr—   p—   pl—n
rel—   cl—   r—sin   p—d   tr—l
compl—nt   dec—   prev—l   f—th   dism—

(1) Draw a conclusion as to what determines the spelling of the diphthong in these words.
(2) You have previously observed another, probably more frequent spelling of the diphthong *ā*. What is it? Illustrate.

b. Write the following words, supplying the appropriate graphemes to represent the diphthong *aù*.

cl—d   n—   someh—   am—nt   gr—l
fr—n   all—   pron—nce   sc—t   m—th
f—nd   comp—nd   end—   t—n   ren—n

Draw a conclusion as to what determines the spelling of the diphthong in these words. Check your findings with the authors' statement.

4. Write the following words, supplying the appropriate grapheme to represent the phoneme /k/.

-ettle   -limax   -onvention   -itten   -rocus
-alculus   -ingdom   -eg   -linical   -ulprit
-ashier   -ennel   -orporal   -itchen

Paul R. Hanna and Jean S. Hanna **94**

What seems to determine the choice of the grapheme to represent the phoneme /k/ in initial position? Are your conclusions in accord with the authors' statement?

5. The spelling of vowels in unstressed syllables presents one of the most difficult spelling problems. One helpful device is to think of the spelling in a variant form of the word in which the syllable is stressed, for the spelling is likely to remain the same in the unstressed syllable even though the vowel may be obscured in pronunciation.

    Write the following words, supplying the omitted vowel grapheme. Mark the stress.

    Example: sýnthesis synthétic

or-gin	or-ginal	influ-nce	influ-ntial
incid-nt	incid-ntal	temperam-nt	temperam-ntal
med-cine	med-cinal	gr-mm-r	gr-mm-rian
emph-sis	emph-tic	practic-l	practic-lity
f-nt-sy	f-nt-stic	r-fer	r-ference
symb-l	symb-lic	an-t-my	an-t-mical

6. Write a short paper in which you explain to an uninformed reader that there are no "silent letters." Illustrate, using these words as well as others that occur to you: *knight, gnaw, bomb, psalm, stuff, crack, bill, glass.* Explain the function of the so-called "silent letters" in your illustrations.

7. Write a short paper in which you explain and demonstrate that the position of a phoneme in a word may influence the spelling of that phoneme.

8. Since English spelling is not only phonemic but also morphemic, some familiarity with the use of roots, prefixes, and suffixes in word formation is an aid to spelling.

    a. Write the words suggested below by supplying the root listed at the left.

Root	*Meaning*	*Illustrations*		
fer	to bear or carry	re—	con—ence	de—ential
		dif—	of—ing	trans—
spect, spec	to look	ex—	re—able	pro—
		—ific	—ulate	per—ive
scrib(e), scrip	to write	—ble	de—	pre—tion
		—ture	sub—	in—tion
duct, duc(e)	to lead, make	in—	pro—	repro—tion
		intro—	via—	con—
tain, ten	to have, hold	re—	in—tion	—ant
		main—	con—ment	—acity

Because suffixes and prefixes are unstressed, one cannot rely wholly upon the regular grapheme-phoneme relationship for vowels. It is important to know what these morphemes are and to what they are added.

b. Write the words formed when the suffix is added.

child + -hood	thought + -ful	lone + -ly	lace + -y
free + -dom	success + -ful	happy + -ness	fame + -ous
thin + -ness	final + -ly	loyal + -ty	engine + -eer
govern + -ment	incidental + -ly	slime + -y	amaze + -ment

The variant spellings of some prefixes may create spelling problems.

c. Discover the variant forms of the negative prefix *in-* by writing the negative forms of the following words.

in- + vulnerable	in- + modest	in- + reverent
in- + probable	in- + moderate	in- + legal
in- + patient	in- + relevant	in- + literate

How many forms of the prefix did you write? If you pronounce the negative words, you will observe that in some instances the phoneme /n/ is lost and that only the phoneme /i/ remains of the prefix. But in writing, the prefix *in-* is always represented by two graphemes. The prefixes *ad-* and *ob-* likewise may lose the consonant in speech, but in writing the prefix is always represented by a vowel and a consonant.

d. Form words by adding the appropriate form of the prefix *ad-*, meaning "to" or "toward," to the bound morpheme or morphemes that follow. Then draw a conclusion as to when each form of the prefix is written.

ad- + mit	ad- + gressive	ad- + nounce
ad- + here	ad- + leviate	ad- + rive
ad- + cept	ad- + pear	ad- + sist
ad- + fect	ad- + point	ad- + tend

e. Add the appropriate form of *ob-*, meaning "toward" or "against," to the bound morpheme or morphemes. What determines when each form of the prefix is written?

| ob- + struct | ob- + cur | ob- + fend | ob- + pose |
| ob- + tain | ob- + cupy | ob- + fer | ob- + press |

9. A homonym is a word identical with another in spelling and in sound but differing from it in origin and in meaning: *bank* (of a river); *bank* (an institution for lending, borrowing, safeguarding money). A homophone is a word identical with another word in sound (not necessarily in spelling) but differing from it in origin and in meaning: *cent, scent*. From the following list of homophones, write the appropriate word to complete each sentence below.

   (a) altar
       alter

   (b) board
       bored

   (c) capital
       capitol

   (d) coarse
       course

   (e) passed
       past

   (f) peace
       piece

   (g) presence
       presents

   (h) principal
       principle

   (i) stationery
       stationary

   (j) rain
       rein
       reign

   (1) Mr. Hodgkins is the _____ of the school.
   (2) We requested his _____ at the party.
   (3) This desk is _____.
   (4) I ate a _____ of pumpkin pie.
   (5) I enjoyed the _____ in botany.
   (6) We admired the dome of the _____.
   (7) The parade _____ our house at three o'clock.
   (8) The lecture _____ us.
   (9) The defeat of the Spanish Armada occurred during the _____ of Elizabeth the First.
   (10) She refused to _____ her plans.

10. Write a personal essay in which you recount your experiences in learning to spell.
11. Write a short evaluation of the usefulness of the spelling patterns that have been introduced. Do you think they would be helpful to someone who was learning to spell?
12. If you have spelling problems, you may find it helpful to keep a list of the words you misspell, group those that represent the same type of spelling pattern, and then work on those patterns.

9
OBSTACLES TO SPELLING REFORM
William J. Stevens

Recent research has made it clear that English spelling is not such a mess as some people have charged. Actually, it has patterns of consistency based upon the phonology and the morphology of the language. Many people argue, nevertheless, that there is a need for spelling reform to eliminate those irregularities that admittedly exist. To these individuals the very title "Obstacles to Spelling Reform" may be discouraging.

If English spelling has not been reformed, it isn't for lack of effort. The movement which began with Orm about A.D. 1200 continued through the years, but with little success. Noah Webster did manage to make a few changes in American spelling, including these: British *-our* in such words as *colour* and *honour* became *-or* on this side of the Atlantic; one *l* became permissible in *travelled*, *labelled*, and so forth; *theatre* was rewritten *theater*.

The most highly organized attempt at revising English spelling occurred toward the end of the nineteenth century, when spelling-reform associations were formed in both England and America. In 1906 a Simplified Spelling Board was organized in America, supported by a grant from Andrew Carnegie. Though the Board was endorsed by prominent people, including Theodore Roosevelt, its results were negligible, and it finally went out of existence. In fact, all efforts to reform spelling have produced only a few minor changes.

Obviously, English spelling has many irregularities despite its phonological and morphological basis. The question is whether a better spelling system can be devised and, if so, whether it could be put into operation. Before anyone supports another movement for spelling reform, he might well consider some of the obstacles which Stevens presents in the following article.

William J. Stevens is associate professor of English at the University of Akron.

> Annd whase wilenn shall þiss boc
> > efft oþerrsiþe writenn,
> Himm bidde icc, þatt het write rihht,
> > swasumm þiss boc himm tæchepþ
> All þwerrtut, affterr þatt itt iss
> > uppo þiss firrste bisne,
> Wiþþ all swillc rime, als her iss sett,
> > wiþþ allse fele wordess,
> Annd tatt he loke wel, þatt he
> > an bocstaff write twizzess,
> Ezzwhaer þaer itt uppo þiss boc
> > iss writenn o þat wise.
> Loke he wel þatt het write swa,
> > forr he ne mazz noht elless
> Onn Ennglissh writenn rihht te word;
> > þatt wite he wel to soþe.[1]

So wrote Orm, the father of English spelling reformers, in his *Ormulen* (about A.D. 1200). The book is dull, but there are scraps of it found in another manuscript—with a normal spelling.

Orm's "reform" was not, so far as I know, followed by anyone else. And this seems to have been the fate of all the well-meaning reformers that have set up the "only proper and sensible way" to spell English. Largely—there have been a few exceptions—whether the reformers' schemes have been minor or all-encompassing, whether their new alphabets are modifications of the one we now use or completely different, based on shorthand or Greek—they really do not make much difference. They write, they somehow get printed, and they are forgotten.

For although the interest seems high (and the publicity good), the way of the reformers has been discouraging. They seem to have had little difficulty in concocting spelling systems and alphabets better than the ones

---

[1] (And whoso will wish to write this book over again, I command him that he write it correctly, just as this book teaches him all the way through, in the way that it is in this first example—with all such rhymes as it is here given, and with just as many words; and that he take care that he write a letter twice, everywhere that it is so written in this book. Let him take care that he write so, for he may not otherwise write the word correctly in English; that he must truly know.)

we now use; but their total effect has been piddling. The feckless Orm set the pattern.

Why so dismal a record? Surely, it is not hard to point out weaknesses in our present spelling system—and the reformers have done so. They have attacked "silent letters" as in "ni*gh*t," there being more than one way of spelling the same sound, as the *sh* sound in "*s*ugar," "*sch*ist," "ti*ss*ue," "ma*ch*ine," "ra*ci*al," "men*ti*on," "se*ssi*on," and the English "conne*xi*on"; and they bemoan the years wasted in learning so illogical a system. (Our spelling, we have been told, accounts for the superiority of the Russians, who have—as we have also been told—a phonetic spelling.)

So both what is wrong with our present English spelling system and what is to be done about it have been made clear: If we spell as we pronounce, English spelling would become regular and simple; therefore, all we have to do is spell as we pronounce.

The logic is unassailable. Alphabets, therefore, have been invented to permit us to write down every sound that the reformer recognizes. Societies have been organized to simplify our spelling. Governments, both Parliament and Congress, and individuals in these governments have from time to time been interested in such reform (in the United States, one thinks of Theodore Roosevelt). Yet our spelling has remained largely unchanged for three centuries.

Could it be, then, that the reformers are in some way mistaken? Possibly English spelling is not very bad after all? Or possibly the reformers and their reforms are not too good? It seems again time to give some of the arguments that led at least one famous linguist to say that he would consider reform "an utter disaster."

1. *The present English spelling system is really not very bad:* For example, "silent letters," such as the *-n* in "condem*n*," may waste space and time. But in the derivative "condemnatory" the *-n-* is pronounced and would have to be restored even if taken away from *condemn*. *Damn* and *damnation* are another pair exactly like this, and there are many others.

Again, the *-gh-* in "ni*gh*t" is not pronounced in the United States; but neither is the final *-e* in the popular *reformed spelling* "nite." For this word the reformer drops two silent letters, picks up one that is equally silent—and for the most part spells *bright, sight,* and *sigh* without much thought of reform.

2. *The present English spelling separates homonyms:* This is one of the most popular arguments of the anti-reformers. But in all fairness it is not a very good one. It assumes that spelling such three different words as *pear, pair,* and *pare* in the same way, say *payr*, would lead to confusion of meaning. But at present one spelling, *plate* covers a multitude of meanings from "dinner plate" to "home plate" to "plate with gold." *Plate* is not at all exceptional; most words in English have more than one meaning, and these meanings are clear from context, as they would be for *payr*.

3. *English makes little use of punctuation for pronunciation:* The most used

symbol we now have is the apostrophe when it shows a contraction: *don't* for *do not* (*dont* would probably be pronounced differently). The "apostrophe for possession" has no effect on the pronunciation, and so often is improperly added or omitted by those weak in punctuation. We also use the hyphen—a few the dieresis—to show the pronunciation of such words as *re-elect* (this hyphen seems to be fading in *cooperative*). English is almost completely free of such marks found in other languages as the acute, grave, and circumflex accents, the cedilla, the umlaut, the tilde, the macron, the breve, and many others.

4. *With a phonetic spelling* we would not only spell the way we pronounce, we might pronounce the way we spell:* At first glance, some would think this all to the good. Even our present system, because of earlier reforms, has led us to discard some historical pronunciations in favor of false etymologies. So we have inserted a *-b-* in "de*b*t," although the word comes into English from the French *dette* (Chaucer has *dette*), not from Latin *debitum*—and now some try to pronounce the *-b-*. Likewise, the *-l-* in "fau*l*t"—another word from French (*faute*) and not Latin (*faltum*)—is now frequently pronounced.

But much more important, a person could force his own habits of pronunciation, if he were in a position of some authority, on others. For example, one grade-school teacher of mine in New York City insisted that we say something like *ah-ten-ti-on* for *attention* because it was "spelled that way." But we knew better; out of her grip, we returned to the usual *uh-ten-shun*. Phonetic spelling might not be very harmful in this way, however. Granted that we could all agree on the same pronunciation.

5. *Previous reforms have not been outstandingly wise:* This last negative argument is all I wish to give in favor of our present system. But, for one, the dropping of the *-e-* in "judgement" has never been fully accepted; the odd combination *-dgm-* and the wide use of *judge* have been too strongly against it. The seemingly more innocent dropping of the *-ue* in the words like "catalog*ue*" has had more success; but even here there is resistance both based on elegance and on the need to restore the *-u-* in "catalog*u*ing" and "catalog*u*er." And picnic is now spelled universally without the original final *-k* although this must be restored in *picnicking*.

Finally, some words ending in *-re* (still so spelled in Britain) have been reformed to *-er*. So we now have *meter*, *theater* (often spelled *theatre* when

---

* A truly phonetic spelling system that attempted to record the many variations in pronunciation would be complicated indeed. The twenty-six letters of the alphabet could not possibly represent the sixty or more phone types present in American speech alone. The International Phonetic Alphabet has been devised to represent such variations, but mastering it requires special training. This is an example of very simple phonetic transcription:

kæn ju rid ðɪs fonetɪk trænskrɪpʃən

Here is the same sentence in more precise transcription—Eds.:

¹k'æˢ n juˇˊ rɪˆˋ ᶦd ðɪ > s fə̣ > ³nɛʃɪk tɹᶦæn³skrɪpʃəˆn³↑

elegance is wanted); but we have to shift the -r- back to its earlier position beside the -t- in words like *metrical*. Surely, the dropping of -re in favor of -er is at best a small gain. Like the dropping of the -u- in such words as "hono*u*r" and "favo*u*r," it serves mainly to separate the written language of the United States from that of Britain and Canada—perhaps more desirable in the time of the War of 1812 than in the days of NATO.

Our present spelling, then, has its virtues. Reformed or "phonetic" spelling has its defects. To begin with the trivial:

6. *There is no real reason to assume that a phonetic spelling system is particularly useful:* The methods and the vocabulary of written English are not very close to those of speech. What I am writing here is not very much like what I would say, and that Cicero spoke the Classical Latin he wrote when he was talking over a hard day at the Senate with his wife is doubtful. Certainly, his Vulgar Latin contemporaries, the founders of the Romance languages, did not.

But vocabulary use is not the only difference between speech and writing. Yet, with their sole interest being in pronunciation, none of the popular "reformers" seems to have considered imitating tone, pauses, and stresses as a part of their reforms. All of these are very important to speech.

7. *No language has ever been spelled purely phonetically:* Indeed, the writing of some languages—Egyptian hieroglyphs, Modern Chinese, Amerindian picture writing—makes no attempt to approximate speech. And none of the languages now using the Roman alphabet is spelled phonetically. It is held that Castilian Spanish comes pretty close to it, and it has been held up to us as a model. But, without going through the whole Spanish spelling system (or investigating Latin-American pronunciation): *v* and *b* are identical in their pronunciation; *u* has two different pronunciations in "*u*no" and "c*u*idado," and it is not pronounced at all in such words as "g*u*erra" and "q*u*erer." It is still true, phonetically, that English spelling is pretty bad.

8. *English has never been spelled phonetically:* This is not, of course, of any particular importance to Modern English, except that some reformers have pointed to the past of our language and give the impression that in spelling, at least, we have degenerated. But in Old English, say around the year 950, the letter *g* was used for three or four different sounds. The different *th* sounds of "*th*is" and "*th*ink" were spelled pretty indifferently with either of the Old English letters ð or þ. It would not be difficult to give more examples.

9. *Phonetic spelling looks queer:* There are some—very possibly the same group that would like to explain nuclear fission with Chaucer's vocabulary —who consider English to be sanctified. On this basis alone, they resist all change. They rage against such spellings as *thru, tho*, and *nite* not because these "reforms" are relatively silly and minor but because they are innovations. Of this breed was Boswell. He—quoting Samuel Johnson who had said that English should have a "Saxon *k*" after a final -*c*—expressed the hope that Johnson's authority would "stop that curtailing innovation by

which we see *critic*, *public*, &c., frequently written instead of *critick*, *publick*, &c." (The Anglo-Saxons, by the way, very rarely used *k*. This letter comes to us mainly from Old Norse.) Boswell's modern kind fume at such advertising eye-catchers as *Kandy Koted Korn Kracklies*. And they have their influence.

10. *Reformed spelling would obscure etymologies, hence the relation of English to other languages:* This is another of those arguments that may seem better at first than it really is. It is true that English has borrowed many words from French, Spanish, Italian, or from their ancestor, Latin (to say nothing of Greek, Old Norse, or Algonquin). Generally, we have changed the pronunciation of the words we have borrowed to conform with our English speech habits, but we pretty much keep the original spelling. Anti-reformists hold that by changing the spelling also we would lose sight of the word's relationship to the original language. Thus, a phonetic spelling would not only make English harder for the foreigner to learn; it would result in making English less useful as a universal language (another vested interest in English), since foreigners now recognize in English many words that are familiar to their original vocabularies.

But this argument overlooks the fact that the meanings of these borrowed words have often changed also, either since coming into English or in the language from which they were borrowed—perhaps as much as the pronunciation. A careful study of what has happened to French words in English (or in French after they had been borrowed into English) might well favor a spelling that obscured a relationship that is as misleading as it is helpful.

11. *Reformed spelling would obscure the relationships of English words to each other:* Within the English language itself, the objections to obscuring the etymology of a word are more valid. There are quite a few series of words of like meaning, now connected by their spellings, that would find themselves widely separated if they were spelled phonetically. The different pronunciations in English of the Greek stem *path-*, for one: "*path*os," "*path*etic," and "tele*path*y" are very different. Likewise, the spelling of the differently pronounced Greek prefix *tele-* in "*tele*pathy" and "*tele*gram" now keeps these words together in a way that reformed spelling would not. In short, our present spelling is of some use for vocabulary building and recognition (as well as for listings in dictionaries); reformed spelling is not.

But the foregoing arguments against spelling reform I have admitted to be minor. I do not consider the rest of these so:

12. *If spelling is to be reformed to reflect pronunciation, whose pronunciation is to be reflected?* Possibly, Americans may choose to overlook the pronunciations of the English, Scots, and Irish; certainly many of our reformed spellings would be no reform for them. Even the "silent *-gh-*" is pronounced in some Scottish dialects, making a "reform" like *nite* for *night* or *tho* for *though* quite useless, even downright confusing. Justly, then, the English or the Scots

might well adopt their own reforms, and a letter to Glasgow, or from, that is now completely intelligible might call for a translator's services. Even Canada could go its own orthographic way; our present minor pronunciation differences, say of words like *about*, seem to be enough to give rise to countless witty remarks.

But within the United States itself there are hundreds of regional dialects and subdialects. Will Tidewater Virginia be content to spell in a way that reflects not its own pronunciations but those of San Francisco? Is there much hope that Texans will spell according to the speech habits of Alaska? We have our regional pride and snobbishness, and we gibe at the "Brooklyn accent," the "Southern drawl," or the Midwestern "hard *r*." Which standard of pronunciation—and one must be set up for a phonetic reform of spelling—shall we follow? For me, in my college classes, the answer will be relatively easy—mine. (Since I am from the East and my classes are made up largely of Midwesterners, this may prove a little hard on my students.)

13. *No one speaker uses the same pronunciation time after time:* There are two major reasons for this: stress and/or tone; context. The oft hit-at "carelessness" has really nothing much to do with it. The whole history of English illustrates the tendency of the language toward becoming a one-syllabled language.

So far as stress goes, I myself vary the phrase spelled *don't you* in three major ways. I may say, rather infrequently, *dohnt you*, but I more usually say *dohn chew* or *dohn chuh*, even—and without apology—*dohn cher*. Our present spelling suits all of these well enough; a phonetic spelling would force me to choose, time after time, from three or four possibilities, or it would not be phonetic. For another example, we generally pronounce *the* in two different ways. The rule is to say something like *thuh* before consonants (*thuh cake*), *thee* before vowels (*thee apple*). But *thee* is also used before consonants when there is a heavy stress: "That was *thee* Mr. Jones, Chairman of the Board!"

So far as illustrating spelling affected by context goes, the rule of *thuh* before consonants, *thee* before vowels offers one good example. An even better one, however, can be found in the pronunciation of the so-called "vowel *r*" of many English, Eastern, and Southern speakers. For some of these speakers, this *r*, found after vowels in such words as "far," "hard," and "word" (not before vowels, as in "red," "scrape") has gone; for these speakers *far* is regularly *fah* or *fa-uh*. For others, mostly those in the Northeastern dialects, including many New Yorkers, this *r* will not be pronounced in some places, but it is pronounced in others. If *car*, for example, is followed by a consonant, these speakers normally say *cah*: "His *cah* was wrecked." But if the next word begins with a vowel, then they say *car*: "His *car is* (or frequently *cah riz*) fixed." Moreover, they use *car* when the word is given heavy stress: "Call that heap a *car*?"

And not only this. For this latter group of speakers any word ending in an unstressed vowel behaves in much the same way. A few years ago, a New York City radio announcer said clearly: "*Novuh* (Lou Nova) comes into the center of the ring." "*Novuh* hits Louis!" "*Nover* is hurt!" The same dialectal trait was shown in President Kennedy's pronunciation of *Cuba*. And when we, for I am of this dialect, get excited, we all say: "What's the big *ideer*!" It is very hard for us to remember that what is called "dropping *r*'s" is considered elegant by many speakers who normally do not drop them, but that the same group usually considers that adding *r*'s to words like *idea* is vulgar and uneducated. Both the dropping and the adding come from the same speech habits.

Further, some like the late Fred Allen will put *r*'s into words that have an "*aw* sound"; they pretty regularly say *orful* (spelled *awful*) and pronounce *orphan* and *often* identically (*orfin*). Most of us in public places try to avoid this; too many do not like it. Probably we could manage to avoid it in our writing also, but not if we spell phonetically.

In such pronunciations as these, it can be hard to tell whether one will be praised or damned. Of our last four Presidents two, F.D.R. and Kennedy, were of the "*r*- dropping, *r*-adding" group; two, Truman and Eisenhower, used the *r*, as Midwesterners would say, "where it belonged."

14. *Reformed spelling can lead to, or increase, linguistic snobbery*: For this, the example I have just given of the "vowel *r*" and of some of the reactions to it might well be enough. But for a couple of examples more. Witness the horror, first, that is occasioned by the "dropping of the -*g*" (which in reality was never there phonetically) in such present participles as "hopi*ng*" (*hopin*). Yet the pronunciations *hopin*, *goin*, and the like, are both ancient and to be expected phonetically. Those who "drop the -*g*" do so in unstressed syllables only, keeping *singin* and *sinnin* quite distinct—in their speech at least.

A like bit of criticism sometimes arises over the question of elegance as opposed to sloppy pronunciation in the beginning sounds of such words as "*wh*ich," "*wh*en," and "*wh*y." Some keep *which* and *witch* distinct; others do not. Largely the preference here seems to belong to one's own pronunciation, permitting the other possibility to be labeled either "over-fastidious" or "Slurvian"—whichever suits one best.

But in all seriousness, must those who are said to sin with *r*, -*ing*, and *wh*- confess their errors in their spelling? Or must they spell "phonetically"— even though it is the phonetics of another's speech—lest they (even those who are Harvard graduates) be considered uneducated by someone from Indianapolis?

15. *Phonetic spelling is difficult*: Perhaps this is obvious by now. But it might be well to keep in mind the new British spelling system, Anglic, that is meant for the use of children. In this, purportedly phonetic, representation, the letter *e* serves for quite different sounds in *red*, *her* and *the*; the letter *o* serves for both *not* and *for*; for most speakers the *or* in *for* and the *eor* in *George* are identical, but in this phonetic spelling *for* is spelled *for*, keeping its -*or*

unchanged; *George*, however, is metamorphosed into *jaudz*, losing both *o* and *r* (but both *r*'s are kept in "Be*r*na*r*d"). Actually, whatever may be its merits Anglic is not phonetic. And it is often misleading, as when it gives *to*— usually *tuh*—the same vowel as *look*; and *day* the same vowel as *their*.

16. *Reformed spelling, even if practical, would be very expensive:* First, we would be faced with the re-education of those who have already finished their schooling, or have the necessity of going on for years publishing two differently spelled versions of a newspaper or a periodical, or have an interim period during which children would learn both alphabets. Probably, children would always have to learn to read both alphabets, unless we reprint the older works—the Bible, Shakespeare, Dickens, Hemingway, and Faulkner—in the new spelling. Then it becomes interesting to contemplate the possible quarrels arising over the phonetic spelling of Shakespeare (preserving, of course, his word play and puns). Even more difficult would be the transcribing of the various dialects attempted by Mark Twain in *The Adventures of Huckleberry Finn*.

It appears then that the only way to ultimate reform—if that is what we must have—will be the acceptance of a gradual infiltration of new spellings as the demand for them becomes overwhelming. Rather than "phonetics" only one thing is really needed to implement this infiltration: the removal of the emphasis we now place on a fixed, "correct" spelling. If Shakespeare could write as he did and still feel free to vary the spelling of his own name, why must we, the slaves of the spelling bee, now place so much weight on *to* versus *too*; *their* versus *thier*? If we cared less, our spelling would improve more.

Or we can continue doing much as we have done, using the dictionary to check our spelling—at least not having to worry over whether we have to look up a word in a spelling that accords with the pronunciation patterns of Massachusetts or Iowa.

QUESTIONS FOR STUDY AND DISCUSSION

1. What do you consider to be Stevens's strongest arguments against spelling reform? Would research supporting the consistency of English spelling lend weight to Stevens's point of view? If so, how? What is your own point of view on spelling reform?
2. a. Advertisers frequently employ a kind of simplified spelling in naming their products. In doing so, to what extent do they employ regular spelling patterns? Consider *Brite, Sprite, Duz, Chocolate Ayds*, and at least five other trade names that have variant spellings of words in the vocabulary.
   b. When trade names are coined, to what extent do they represent

regular spellings? Consider *Prell, Teflon, Tetron, Dacron,* and at least five other trade names.

3. These invented words do not follow the usual English spelling patterns. Would you be in doubt as to how to pronounce them? If not, why not?

   glight, clissue, gremn, gremnation, knoster, philathic, gnuff, creigh

4. What objection would Stevens make to spelling *autumn* as *autum* and *resign* as *resine*?
5. Suppose we had only one spelling (*ile*) for the homophones *isle, aisle, I'll*. How could the meaning be determined? Include each word in a sentence, using the common spelling *ile*. Then try out the sentences on your classmates and ask them to supply the correct spelling. Do you agree with Stevens that the need to tell one homophone from another is a weak argument against spelling reform? Cite illustrations to support your position.
6. How would Stevens account for these pronunciations?

   oftən   salm   lejislātōr   səndā   glistən

7. The words listed below represent American reformed spelling. Add the suffixes indicated and weigh the advantages and disadvantages of the change from British spelling.

   meter + -ic + -al   center + -al

   theater + -ic + -al   fiber + -oid

8. Listen to your own speech and to that of other people. Is it true that /n/ is substituted for /ŋ/ only in unstressed syllables? How frequently do you hear this substitution made? Do you hear *ringin* but not *rinnin*; *bringin* but not *brinnin*; *clingin* but not *clinnin*?
9. What is the meaning of the Greek root *path* in *pathos, pathetic, telepathy*? List other words formed on this root.
10. Suppose the letter *s* were to be used consistently to represent the phoneme /s/: *see, list, listen, cell, cent, cement, city, cinnamon, ice, face, cease.* Why would it be impossible to extend this procedure so that every grapheme would represent *one* and *only one* phoneme?

SUGGESTED ACTIVITIES

1. Read the following word pairs aloud and listen to your pronunciation.

   a. which   e. whether
      witch   weather

Obstacles to Spelling Reform   **107**

   b. when   f. why
      wen   Wye

   c. where   g. while
      wear   wile

   d. white   h. wheel
      wight   we'll

Is your pronunciation of the words in each pair the same or different? Listen to the speech of others. Do their pronunciations of these words differ? Check the pronunciation of the first word in each pair in *Webster's Third International Dictionary* or in *Webster's New Collegiate Dictionary*.

2. Stevens points out that the pronunciation of any speaker varies with "stress" and/or "tone" and "context." Test this assertion by reading these sentences and phrases aloud and listening to your pronunciation of the italicized words.

   a. The appropriate conjunction is *and* not *or*.
   b. bread *and* butter.
   c. cake *or* pie.
   d. *The* young man was with *the* old man.
   e. This is *the* Jarvis Eklund, famous captain of the football team.
   f. *Won't you* stay?
   g. You'll stay, *won't you*?
   h. I begged him not to *hit you*.
   i. Go away or I'll *hit you*.

3. Phonetic spelling would obscure the relationship between words formed on the same stem, Stevens states. As you read the following words aloud, contrast the sound of the vowel in the stressed syllable in the second form of the word with the sound of the vowel in the unstressed syllable in the first form of the word. Note that both vowels are represented by the same grapheme.

popular	popuĺarity	integer	int́egrity
universal	univerśality	orient	orí ental
organ	ordínic	parliament	parliaméntary
tyranny	tyŕannical	person	pers´onify
benefit	benéficent	lithograph	lith´ography

4. Add the suffixes indicated to the following words. Pronounce each word. What happens to the so-called "silent letters"?

solemn	+ -ity	+ -ize
column	+ -ar	+ -ist
hymn	+ -al	+ -ody
damn	+ -able	+ -ation
sign	+ -al	+ -atory
malign	+ -ant	+ -ancy
design	+ -ate	+ -ation
condemn	+ -atory	+ -ation
phlegm	+ -atic	+ -asia

Would it be a good idea to change the spelling of the first form to make it conform to the pronunciation?

5. Consult a dictionary and record the various pronunciations of the following words: *calm, card, coffee, dew, either, farm, greasy, root, textile.* How do you pronounce these words? What problem would arise if phonetic spelling were applied to these words?
6. Students of Spanish might explain to the class the degree of regularity of spelling in that language.
7. If you or your younger brothers and sisters have used the Introductory Teaching Alphabet (ITA), write a short paper in which you analyze the advantages or disadvantages of this expanded alphabet from the point of view of the child.
8. Write a short essay in which you summarize and illustrate Stevens's strongest arguments against spelling reform. Have these arguments convinced you that spelling reform has serious drawbacks and would be almost impossible to accomplish? Present your point of view clearly and logically and with sufficient evidence to convince the reader with an opposite point of view.

Part Four

GRAMMAR AND GRAMMARS

10
GRAMMAR DOWN THE AGES
Janet Rankin Aiken

In spite of the shudders of remembered anguish and dismay which the word *grammar* often summons, the fact is that civilized men have long regarded the study of language structure as a very important part of education. Not too long ago elementary schools were still called "grammar schools," a clue to value placed upon the skillful use of language.

The first known grammars were servants to religious needs, as Aiken points out in earlier deleted portions of this chapter. Sanskrit grammars were developed and memorized so that the sacred Hindu texts, the Vedas, would not be corrupted by error. Early Greek grammars, the ancestors of our modern grammars, were more likely to be philosophical than religious. Aristotle, however, generally a rather practical man, was interested in detail as well as principle. For example, he differentiated parts of speech.

When the Romans decided to describe the grammar of Latin, they appropriated the Greek models. Throughout the Middle Ages, Latin grammar was dominant, and its rules became dogma. In this excerpt, Aiken explains how Latin grammar became the ineffective model for the "school" grammar of English, the grammar which has been widely taught in England and America. It is this grammar (and the way it has been presented) which has led to the popular dislike of language study.

Aiken also mentions the beginnings in the nineteenth century of the historical and scientific study of English, which unfortunately did not greatly influence prescriptive textbooks until the twentieth century, when the new science of linguistics challenged the "legislating" grammars.

Janet Rankin Aiken was a member of the English Department of Columbia University when *Commonsense Grammar* was published in 1936.

Source: *Commonsense Grammar* by Janet R. Aiken. Copyright 1936 by Janet R. Aiken; © 1964, 1972 by Thomas Y. Crowell Company, Inc., publishers. (Revised as *Commonsense Grammar and Style* by Robert E. Morsberger.), with permission of the publisher.

In England grammarians began stirring early. Perhaps the first was Alcuin (735–804), advisor to Charlemagne, who wrote his grammar (a Latin grammar, of course) in the form of a dialog between the emperor and himself. Later, about 1000 A.D., Aelfric surnamed the Grammarian was writing of Latin declensions and conjugations for the benefit of small Saxons and perhaps for the family of Canute the Dane as well. And so went on the course of Latin grammars for English pupils, on to that most famous of all Latin grammars, by William Lily, a book which had literally monopolized the textbook trade before 1600, and which continued in use—perhaps still continues in use in English schools.

The story of this famous grammar is an extraordinary one. Its author, born in 1468, learned his Latin, Greek, and Hebrew at first hand on extensive journeys to Jerusalem, to Rhodes, to Rome, after being graduated from Oxford University. By 1512 he had been appointed high master of St. Paul's Cathedral School, and his biographers have ever since been busy asserting or refuting stories of "cruel and inhuman severity" toward his pupils. Of Lily's own fifteen children, only two were living at the time of his death in 1522, following an injudicious operation for a carbuncle on the hip.

The famous grammar made its first appearance at some time after the year 1509, but only as a part of Colet's "Aeditio," called also "Grammatices Rudimenta." It was a brief statement of Latin syntax, its rules being in English. Later, about 1513, this same syntax, with rules in Latin instead of English, was published anonymously as the "Absolutissimus de Octo Orationis Partium Constructione." The lack of an author's name was probably owing to the fact that Erasmus had a large share in the work.

About 1540 the "Aeditio" and the "Absolutissimus" were merged into one, and a special copy on vellum was later made for Edward VI. Now with royal prestige assured, the little seed William Lily had sown soon became a great plant. But the grammar did not reach its final form until the revision of 1574, over half a century after its half-author's death, when it was called in plain English, "A Short Introduction of Grammar." Bills were more than once introduced into Parliament to make it the official textbook for all schools, but it was so in fact if not by process of law. That Shakespeare learned Latin from it is proved by tags in *Love's Labors Lost* and other plays. No grammar, it is safe to say, has ever been more universally used than this one with its title page paying acknowledgment to the dead and gone master of St. Paul's, whose share in it was by this time slight indeed.

Grammar to the Elizabethan was of course Latin grammar; if English had a grammar it was thought scarcely worth study. In connection with English, however, two linguistic problems puzzled the scholars of the sixteenth century. One was the extent to which foreign (particularly Latin) terms should be allowed to enter the native speech, and the other was orthography or the correct spelling of English. Many books and pamphlets on these two timely topics appeared, but almost nothing which could be called a grammar of the English language. The genesis of English grammar is to be found first in the Latin grammars of the fifteen hundreds, and second, in chance observations made in books concerned with related subjects.

The seventeenth century opened with a brief English grammar by no less a writer than Ben Jonson, and later John Milton carried on the literary tradition by writing a treatise on the same subject. These as well as other early grammars of English were little more than Latin terms and classifications applied to English words. From five to seven "cases" were ascribed to the English noun, and long "conjugations" like "I went, we went, you went, they went" were set forth. In 1653 John Wallis in his Grammatica Linguæ Anglicanæ ventured to protest that English was a language different from Latin and that it required different treatment for that reason; but the protest went largely unheeded. It was not so much that men consciously idealized the Latin language patterns as that these were so much a part of their minds that English naturally took form in their image.

The sixteen and seventeen hundreds saw English grammar handled not so much from the scientific as from the moralistic or regulatory angle. English was like a garden whose luxuriant growth had never been pruned. English must be inventoried and stabilized. It must be standardized so as to separate the good from the bad, the correct from the incorrect.

John Dryden, arbiter of matters poetical toward the end of the sixteen hundreds, was among those men of letters who interested themselves in proposals to establish an Academy to set up such a standard of correct English, very much on the order of the French Academy inaugurated by Cardinal Richelieu in 1635. Perhaps fortunately for the English language, these proposals never came to fruition, though they persisted well into the next century.

Failing an official body of men to regulate and codify English, the next best solution might be an authoritative body of books; and the seventeen hundreds saw a succession of regulatory grammars, legislating on hundreds of expressions, most of them minute and unimportant. Of these the most popular were Lowth's *Short Introduction to English Grammar* (1762) in England, and Noah Webster's *A Grammatical Institute of the English Language* (1784) in America; the most progressive and sensible was Joseph Priestley's *The Rudiments of English Grammar* (1761).

While Priestley recognized that English must and should grow, change, and develop as any living language does, Lowth and his many successors and imitators sought not only to describe but to "fix" or stabilize English, setting up a body of rules as final authorities to govern the language for all time to come. These rules were not determined by any great scientific knowledge of the character and history of English; many of them were unconscious analogies from Latin, others based on observations of actual cultivated usage, and too many others mere matters of personal prejudices.

Back in 1710 Jonathan Swift had published a paper in the *Tatler* in which he had vented a long series of personal prejudices, against certain words such as *sham, banter, bubble, shuffling*; against abbreviated words such as *mob, rep* (*reputation*) and *incog*; and against contractions like *shan't, he's, disturb'd, rebuk'd*, the last two of which he would pronounce with three syllables. None of Swift's prejudices seems actually to have succeeded in modifying the course of English, but Lowth is probably responsible for the present-day use of *have written* rather than *have writ* (the form used by Shakespeare) or *have wrote*, a form popular in the seventeen hundreds.

During the century following, one grammarian typifies the general temper of all. Lindley Murray wrote textbooks probably surpassing in popularity any other English grammars before or since, and current in schools both in England and America. Of Quaker stock, Lindley Murray early removed from Pennsylvania to New York, to the locality which yet bears the name of Murray Hill, so called after his family. A lawyer and then a merchant, Murray amassed a small fortune and retired, first to Long Island and then to Yorkshire in England, where his gardens are said to have surpassed the royal gardens at Kew in beauty and rarity. As a diversion Murray occupied himself in teaching at a nearby school, and it was for this school that the famous English grammar was produced, to be followed later by *English Exercises*, with a key, the *English Reader*, the *Spelling Book*, and other similar textbooks, as well as certain religious works and an autobiography. The grammar followed in the path marked out by Lowth, of dogmatic rules with no exceptions, of prejudices magnified into rules. If anything could have "fixed" the English language, it would have been such widely used books as these of Lowth and Murray.

The eighteen hundreds, however, saw also the beginnings of the historical and scientific study of English, and such knowledge was bound to undermine the authority of dogma. Linguists like Sweet, Ellis, Max Muller, and Whitney began to study grammar from a new point of view, that of the explorer rather than the legislator. It was not until the twentieth century that this new science of linguistics began to come into actual conflict with the legislating grammars; today the conflict is joined and seems to be increasing rather than decreasing.

Today grammar is not one study but four or five. In contrast to the six domains of grammar marked out by Dionysius Thrax* (accentuation and phonology, the explanation of figures of speech, definitions, etymologies, the rules of flexion, and the canons of criticism) we now recognize as varieties of grammar the historical, the comparative, the descriptive, the corrective, and the explanatory. The first, historical grammar, is the theme of the present chapter; it traces linguistic facts and their discoverers from Panini†

---

* In Alexandria, Egypt, about 100 B.C., Dionysius Thrax wrote a Greek grammar for Roman schoolboys.—Eds.

† Pāṇini wrote a Sanskrit grammar, 700 to 200 B.C. Robert C. Pooley is a twentieth century grammarian.—Eds.

to Robert Pooley. Textbooks of historical grammar are few, and classes are far between. Perhaps some day it will not be so, and pupils will learn the historical background of grammar as they now learn the history of music or of education.

But if historical grammar is not formulated and taught, what shall we say of comparative grammar, which makes a synthesis of the grammars of all languages—the most complicated study in the world? Comparative grammar is not for the pupils but for the masters of learning; it is the sport and preoccupation of mighty minds at Oxford, at the Sorbonne, at Copenhagen, at Heidelberg. Sapir of Yale and Boas of Columbia reach out from the endless grammars of the American Indians; Meillet of Paris searches Indo-European dialects, Lithuanian and Zend, Tokharian and Walloon. It is what keeps such men interested in life despite their classes. It is to construct and to pore over formidable charts and tables of sounds and syllables. It is at once as comprehensive and as minute as any research ever pursued by the mind of man.

From comparative to merely descriptive grammar, that giving the plan or pattern of the structure of some one language, is a long descent; yet the former is built upon the latter, as the coral reef on the humble polyp. Unquestionably the first of all grammars was descriptive; and today, if you ask in a bookstore for an English grammar, it is a descriptive textbook that you will get. Descriptive grammar takes account of parts of speech, of subjects and complements, of infinitives and gerunds. It is the trunk of the grammar tree; it constitutes grammar in the eyes of most of us.

Corrective grammar is the stepsister of descriptive. . . . The purist is its prophet, and it comes but little within the purview of graduate schools and professorates. These avoid even the terminology of the corrective grammarian. What he calls vulgar they term popular usage, and what he praises as right they call traditional or literary. Corrective grammar tells submissive students plainly what they must or must not say.

Explanatory grammar, our fifth and last branch, is not so intellectually lofty as comparative, but it has enlisted some able minds, particularly among the linguistic psychologists. It seeks to find, perhaps in the workings of the human mentality, the reasons for changes in grammatical constructions. Its chiefest reliance is analogy, that principle which leads children to say *mans* for *men*, the conforming instinct which fits into a single pattern all things felt to be similar in idea. To give an example, it is obvious that such an expression as *It's me* originated as a construction analogous to *teach me*, *answer me*, etc., where the objective rather than the nominative follows the verb. The modern mind is not naturally alive to inflectional variations, most inflections being lost in modern English; and as *me, him, them,* and so on are used in most sentences after verbs, they naturally come to be used in all. Such a change, from *It is I* to *It's me*, is probably a benefit to the English language. It involves no ambiguity, simplifies grammar, and is intrinsically as euphonious as the alternative form. Such analyses and evaluations are the stuff of which explanatory grammar is made.

Of these five branches or types of grammar, only the descriptive and the corrective have any very long history. And these, like all things mortal, have suffered many changes as years have slipped by. Things which were wrong to one generation became right to the next, or vice versa. Words which meant one thing in 1800 mean something else today. Textbooks framed on one plan yielded to others, differing in sequence, in content, in doctrine.

Almost any grammar published in the seventeen and eighteen hundreds was fairly sure to be divided into four parts, which were orthography, etymology, syntax, and prosody. But orthography to these grammarians meant not spelling but phonetics and pronunciation; etymology meant not word derivations but a setting forth of the parts of speech. Syntax was largely concord or agreement and usage; and prosody was for the most part an exposition of figures of speech.

Words like *sentence, clause, case, grammar* itself, are subject to the shifting winds of opinion, and it is impossible to predict what they will mean a century hence. Yet below the terms used for naming the elements of grammar lies something deeper—the language itself. Every attempt to understand this growing, expanding mechanism is worthy of respect; every grammar from the earliest to the latest is worthy of our attention. But the language itself is greater than all.

QUESTIONS FOR STUDY AND DISCUSSION

1. "Grammar to the Elizabethan was of course Latin grammar," writes Mrs. Aiken. What historical events explain the great influence of Latin grammar? Refer to the articles by Myers and Hungerford.
2. What is the French Academy and what are its functions? If John Dryden had succeeded in establishing an English Academy patterned after the French, what influence might it have had on the development of English?
3. a. Aiken lists five varieties of grammar. In which kind of grammar would each of these statements be most likely to occur?
   (1) All Germanic languages contain weak verbs—verbs that form the past tense and the past participle by adding the past tense morpheme (*-ed*).

   Example: *English* learn   learned   (have) learned

   German lernen lernte   gelernt

   (2) A preposition sometimes occurs at the end of an English sentence.
   (3) Do not end a sentence with a preposition.
   (4) In Old English there were five different ways of forming the

plurals of nouns. Today most English nouns have plurals in /s/ or /əz/: *books, churches*.
      (5) The process by which the /s/ or /əz/ form became dominant was analogy (a process emphasized by Hungerford).
   b. Of these five varieties of grammar, which is the most familiar to you?
4. In the preface to his grammar, Bishop Lowth said: "The principal design of a Grammar of any Language is to teach us to express ourselves with propriety in that Language, and to enable us to judge of every phrase and form of construction, whether it be right or not."
   a. Explain what Lowth considered to be the purpose of a grammar.
   b. To which of the five varieties of grammar listed by Aiken does this preface seem to belong?
   c. Reconsider the essential nature of language as presented in part one of the book and then evaluate Lowth's premises about language.
   d. Cite instances to show the influence of Lowth's grammar.
5. "The most progressive and sensible" of the eighteenth-century grammars was *The Rudiments of English Grammar* by Joseph Priestley, Aiken states. Does the fact that Priestley was a scientist (the celebrated discoverer of oxygen) help to explain the difference between his grammar and Lowth's?
6. What definition have you learned for the term *sentence*? As you read the next two articles, look to see whether the same definition is used in structural and in transformational grammar.

SUGGESTED ACTIVITIES

1. Here is a paradigm, or model, which explains the five cases, singular and plural, for a group of Latin nouns. *Puella* means *girl*.

	Nominative	*Genitive*	*Dative*	*Accusative*	*Ablative*
Singular	puella	puellae	puellae	puellam	puella
Plural	puellae	puellarum	puellis	puellas	puellis

List the distinctive forms for *girl*. What grammatical ideas are represented in both the Latin and the English forms? You have read that the first English grammars were modeled after Latin grammars. How useful is the Latin paradigm above for English grammars?

2. Here is a paradigm for the first person singular of the Latin verb for *see*:

Present tense	video	I see
Past tense	videbam	I saw
Future tense	videbo	I (shall, will) see

Present perfect tense	vidi	I have seen
Past perfect tense	videram	I had seen
Future perfect tense	videro	I (shall, will) have seen

How many separate forms of *see* are there in comparison with the six forms of the Latin verb? Can English incorporate the personal pronoun subject in the verb form as Latin does? Is this a good model for English verbs? What grammatical idea is represented in both the Latin and the English paradigms?

3. Noah Webster, whose name is almost synonymous with *dictionary* in the United States, also wrote an important book on American spelling and grammar called *A Grammatical Institute of the English Language* (1784). In 1785 he began a thirteen-month journey to urge a strong centralized government for the new country and to lecture on the English language and on American education. These lectures are published in *Dissertations on the English Language* (1789). Read a biographical account of this amazing American, who was inspired not only by nationalistic fervor but also by eighteenth-century "enlightenment," and summarize his contributions to American English. If you can locate copies of the books mentioned, you will find them curiously modern in many ways.

4. In *A Short Introduction to English Grammar*, Lowth wrote: "A sentence is an assemblage of words, expressed in proper form, and ranged in proper order, and concurring to make complete sense. The Construction of Sentences depends principally upon the Concord or Agreement, and the Regimen or Government, of Words. . . . Sentences are Simple, or Compounded." Is this a helpful definition? Write a paragraph—humorous, if you wish—in which you point out the vagueness and weaknesses in Lowth's statements.

5. Write a personal essay narrating your most interesting, mortifying, terrifying, or boring experience with some area of English grammar.

6. Write a chronological account of your personal study of English grammar. When and how was the discipline introduced? Over how many years did it extend? Specifically, what did it include?

11
ENGLISH GRAMMAR AND THE GRAMMARS OF ENGLISH

Kenneth G. Wilson

" . . . [E]very grammar from the earliest to the latest is worthy of our attention," concludes Aiken. "But the language itself is greater than all." In other words, the quest continues for the all-encompassing theory which will explain the structure of our language, even though most people using and responding to language are unaware of this scholarship.

The last two decades have reflected the restlessness in the search for an adequate grammar. Textbooks have begun to include strange-looking "layers" and "trees" characteristic of the analytical approach of the so-called New Grammars. Obviously, there is no universal definition of the term *grammar*, and as yet no universal grammar.

In this introduction to a longer essay, Kenneth Wilson attempts to identify some of the misconceptions about the nature of grammatical study. He distinguishes between *the* grammar of a language (the system which is inside the language) and *a* grammar (a description of that system). *The* grammar is inherent in the language and is subject only to historical change. Every speaker of a given language is automatically forced to use the grammar of that language. Grammars can be many and varied. Aiken mentions five broad varieties of grammatical study. Wilson concentrates on three grammatical approaches: traditional, descriptive, and generative. All three have had a significant impact upon textbooks.

Articles which follow Wilson's introduction will present the approach of the descriptive (structural) and generative (transformational) grammars. Wilson uses the term *traditional* to describe the grammars that are based primarily on meaning rather than on form or syntax. These grammars spend a great deal of time defining parts of speech. Although

---

Source: "English Grammars and the Grammar of English," in *Standard College Dictionary*, Text Ed., pp. xiii–xiv. Copyright © 1963 by Funk & Wagnalls Company, Inc. Reprinted by permission of Harcourt Brace Jovanovich and the author.

many of them meticulously record details about the language, they do not try to explain how sentences are produced. As modern grammarians began to associate their discipline with the science of linguistics, the inadequacies of traditional grammar became apparent.

Kenneth G. Wilson is professor of English at the University of Connecticut as well as dean of the College of Liberal Arts and Sciences.

The word "grammar," used loosely, can refer to nearly everything about a language from its sounds and spelling to syntax and semantics. We often use it to mean usage in speech or writing compared with current standards of correctness: "Her grammar was awful." Or a grammar can be a book, usually a textbook, on any of these aspects of a language. Modern students of the language, however, also understand two narrower meanings, which are our particular concern in this essay:

1. *The grammar* of a language is the system of devices which carry the structural "meanings" of that language in speech and writing. This system specifies the way words in a given language are related to each other, so that we may extract meaning beyond the relatively simple lexical or dictionary meanings of the words themselves.

2. *A grammar* is a description of *the* grammar of a language. That is, any full description of the patterned system of signals employed by a language is a grammar of that language. Although the system itself (*the* grammar) may remain relatively constant, our grammars—our descriptions of the system—may improve. We may come to write more accurate, more efficient descriptions.

This distinction between *the* grammar as the system itself and *a* grammar as any description of the system is the source of much confusion when linguists address laymen, and often when grammarians address each other. A few statements about the grammar of English will help to clarify the problem.

The grammar of a language changes in time, but the rate of change is relatively slow when compared with that of words and meanings. Since the grammatical system is not fixed while the language is in use, we can expect to have to redescribe it periodically in order to keep abreast of the changes. For example, the grammar of English during the Renaissance included a question pattern which reversed the subject and verb: *Feels the king sick?* We still retain that pattern with *be* and *have* (*Is the king sick?*), but we rarely use it with other verbs. Instead, we have a relatively new pattern with the word *do*: *Does the king feel sick?* Since changes like this come very slowly, however, *a* grammar of *the* grammar will, if accurate, be useful on most counts for many years, though not for centuries.

The English grammatical system is peculiar to English. No other language has a grammar quite like it, though closely related languages such as

Norwegian and Dutch show many points of grammatical similarity, and other Indo-European languages such as Latin and French display at least a few. But descriptions of none of these languages will fit the English grammatical system, any more than descriptions of English will fit theirs. There may be some grammatical devices which every known language shares with every other, but so far we do not know what they are. For example, German and Finnish have case, and so does English, but there are languages which lack case entirely. Comparing the grammars of various languages is instructive, but each grammar is unique; each belongs only to its own language.

The system of English grammar, then, is the object for study—the same system that little children usually master with no formal instruction by the age of four or five. By imitating the speech they hear, and by trial and error, they learn to use the language; they come to "know" English grammar. They cannot talk *about* it, perhaps, but they know it at least to the extent of being able to use it unconsciously and with great precision.

That the system exists and that every native user responds to it are perhaps most quickly illustrated by a nonsense sentence: *These foser glipses have volbicly merfed the wheeple their preebs.* Although we do not know what most of the words mean (except for the "empty" words, *These, have, the*, and *their*), we "know" the grammar of the sentence. We can identify every part of speech; we can assert that *glipses* is a plural noun and a subject, that *volbicly* is an adverb modifying the verb phrase *have merfed*, and that *wheeple* is probably an indirect object. We know this, even though we do not know the "full," lexically meaningful words. The words we do recognize contain very little lexical meaning (try to define *the*), but give us considerable grammatical "meaning."

We have learned objectively a great deal about this grammatical system, about the features which signal the grammatical meanings to which we respond. In what follows, we shall examine three different grammars of English, three different methods of describing the grammar of contemporary English: *traditional grammars, descriptive grammars, and generative grammars.* We can learn a good deal about our language from each, because each has certain advantages over the others, just as each has certain flaws. But examination of all three should lead us closer to the ultimate goal, a clear view of the system itself.

Underlying each of these three kinds of grammar is the single purpose of describing in rules and generalizations the contemporary system of signaling grammatical meaning in English. The best of these grammars, obviously, will be the one that is most accurate and most efficient. It will need to be accurate because of course we want our description to be right, no matter how complicated this may make it. Ideally, we would like the description to be efficient, too, because we want our grammar to be teachable. We want to be able to teach English to foreigners, and we want to be able to help the native user of the language make better choices among the possible alternative grammatical structures English affords. To do this, we will need to be able to give him rigorously accurate information about where these choices lie, and we will also need a description efficient enough to permit him to learn quickly what he needs to know.

Finally, however, there is an even more important reason for seeking the best description of the English grammatical system. Language is perhaps the most distinctive and most basic of all human activities; it sets us apart from all other animals. As a humane study, as an end in itself, therefore, language merits our every effort to understand what it is and how it works. The liberally educated man will find all his attempts at following the Socratic injunction, "Know thyself," leading him sooner or later to the study of the language he uses. This means, among other things, studying its grammar.

QUESTIONS FOR STUDY AND DISCUSSION

1. The devices of Modern English that carry the structural meanings are broadly defined as word order, structure words, and word forms. (Structure or function words include articles, prepositions, conjunctions, etc., which help to show the relationship between parts of a sentence.) When the devices are operating smoothly, a native speaker of a language understands a sentence to be grammatical; that is, well formed. If he feels that a sentence is ungrammatical, usually some disordering in the system can be detected. Evaluate the grammaticality of the following word groups. If the necessary grammatical signals are missing or misused, explain.

    a. I gave a book my sister.
    b. Pogo is secretary of the Advancement Society for the Protection of Little People.
    c. These are the people I ride with.
    d. Ring bells loudly the.
    e. Three woman is in the bus.

2. By supplying the necessary structure words, try to group these words to form a sentence:

    generation   music   stereo   beat   defining   blared
    house   raucously   "now"

3. Some of the fun of Lewis Carroll's *Through the Looking-Glass* lies in his nonsense rhymes, like this one:

    'And hast thou slain the Jabberwock?
        Come to my arms, my beamish boy!
    O frabjous day! Calloh! Callay!'
        He chortled in his joy.

Which words carry little or no lexical meaning for you? (You might check a dictionary to see whether or not they are in the English lexicon.) Do the sentences sound grammatical? For example, is the word order normal? Are the necessary structure words present? What suffixes do you recognize, and what parts of speech do they signal?

4. The grammar of a language changes slowly. Translate these passages from *Julius Caesar* into Modern English and explain the grammatical changes you found it necessary to make.

   a. Thou art a cobbler, art thou?

   b. Wherefore rejoice? What conquest brings he home?

   c. Dwell I but in the suburbs of your good pleasure?

   d. O mighty Caesar, dost thou lie so low?

   e. This was the most unkindest cut of all.

   f. Think not, thou noble Roman,
      That ever Brutus will go bound to Rome.

SUGGESTED ACTIVITIES

1. If you are reading a Shakespearean play, make a list of sentences containing grammatical structures different from those we use today. These sentences might include questions, negatives, commands and inflectional endings and word order no longer in use.

2. Write two or three nonsense sentences which will show that you understand the English grammatical system because of the conventional use of word order, structure words, and word forms (inflectional endings and derivational suffixes).

12
THE STRUCTURAL REVOLUTION
Miriam Goldstein Sargon

The revolution in mathematics has its counterpart in the revolution in grammar. The scholarly grammarians started the revolution in the early twentieth century, the structural grammarians gave it new direction during the second quarter of the century, and the transformational-generative grammarians followed close in the third quarter with what has been called a "counterrevolution." And waiting in the wings, hoping to come on the scene, are at least two other groups—the tagmemicists and the stratificationalists.

Structural grammarians view an English sentence as a systematic arrangement of structures within structures. In analyzing a language, structuralists work primarily with speech (often with actual utterances of native speakers) and generally proceed from the smallest units of language (speech sounds, or phones) to phonemes, morphemes, words and their classification, then to smaller structural units within a sentence, and finally to the sentence itself. (This method is almost essential in the analysis of a language that has not been put into writing.) Structuralists move from these formal characteristics of a language, which can be observed objectively, to meaning and function, reversing the method of traditional textbook grammars, which begin with meaning.

Because structural grammar emphasizes speech, intonation plays an important part in it. For example, rising intonation can turn a statement into a question.

Jim won the election ↘   Jim won the election ↗

The slight pause between words sometimes differentiates meaning.

I + scream   ice + cream   a + name   an + aim

In some words stress is an indicator of the part of speech: cóntrast (n),

---

Source: *The Teaching of Language in Our Schools* (New York: Macmillan, 1966), pp. 80–88; 90. Copyright © 1966 by the National Council of Teachers of English. Reprinted by permission of the National Council of Teachers of English and the author.

contrást (v). And a shift in stress may even mark a different meaning of a sentence: "Give him the boók"; "Give hím (not someone else) the book."

Miriam Goldstein Sargon is an instructor in English and linguistics at Newton North High School, Newtonville, Massachusetts.

Both revolution and counterrevolution have had a healthy effect on language study. There is a good deal of questioning, bewilderment, and debate; a good deal of unlearning and learning going on these days. No one text or school of grammar provides all the answers; but the general direction has been away from the arbitrariness and prescriptiveness of schoolroom grammars to the reasonableness and descriptiveness of scholarly traditional grammar, structural grammar, and transformational grammar; from sentence analysis to sentence building, from rote memorizing to problem solving. As a science, grammar's unsolved problems and new frontiers challenge teacher, student, and theoretician.

The grammar underlying the wonderful feat of language is yet to be presented in its entirety. Meanwhile there are several grammars. *A* grammar is to *the* grammar as a map is to the landscape. The road map serves one purpose, the contour map another. So is it with the various kinds of grammar now being offered. Each attempts to describe the rules underlying an English sentence; each can be evaluated in various ways; for example, by seeing how well it corresponds to the given data. Traditional classroom grammars, in their prescriptions, described how English conformed to the logic and perfection of Latin and how we might perpetuate that perfection. If, for example, you could not split an infinitive like *amāre* into two words in the Latin language, then you should not hasten the deterioration of English which (alas!) has a two-word infinitive (to love). You should try not to further split the poor English infinitive. Scholarly traditional grammar, a natural outgrowth of traditional descriptive linguistics, is our richest source of detailed and varied examples of English sentence structure. It neatly organizes these examples, comments on them, and suggests how the student may construct similar sentences. All modern grammarians are still mining Otto Jespersen's seven-volume English grammar, one of the richest storehouses of examples of English sentences, one of the most provocative sources of modern theorizing. Jespersen's summary chapter in his *Essentials of English Grammar*,[1] for example, anticipates Charles C. Fries' analysis of grammatical devices. His chapters on junction and nexus have been picked up and expanded by transformationalists. The first stage of the revolution, then, is reflected in these early twentieth-century scholarly grammarians like

---

[1] Otto Jespersen, *Essentials of English Grammar* (University, Ala.: University of Alabama Press, 1964). Originally London: George Allen & Unwin Ltd., 1933.

Jespersen, Curme, Poutsma, and Palmer. Although some of these grammars originally taught English to foreigners, they still enlarge the understanding and appreciation of a language already known to many readers. Porter Perrin's texts (e.g., *Writer's Guide and Index to English*) incorporate much of this traditional grammar.[2] In many schools grammar is being quietly well taught through them. In others teachers are adapting to their students' level the rich fund of knowledge in Ralph B. Long's *The Sentence and Its Parts*, which incorporates contemporary scholarship in a traditional grammar.[3] What characterizes the best teaching of traditional grammar is the reformulation of knowledge. Scholarly traditional grammars always base their appreciation and prescription on an exhaustive description of spoken as well as written English.

The second stage of the development of linguistics—an outcome of the awareness of linguistic relativity, of differences in languages—sought to explain the uniqueness of each system. Structural linguists collected, classified, observed stretches of physical events called utterances as the botanist collects, observes, classifies plant life. The most subjective element in language making is obviously meaning; hence the structuralist not only refused to rely on meaning but he tried to exclude meaning from his analysis. The words "You drive me wild" may be a plea to a coy mistress or a blast at a termagant wife. The shift in meaning may interest all the neighbors, each of whom may have his theory as to how the transformation occurred. The grammarian also wants to find out how the change took place. In investigating the change, he cannot ignore the fact that speech is primary and has more signals of meaning than the written word has. Thus, though the written words remain the same, the spoken words have reversed their original meaning. But meaning is the outcome, not the method, of the structuralists.

Closely related to the problem of meaning is that of criteria for classifying elements of the sentence. Here the classroom grammars proved only circular, contradictory, and confusing. A sentence, we were told, is a group of words expressing a complete thought. But who tells the child what a complete thought is? How does he know? And if he already knows, of what further use is the definition? Or a sentence is a group of words beginning with a capital letter and ending with a period. The child can accept or recognize this in his reading. But how is he to use this definition to help him in his writing? Yet we speak and are understood without punctuation. The pupil who writes sentence fragments and run-on sentences has no trouble communicating orally. He knows more about a sentence than its traditional definition.

We can readily see *why* grammarians relied so heavily on meaning for

---

[2] Porter G. Perrin, *Writer's Guide and Index to English* (4th ed.; Chicago, Ill.: Scott, Foresman and Company, 1965).

[3] Ralph B. Long, *The Sentence and Its Parts* (Chicago, Ill.: University of Chicago Press, 1961).

classifying words as parts of speech. Since so many of our words had lost their characteristic inflections (case endings for nouns, personal and tense endings for verbs), we could no longer define them by form and meaning, as the Latinate grammars had. So we were left with meaning. *A noun is the name of a person, place, or thing.* Again, because the native speaker unconsciously knows more than this definition tells him, he rarely gets into trouble. Is a thing an action like *explosion*, an event like *revolution*, a quality like *mercy*, an animal like *dinosaur*, an object like *protoplasm*? Then why are *set* and *function* nouns? Note that my question does not include the possibility that *set* and *function* are nouns. It simply makes me seek a better definition of noun than the semantic one. And if a verb shows action or a state of being, where shall we draw the line between showing an action and naming it? In *They saw the fireworks*, where is the action? The interjection, according to prescriptive grammars, shows strong feeling. In *She adores him*, *adores* certainly expresses her strong feeling. Is it therefore an interjection?

If meaning was an unreliable criterion for some parts of speech, might overlapping the categories of function and meaning clarify our definitions? An adjective is a word that modifies a noun or a pronoun. But when *A bee stung Johnny and me*, both of us were modified by that bee. Is *bee* therefore an adjective? What does *modify* mean? An adverb is a word that modifies a verb, adjective, or another adverb. In *What did your brother's keeper use last year instead of his own money?* *brother* becomes an adjective, *your* an adverb, *year* an adverb, *last* an adverb. A pronoun takes the place of a noun. In *She and I are friends*, what noun does *I* replace? In *Nelson is my hideaway; I do my writing there*, is *there* a pronoun? If a conjunction is a word that connects words, phrases, or clauses, what shall I label conjunction in *He went from pillar to post?* And if a preposition is a word that shows the relationship between its object and some other word in the sentence, then in *John loves Mary*, *loves* must be a preposition. Since all of these definitions combine function and meaning, we do not know which takes precedence—according to the definition. Yet you know and I know in spite of the definition.

Because of these problems, structuralists decided that form and position were more reliable guides to function and meaning. Word order was paramount: *Man bites dog* makes headlines; *Dog bites man* is hardly news. But word order in turn demanded classification or identification of words. Structuralists recognized four large unlimited form classes (noun [and pronoun], verb, adjective, and adverb) and called the rest structure or function words (including determiners [such as *a, an, the*], auxiliaries, intensifiers, prepositions, conjunctions). We memorize function words naturally because they are limited in number and rarely change, yet through their position in the sentence they show structural relationships among the form classes that signal meaning. The ambiguity of headlines or telegrams disappears when we insert a function word like *the*: *Jam sticks in his throat* or *Police walk nightly*. So form and word order give a sentence its structure or grammatical meaning, which in turn is the basis for its lexical meaning.

In a sequence like *A raglump propagoodle hieraddles the aleurest ptolomaniacs ptaly*, the only two words that are unmistakably English are *a* and *the*, the only recognizable suffixes *est* and *ly*. Though there is an antique flavor about the roots of some of the other words, and *gl*, *mp*, and *dle* suggest the tone, we don't know what the sentence means. Yet the structural meaning is not so elusive. We can assume that what follows *a* and *the* are either nouns or noun phrases. Furthermore, the first noun phrase has to stop before *hieraddles*, because *a* signals a singular noun. So although *hieraddles* might have been a plural noun ending in *es*, and preceded by two adjectives (or what else?), it is more probably a singular verb ending in *es* with the preceding three-word noun phrase as subject. What follows *hieraddles* now looks like another noun phrase used as an object. *Aleurest* looks like an adjective in the superlative degree just as *ptaly* looks like an adverb; its position before the noun phrase used as object confirms our suspicion. We can assume all these things if the stress and pitch and pauses go along with this analysis. We can assume that the sentence consists of subject and predicate; that the subject consists of a noun phrase, the predicate consists of a verb, noun phrase used as object, and finally adverb, as in the sentence *A rabid demagogue addles the weakest voters usually*. Given punctuation, we might also see in these words a noun series consisting of *A raglump propagoodle*, (some) *hieraddles*, *THE aleurest*, (some) *ptolomaniacs*, and (a little bit of) *ptaly*, as in *a Santa Claus, gifts, the tree, cones, holly*.

To parse this sentence or noun phrase we have availed ourselves of the structuralists' criteria: inflectional endings, derivational prefixes and suffixes, word order, associated function words, and the suprasegmentals known as stress, pitch, and juncture or pause. In other words, by substituting the form classes and structure words in a test frame, we have arrived either at the sentence pattern or at the noun phrase pattern. These problems were clearly faced in such revolutionary texts as Smith and Trager's *Outline of English Structure* in 1951[4] and in Fries' *The Structure of English* a year later.

Inflectional endings alone are no guide, but combined with other criteria, they confirm our intuitions about the way an English sentence goes. Nouns, for example, remain unchanged except for the possessive *'s* or *s'* and they usually form their plurals by adding *s* or *es* to the singular. In some words, replacement of an internal vowel by another (m*a*n, m*e*n) functions as a grammatical signal for the plural. Verbs are usually identified by their *ed*, *t*, and *d* endings for the past tense (or by the vowel replacement as in s*a*ng and s*i*ng) and by *s* or *es* for the third person singular in the present. When adjectives form their comparative and superlative by inflectional endings, those endings are *-er* and *-est*. Adverbs add the inflectional ending *-ly* to the adjective and *-er* or *-est* for comparative and superlative.

---

[4] Henry Lee Smith, Jr., and George L. Trager, *Outline of English Structure* (New York: American Council of Learned Societies [Columbia University Press], 1951).

In addition to inflectional endings for case, number, person, tense, and degree, the four form classes have characteristic derivational endings: prefixes or suffixes. The most common noun endings are *-hood, -acy, -tion, -age, -al, -ant, -ism, -ness, -ess, -ist, -ster, -dom, -ment, -ence, -or,* and *-er* as in *motherhood, democracy, attention, portage, survival, informant, totalitarianism, kindness, actress, jurist, youngster, kingdom, judgment, competence, actor,* and *teacher.* Verb prefixes may be *un-, be-, de-, re-, pre-,* or *dis-* as in *UNdo, BEdevil DEcontaminate, REsell, PREview,* or *DISapprove*; suffixes may be *-ize, -ate, -fy, -en* as in *agonIZE, activATE, rareFY, threatEN.* Adjectives have a long list of derivational suffixes, identifiable in words like *ghostLY, attractIVE, goldEN, cloudY, cloudED, hesitANT, competENT, beautiFUL, courageOUS, personAL, stationARY, argumentaTIVE, childISH, fashionABLE*; the commonest prefixes are *un-, a-, in-* as in *UNkind, Amoral, INeffectual.* The commonest derivational endings for adverbs are the suffixes *-ward, -time, -wise,* and *-ly* as in *homeWARD, someTIME, otherWISE,* and *heavenLY.* All of these derivational endings show us how a part of speech is derived from the root of the word: *agonY, agonIZE, agonizING, agonizingLY,* or *rariTY, rareFY, rare, rareLY.* In *rare* the adjective shows no derivational ending. These formal contrasts signal different meanings in *The dog's friendLY arrivAL* and *The dog's friend arrivED.*

But beyond inflectional and derivational ending, the four form classes can be identified by their position in the sentence and by associated function words. The usual patterns for nouns are shown in *The BABY woke, The BABY woke his MOTHER, The BABY woke his MOTHER at NIGHT, His MOTHER called the BABY a BRAT,* and *His MOTHER gave the BABY a BOTTLE. DICKY cried* and *MOTHERHOOD bored her* suggest some modifications to our tests for noun, since they do not ordinarily form plurals or take determiners like *a* or *the. A criminal lawyer* loses its ambiguity when we hear the stress.

The most common verb patterns are *The baby DRANK his milk, The baby CRIED loudly, The baby IS hungry.* If nouns are usually signaled by determiners, verbs are often preceded by auxiliaries like *be, have, do, can, will, may, shall, must,* and *ought.* Another way to distinguish noun from verb is stress. Listen to the difference between *con'duct* and *conduct', im'port* and *import'.* Noun compounds seem to follow the pattern of initial stress, as in *mad'house, egg'head, gun'powder, air'port, mas'termind.* Verb auxiliaries have weak stress except for *may, ought,* and *do.* Pause makes further syntactic distinctions. For example, it tells whether Herman is being spoken to or about in *Herman, the hermit is gone* and *Herman the hermit is gone.*

Similarly adjectives and adverbs are identified by position, associated words, and stress. Adjectives usually occupy positions as in *The dog is FIERCE. The FIERCE dog snarled. They thought him DANGEROUS.* Adjectives are often preceded by intensifiers; the same is true of adverbs. Stress frequently marks the difference between adverb and preposition: *He went up.*

He went up the stairs. Or adverb and conjunction: *Speak to him; however, you'll offend him. However you speak to him, you'll offend him.*

Thus youngsters nowadays discover the word order or patterns which characterize the most common English sentences and which form the basis for more complicated sentences. Drill in such patterns is particularly helpful to those who are learning English as a second language. In these patterns, parts of speech appearing in parentheses may or may not appear in the sentence. Contrast, for example, *Experience* in pattern 1 with *(The) Experience* in patterns 6 and 7.

1. (Det) Noun   +   Intransitive Verb   +   (Adv.)
   Experience   *teaches*   *occasionally*

2. (Det) Noun   +   Verb   +   (Det) Noun
   Experience   *teaches*   *a lesson*

3. (Det) Noun   +   Linking Verb   +   (Det) Noun
   Experience   *is*   *a teacher*

4. (Det) Noun   +   Linking Verb   +   Adjective
   Experience   *is*   *costly*

5. (Det) Noun   +   Verb   +   (Det) Noun +   (Det) Noun
   Experience   *taught*   *the boys*   *a lesson*

6. (Det) Noun   +   Verb   +   (Det) Noun +   (Det) Noun
   (The) Experience   *made*   *the boys*   *men*

7. (Det) Noun   +   Verb   +   (Det) Noun +   Adjective
   (The) Experience   *made*   *the boys*   *cautious*

The child learns to identify clusters of nouns consisting of a headword and various modifiers—such as determiners, adjectives, participles, adverbs, prepositional phrases, and clauses—each of which occupies a fairly predictable position in the sentence. Thus we say *A certain pretty little green-eyed girl with tawny skin that suggested her creole background,* and we know that the same details in another order alter the meaning: *A pretty certain green-eyed little tawny creole girl with skin that suggested her background.* The structuralists get at the complexity of analyzing and writing mature sentences by isolating layers of structural relationships from the largest cluster (or groups of words) to the smallest morpheme (units of meaning within the word), always correlating form with order.

Two great virtues of this grammar are the stress on inductive rather than deductive reasoning and the emphasis on synthesis rather than analysis. The pupil decides why he is calling a certain word a noun; he can account for his choice; he does not resort to rote memorizing or to unintelligent guessing. He also builds sentences from slots and patterns rather than takes given sentences apart. These sentences can grow in complexity as his need for expression develops. Sometimes, to wean him from earlier notions about parts of speech, he uses numbers rather than letters: 1—noun, 2—verb, 3—adjective, 4—adverb, A—auxiliary, D—determiner, P—preposition.

To make for sharper distinctions, nouns are indexed a, b, c, and so forth. The first noun in a sentence is indexed "a." All other nouns which refer back to this noun are also indexed "a." (*Mother is a teacher*: 1a 2 D 1a; but *Mother saw the teacher*: 1a 2 D 1b.) When he has almost completed a standard text like Paul Roberts' *Patterns of English* (written for college freshmen but now used in junior high grades),[5] he can write sentences from formulas, for example:

A	D	1^a	2	D	1^b	D	1^c
Does	the	doctor	give	every	patient	these	pills?

or

let's	2	P	D	1^a	S	D	1^b	↔	2	4
Let's	get	to	the	theater	before	the	feature		starts	tonight.

where S = subordinator and ↔ ties units into agreement. We need only compare the definitions of *adjective, modify,* and *exclamatory sentence* in a book like James Sledd's *A Short Introduction to English Grammar*[6] with those in another text for teachers, Robert Pooley's *Teaching English Grammar*,[7] to see the structuralists' enormous advances in consistency and precision.

The pupil notices the effect of various kinds of sentences—statements, questions, and requests—on the hearer. He traces these responses back to their cause in the different structure words that have signaled the sentence pattern.

These criteria of word order, inflectional and derivational endings, associated function words, suprasegmentals, and sentence patterns account for the different meanings of the same word. As native speakers, we know intuitively that *about* has several different meanings in the following sentences. We don't even need to refer to a dictionary:

1. He is *about* to jump.
2. She is *about* ten years old.
3. We talked *about* ten cave men.
4. We were given instructions *about* the work.
5. We wandered *about* the cave.
6. The railing *about* the tower is rusty.

---

[5] Paul Roberts, *Patterns of English* (New York: Harcourt, Brace & World, Inc., 1956).

[6] James Sledd, *A Short Introduction to English Grammar* (Chicago: Scott, Foresman and Company, 1959).

[7] Robert C. Pooley, *Teaching English Grammar* (New York: Appleton-Century-Crofts, 1957).

7. I'm *about* ready to leave.

8. We moved the furniture *about* the room.

9. I spun *about*.

But in order to explain this intuitive knowledge, we need only examine the forms of words and their positions in these different contexts. Then we see how grammatical structure eliminates ambiguity. For example, *about* means *ready* only when it is followed by an infinitive. *About* means *approximately* when it is preceded by *is* and followed by countable nouns. When preceded by a verb of mental action like *talks* and followed by countable nouns, *about* means *concerning*. When preceded by a verb of physical action like *moved*, *about* means *around*. Grammatical structure, in other words, is an important part of what we loosely call *context*. . . .

Structural grammar had not answered all the questions it set out to answer as to how we recognize and produce sentences, nor had it avoided all the pitfalls of semantically based grammar; but it liberated pupil and teachers from dull repetition and arbitrary routine. Structural grammar replaced the fictitious simplicity of a dead language with the complex reality of a living language. Careful observation, classification, and verification were beginning to make order out of chaos.

QUESTIONS FOR STUDY AND DISCUSSION

1. a. Here are some quotations from "The Structural Revolution." Do they qualify as sentences on the basis of the usual textbook definition that "a sentence is a group of words expressing a complete thought"?

    Example: "So is it with the various kinds of grammar now being offered."

    Clue: Since *so* refers to what has been said before, can this sentence be considered to offer a "complete" thought?

    (1) "Here the classroom grammars proved only circular, contradictory, and confusing."

    (2) "How does he know?"

    (3) "And if he already knows, of what further use is the definition?"

    (4) "So we were left with meaning."

    (5) "Is it therefore an interjection?"

    (6) "Yet you know and I know in spite of the definition."

    (7) "We can talk about this fact, and use this fact in interpretation, not vaguely but precisely."

    b. How did these sentences acquire meaning in the essay?
    c. What additional information would have to be supplied to make each sentence meaningful in isolation?
    d. How useful is the definition in determining whether a particular group of words is a sentence?
2. Compare the structuralists' classification of parts of speech with that of the textbook grammars you have studied. What is the basis for each classification? Which classification seems preferable to you? Why?
3. What are the inflectional endings in these sentences, what part of speech does each inflection identify, and what is the grammatical meaning of the inflection?

    a. The mayor's secretary invited the students to visit the latest exhibit in the city hall.
    b. The team wants a larger crowd at the next game.
    c. I have written a letter and am waiting for a reply.

4. Select the nouns, verbs, adjectives, and adverbs in this nonsense sentence and be ready to present the evidence for each classification. Use as many of the following criteria as apply: word forms (inflectional and derivational endings); associated structure, or function words; and word order. Then supply English words for the nonsense words.

    The trummest phlatesters antrugonized the more fensantive flohences flatally.

5. a. If someone addressed these sentences to you, what would your response to each sentence be?

    (1) Have you read *Lord of the Flies?*
    (2) What do you plan to do next summer?
    (3) Open the door, please.
    (4) Something funny happened this morning.

    b. Classify each sentence on the basis of your response.
    c. How do traditional textbooks classify the sentences? Can you support the criticism that, because they are circulatory, the definitions do not really define?
    d. Show how word order (and possibly other signals) helps to identify these three kinds of sentences.
6. Read the following sentences aloud and note the change in meaning as the stress shifts.

    a. My lawyer was an honest mán.
    b. My lawyer was an hónest man.

c. My lawyer wás an honest man.

d. My láwyer was an honest man.

e. Mý lawyer was an honest man.

SUGGESTED ACTIVITIES

1. Write a sentence composed of nonsense words (except for structure words). Classify the words as noun, verb, adjective, or adverb and be ready to point out to the class the formal signals that identify the part of speech.
2. a. Classify each of these words as noun, verb, adjective, or adverb on the basis of its derivational suffix.

commutative	imperviable	predacity	crosswise
necromancy	transcription	fructify	hypothetical
dicephalous	lethargize	contrary	enlighten
matriculate	disestablishment	sententiousness	reluctant
prohibitively	backwards	antagonist	totalitarianism

   b. Could you have classified these words readily on the basis of meaning?
3. The experimental character of E. E. Cummings's poetry is apparent not only in the obvious mechanics of writing—the reduction of capital letters and underpunctuation—but especially in his "sprung" syntax—the disassociation of grammatical forms from their usual slots. You can find some of Cummings's poems in anthologies of American literature or of modern poetry. Write an analysis of Cummings's sentences in "My Father Moved Through Dooms of Love" or "Anyone Lived in a Pretty How Town" by enumerating the parts that are technically ungrammatical, explaining why they are ungrammatical, and commenting upon the effect these passages have upon the total meaning of the poem. For example, in the first title *dooms* is not normally used in the plural; in the second, *how*, usually classified as an interrogative adverb, occurs in an adjective position.
4. a. Arrange the following words in different ways to form as many sentences as possible.

carrying	gold-headed	with	student
who	met	Dogpatch	dachshund
bone	leading	cane	haughty

| man | was | from | a, a, a, a, an |
| old | young | | |

b. What makes the differences in meaning in the sentences?

5. a. Write two sentences to illustrate each of the seven sentence patterns on p. 130. In Pattern 4 not only *be* but such other linking verbs as *seem, appear, become, remain* can be used.

   b. Expand one sentence in each pattern by making additions to the skeleton sentence.

   Example for Pattern 2: The students read *Barn Burning.*

   The twenty enthusiastic students in the Honors section of senior English recently read *Barn Burning,* a short story by William Faulkner, a Nobel Prize winner.

6. a. A sentence is not just a string of words. It is made up of structural units within structural units, like a set of Chinese boxes. The component parts, or immediate constituents, of most sentences are subject and predicate. These immediate constituents can then be divided into smaller units, each with its immediate constituents, until no further division can be made. To cut the following sentence in two, one would make the break after *Pittsville.* The immediate constituents of the subject are *in Pittsville* and *an old shack*; the immediate constituents of the predicate are *last night* and *burned to the ground. In Pittsville* is a unit because *there* could substitute for it, and *to the ground* is a unit because *down* could substitute for it; but *burned to the* is *not* a unit because no substitute can be found for it, etc. The subject contains four layers of structural units and the predicate five layers as illustrated in the open boxes below.

Layer 5 An | old | shack | in | Pittsville | burned | to | the | ground | last | night.
Layer 4
Layer 3
Layer 2
Layer 1

   b. Show the successive immediate constituents of these sentences, following the illustration above.

   The neglected dogs on the corner barked incessantly at night.

   These fat members of the club jog conscientiously every day.

13
HOW LITTLE SENTENCES GROW INTO BIG ONES

Kellogg W. Hunt

Any native speaker of a language has an intuitive knowledge of the grammar of his language. He immediately recognizes that "The parade marched down the street" is a well-formed sentence and that "The parade the street down marched" is not. He constantly hears and utters totally new sentences and can pack several messages into a single sentence, all within the limits imposed by a particular language system. This flexibility of language is emphasized by Chafe in "The Nature of Language."

The purpose of a generative-transformational grammar is to account for the intuitions of the native speaker by setting up a system of rules, or specifications, that clearly describe the structures of all the possible sentences of a language. The number of sentences in a language and the length of the sentences are theoretically unlimited, but the language system is limited and can be described.

Generate, a term borrowed from mathematics, means "to characterize explicitly." The generative part of the grammar consists of specifications for rewriting the concept Sentence into smaller and smaller structures to show the component parts (immediate constituents) of a sentence. The first division is into Noun Phrase (Subject) and Verb Phrase (Predicate). In similar fashion the number 6 can be rewritten to show that it contains 2 + 4; 2 can be rewritten as 1 + 1; 4 as 1 + 3, etc. Though the words in two sentences are different, the underlying grammatical structures may be the same as in "The cat will drink milk," "The student may read the novel," "The legislature should pass the bill." In generative-transformational grammar an upside-down tree is used to represent the immediate constituents of a sentence as layered lines are used in structural grammar.

Source: Alexander Frazier, ed., *New Directions in Elementary English* (Champaign, Ill.: NCTE, 1967), pp. 110–121; 123–124. Copyright © 1967 by the National Council of Teachers of English. Reprinted by permission of the National Council of Teachers of English and the author.

Though it would be possible to describe the structures of all sentences in a language with formulas, as on p. 138, it would become needlessly cumbersome for long sentences. So a process called transformation is employed. We have all sensed a relationship between sentences differing in structure but having approximately the same meaning: "Our team won the game" and "The game was won by our team"; "I like pickles that are sweet" and "I like sweet pickles." The second sentence in each instance is produced by performing a transformation upon the string of grammatical structures underlying the first sentence. For anyone who has not studied transformational grammar, however, it is simpler to proceed as though the transformations were performed on the sentences themselves; and Hunt uses this method as better adapted to his audience. The transformations that are introduced in this article can be used to good advantage by students who are trying to construct more sophisticated sentences.

Genertaive-transformational grammar is relatively new, dating back to 1957 with the publication of *Syntactic Structures*, a monograph by Noam Chomsky, professor of modern languages and linguistics at the Massachusetts Institute of Technology. Since then, Chomsky and other scholars have further developed this theory of grammar.

Kellogg W. Hunt gave the following address to language arts teachers as an introduction to transformational grammar when he was professor of English at Florida State University. He is now engaged in research at the East-West Center, Honolulu.

. . . The newest model in grammar is called generative-transformational. It is called generative because it aims to be as explicit as the mathematical formulae that generate a circle or a straight line on a sheet of graph paper. An explicit formula is capable of being proved true or false. A vague statement is not capable of being proved either true or false. So generative grammar aims to say explicitly many of the things that traditional grammars have said only vaguely. It tries to generate the same sentences that people generate, and it tries to generate none of the nonsentences. This grammar is by no means complete, but no other grammar is complete either, as any experienced grammarian knows. (The second half of the generative-transformational label will be touched on later in this paper.)

NATURE OF GENERATIVE-TRANSFORMATIONAL GRAMMAR

I will call the grammar by its initials, g-t. Ordinarily, g-t grammar is presented as a series of formulae that to many people look horribly scientific.

Sample formulae look like this:*

S → NP + Predicate

Predicate → Aux + VP

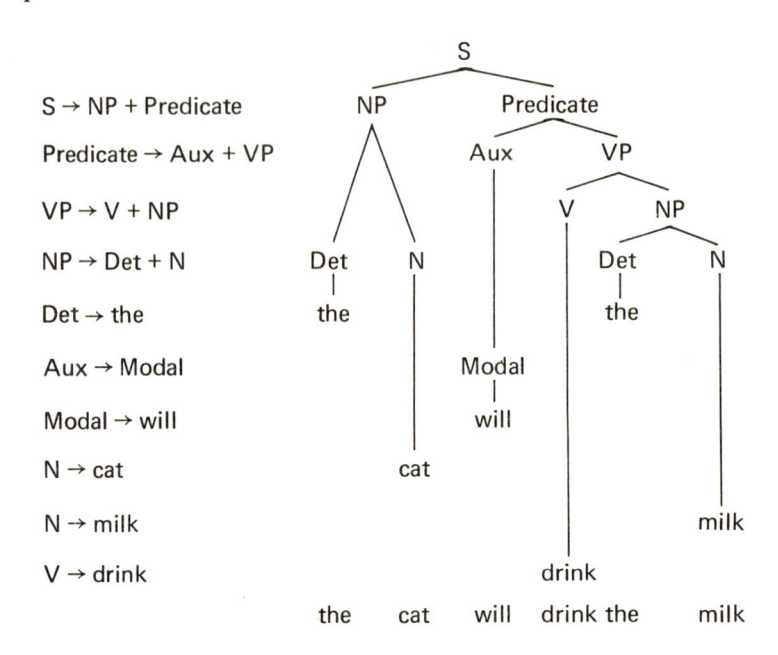

VP → V + NP

NP → Det + N

Det → the

Aux → Modal

Modal → will

N → cat

N → milk

V → drink

```
                    S
              ┌─────┴─────┐
             NP         Predicate
            ╱ ╲         ┌───┴───┐
          Det  N       Aux      VP
           │            │      ┌─┴─┐
          the          Modal   V   NP
                        │      │  ╱ ╲
                       will    │ Det  N
                               │  │
                              drink the
          cat                          milk

          the  cat   will  drink  the  milk
```

But what these formulae mean is not at all strange and forbidding. In fact it is so familiar to language arts teachers that I am afraid I will be dull and commonplace for the next several pages. I am going to talk about some things you know so well that you may never have noticed them. First, I will talk about little sentences. These formulae would produce or generate the one little sentence *The cat will drink the milk*. They also ascribe a structural description to that sentence. A structural description is somewhat like a sentence diagram, though it is also different in some respects. The structural description says that the sentence can be broken first of all into two parts: *The cat* is one part and *will drink the milk* is the second. It also says that the second part is composed of two subparts, *will* and *drink the milk*. It breaks

---

* Generative-transformational grammars are in a state of development. It is now more usual to construct tree diagrams without *Predicate* and to have *Aux* (auxiliary) directly relate to *S* (sentence) in this way:

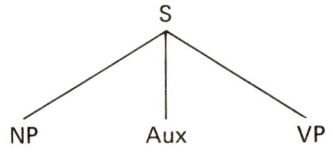

```
            S
         ╱  │  ╲
       NP  Aux  VP
```

NP stands for noun phrase; *VP* for verb phrase. Professor Hunt has stated that he would now present his analysis somewhat differently, although the basic theory remains constant. —Eds.

the second subpart into two sub-subparts *drink* and *the milk*. It breaks *the milk* down into its two parts, *the* and *milk*.

Who cares what the structural description of a sentence is? Why have we been analyzing sentences all these years? Have we known why? Actually there are several reasons. First, the meaning of the whole sentence is made from the meaning of exactly those components, not other components. That is, one *the* forms a meaningful unit with *milk*, but not with any other one word in the sentence: *drink the* is not a meaningful unit, nor is *will drink the*. Furthermore, *the milk* next forms a meaningful unit with drink: *drink the milk*. But *the cat the milk* is not a meaningful unit. This larger unit *drink the milk* forms a meaningful unit with *will* to produce the next unit, and finally *will drink the milk* joins with *the cat* to give the meaning of the whole sentence. Here we happen to have worked from the small units to the large unit, but we could have worked from large to small as we did in the formula. When you listen you work from large to small, but when you speak or write you work from small to large.

REASONS FOR STRUCTURAL DESCRIPTION OF SENTENCES

One reason to give the structural description of the sentence, then, is to show which are the meaningful parts and what is the order in which those parts are joined together one after another to give the whole meaning of the sentence.

When I used to assemble model airplanes with my son, we had to learn about subassemblies and sub-subassemblies. We had to glue the parts together in the proper order or some part would be left over and we would have to tear the whole thing apart to get it in. Sentences too have their subassemblies, and the order of assembly is no chance matter.

There are two other reasons to show the structural description of a sentence. Some words are called nouns in this description and some are called verbs and some are called modals. Which names we use for these sets of words would not matter, except that these names have been used for two thousand years. We could call them class 1, class 2, class 3 words instead if we gained anything by the change. One reason we group words into those various classes or sets is to show that thousands of English sentences can be made simply by substituting one noun in the same place as another noun and some new modal in place of another modal. But we never can substitute a noun for a modal or a modal for a noun. For instance if it is English to say

The cat will drink the milk.

we know it will also be English to say

    John will drink the milk.
The dog will drink the milk.
    Mary will drink the milk.

One animate noun substitutes here for another animate noun. Similarly one modal substitutes for another.

The cat   can   drink the milk.
The cat should drink the milk.
The cat   may   drink the milk.
The cat might drink the milk.

But we know too that a modal cannot be substituted for a noun. It is not English to say

Could will drink the milk.
The cat John the milk.

Regularities such as these make a language easy enough that people can learn it. When we learn a new word we unconsciously learn whether it is a noun or a verb, and so we unconsciously learn countless thousands of new sentences in which it can be used. So this is a second reason why the structural description of a sentence helps to show what we know when we know our language.

A third reason to show the structural description is to show what can be conjoined. For instance we said earlier that *the cat* is a grammatical unit, but that *drink the* is not. That tells us that it will not be English to conjoin *drink the* and *taste a* as in the sentence.

The cat will drink the and taste a milk.

However, it will be English to say

The cat will taste and drink the milk.

for *taste* and *drink* are both V's. But words are not all that can be conjoined. Larger structures can be too.
Here two VP's are conjoined though there is only one NP and one modal:

The cat will drink the milk and go to sleep.

But only the components generated by the rules can be conjoined. Words cannot be conjoined at random.

Just as one noun phrase can be substituted for another noun phrase but for nothing else, so one noun phrase can be conjoined with another noun phrase, but not with anything else. Just as a VP can be replaced by another VP but not by a modal or an NP, so one can be conjoined to another bearing the same label in the formulae.

So when we give the structural description of a sentence, we are simply pointing out explicitly some of the things we know unconsciously when we know our language.

That is not all that a g-t grammar shows about little sentences. It also assigns certain functional relations to certain components. What are here called functional relations are not the same as the grammatical categories. For instance, *the cat* is an NP and *the milk* is another NP. But one is subject and the other is object. And the subject NP does not mean the same as an object NP. In the following sentences both *John* and *Mary* are NP's, but in one sentence *John* is the subject, and in the other *Mary* is the subject. Any youngster knows the difference between the two.

John hit Mary first.
Mary hit John first.

One NP is often substitutable grammatically for another NP, whether subject or object, but an NP which is subject does not mean the same as it does when it is object.

Take another simple example.

The boy is easy to please.
The boy is eager to please.

In one sentence, the boy pleases other people and is eager to do so. In the other sentence, other people please the boy and to do so is easy. In one sentence, *the boy* has the subject meaning relationship to *please*. In the other sentence, *the boy* has the object meaning relationship to *please*. But in both sentences, *boy* is the formal subject of the verb *is*.

The g-t grammarian makes further distinctions between the formal subject and the formal object and the semantic subject and the semantic object. For instance, the two following sentences mean the same thing (that is, if one is true the other is true, and if one is false the other is false).

The boy pleases other people.
Other people are pleased by the boy.

The semantic subject in both sentences is *the boy*: the boy does the pleasing. But one verb agrees with the formal subject *the boy* which is singular, *the boy pleases*. The other verb agrees with the formal subject *other people* which is plural: *other people are pleased*. So in this sentence the semantic subject is not the same as the formal subject. The verb agrees with the formal subject and that may not be the semantic subject.

FORMULAE FOR MAKING BIGGER SENTENCES

The sentence we started out with was extremely simple. A g-t grammar gives formulae to produce all these different simplest sentences: sentences with direct objects, predicate nominals (John is a hero), predicate adjectives (John is heroic), indirect objects (John gave Mary a book), and many constituents which are not named in school book grammars. These simplest sentences used to be called kernel sentences by the g-t grammarian. That term is not being used in recent publications, but I shall continue to use it here.

A g-t grammar also gives you explicit directions on how to make big sentences out of little ones. Of course, being a native English speaker you know that, but you know it unconsciously without even knowing how you learned it. The grammar merely tries to describe what you know and what you do. But before I talk about how we make big sentences out of little sentences, I want to take a couple of minutes to give you a sample of how we make question sentences and imperative sentences and passive sentences out of statement or declarative sentences.

If you have a statement sentence with a modal, all you have to do to make it into a yes-no question sentence is to put the modal before the subject:

The cat will drink the milk.
Will the cat drink the milk?

The cat with the tiger markings and the ragged ears will drink the milk.
Will the cat with the tiger markings and the ragged ears drink the milk?

The formulae for other questions are almost as simple.

The inversion of modal and subject signals that a yes-no question is being asked. What is the meaning there signaled? It is simply "The speaker requests the listener to affirm or deny the following sentence." All yes-no questions bear that same relation to the statements from which they are formed. *Will the cat drink the milk?* means "The speaker requests the listener to affirm or deny the sentence, *The cat will drink the milk.*"

To produce an imperative sentence you must begin with a sentence that has *you*, meaning the listener, as the subject, and *will* (the volitional *will*, not the future tense *will*) as its modal: *You will be here on time tomorrow.* The verb following *will* is always in the uninflected form, and that is just the form we always want. We say *You are here, You will be here*, and consequently we say in the imperative *Be here*, not *Are here*. To form an imperative sentence from such a declarative sentence, all you have to do is delete the *you will*: *Be here on time tomorrow.* The absence of the subject and the uninflected form of the verb are the formal signals that an imperative has been uttered. We say that *you will* has been deleted, because if we add a tag question at the end of the imperative, we put the *you* and the *will* back in, though in negative form.

Be here on time tomorrow, won't you?

The meaning signaled by the imperative is "The speaker requests that you will: Be here on time tomorrow."

Passive sentences are formed from kernel sentences by as simple a formula. Take this example: *The cat will drink the milk*: *The milk will be drunk by the cat*. (1) Whatever expression functioned as semantic direct object now becomes formal subject. (2) Whatever expression functioned as semantic subject now follows *by* (or is deleted along with *by*) at the end of the sentence. (3) The proper form of *be* is inserted before the main verb and the main verb takes the past participle form. Thus:

(1) The cat will (2) drink (3) the milk.

(3) The milk will (2) be drunk by (1) the cat.

These are the formal signals of the passive. The meaning of the passive does not differ from that of the active, but in a passive sentence the semantic subject does not need to be mentioned. Instead of saying "Someone hurt him" we can say "He was hurt."

VARIETY OF TRANSFORMATIONS

These changes which we English speakers make on active declarative sentences to turn them into questions and imperatives and passives are called singulary transformations, because they change a single sentence of one sort into a single sentence of another sort. Children before they ever get to school can form questions and imperatives in an endless stream, though they have no conscious notion of the general rules which they have learned to follow.

. . . . .

But the statement comes before the question in a thoroughly different sense. It is simpler to write a grammar which generates first the form and meaning of statements than to write one which generates questions first and then transforms them into statements.

In many elementary grammar books, I see questions and statements mixed together indiscriminately, though the relation of one to the other is never explained.

Far more useful for the language arts program, however, are the transformations which have been called sentence-combining. They take one sentence of a certain sort and another of a certain sort and combine them to produce one new sentence. The g-t grammar tries to tell exactly what changes are made in the process. The process of combining little sentences into bigger ones can be repeated an indefinite number of times so that two, three, four, five, and even ten or twenty can be combined into one complicated sentence.... Furthermore, the meaning of the complicated sentence is the meaning of all the simple sentences put together.

This process is particularly interesting because apparently the ability to combine more and more kernel sentences is a mark of maturity. The older a child becomes, the more he can combine. Apparently, too, the higher the IQ, the faster children learn to do this, so that by the time they are in the twelfth grade, the students with superior IQ's tend to be well ahead of students with average IQ's.

THE PROCESS OF COMBINING SENTENCES

I want to sketch for you that process of combining sentences.

Very young children combine two sentences into one by putting *and's* between. We can call this sentence coordination. Children in the earlier grades do this far more often than adults. In writing, fourth graders do so four or five times as often as twelfth graders in the same number of words. As they get older, they learn not to use sentence coordination so much. Also children use sentence coordination more often in speech than in writing. In fact, Dr. Griffin and his associates at Peabody have found that fifth graders use two or three times as much sentence coordination in their speech as they do in their writing for the same number of words.[1] So we may think of sentence coordination as a relatively immature device for joining little sentences into bigger ones. It is a device which they will outgrow, or, better yet, which they will replace with the other devices I will now describe. Sentence coordination is the only transformation that we know to be used *less* frequently by older students.

Often two adjoining sentences have a certain relation between them such that the event recorded in one sentence happened at the same time as that in the other. When such is the case, *when* can be put in front of one sentence, making it an adverbial clause with the other as the main or independent clause:

My mother came home and I got spanked. (*When* my mother, etc.)

We climbed out on the end of the limb and it broke. (*When* we climbed out, etc.)

There are many subordinators besides *when* which introduce movable adverbial clauses, and, in writing, students use a few more of them as they get older. Dr. Griffin finds that in the speech of students from kindergarten

---

[1] Roy C. O'Donnell, William J. Griffin and R. C. Norris, *Syntax of Kindergarten and Elementary School Children: A Transformational Analysis* (Champaign, Ill.: National Council of Teachers of English, 1967).

to seventh grade, there is a general increase in their number. I find that in writing there is also a slight increase from the fourth grade up to the twelfth.[2]

So-called adjective relative clauses are also produced by sentence-combining transformations. They can be formed when one sentence contains the same noun or the same adverb of time or place as another sentence contains. Let me take as my main clause *The man did something* and then combine with it a number of different sentences in the form of adjective clauses. At the same time, we will notice that in all the examples I happen to have chosen, the adjective clause can be reduced by deletion to a single word modifier of a noun or to a phrasal modifier of a noun.

The man did something.

The man was big.
The man (who was big) did something.
The (big) man did something.

The man was at the door.
The man (who was at the door) did something.
The man (at the door) did something.

The man had a derby.
The man (who had a derby) did something.
The man (with a derby) did something.

The man was swinging a cane.
The man (who was swinging a cane) did something.
The man (swinging a cane) did something.

We find that as students mature they use more and more adjective clauses in their writing. Furthermore, as students mature they use more and more of these single-word or phrasal modifiers of nouns. So we see that the ability to combine sentences into adjective clauses and to delete parts of the clause to produce single word or single phrase modifiers is indeed a mark of maturity.

Now let us see how a twelfth grader can combine five sentences into one. You will see that the twelfth grader is telling about a sailor. In fact the word *sailor* is subject of each of the sentences which he has consolidated into one.

The sailor was tall.
The sailor was rather ugly.
The sailor had a limp.
The sailor had offered them the prize.
The sailor finally came on deck.

---

[2] Kellogg W. Hunt, *Grammatical Structures Written at Three Grade Levels* (Champaign, Ill.: National Council of Teachers of English, 1965).

There are lots of bad ways to combine these sentences. One is with sentence coordinators:

The sailor was tall and he was rather ugly and he had a limp and he had offered them the prize and he finally came on deck.

I have seen fourth graders who wrote almost that way.
Another bad way to combine the sentences is to produce a great number of relative adjective clauses all modifying the word *sailor*. No one would ever write like this:

The sailor who was tall and who was rather ugly and who had offered them the prize finally came on deck.

Rarely do we let more than one full adjective clause modify a single noun. Instead we reduce the potential clauses to single word modifiers or phrasal modifiers.

I fancy most of you are way ahead of me already. You have been so uncomfortable with these bad sentences that you have already rewritten them as the twelfth grader did. But even so I am going to ask you to combine these sentences with me, one by one, slow motion, so we can study the process.

Below, I have numbered the minimal sentences S1, S2, etc. The procedure will be as follows. First, I will state a general transformational rule for English sentences. Then we will apply that rule to two of the sentences and see what we come out with. Next I will state another transformational rule, or the same one again, and we will apply that rule to the third sentence plus what we produced the previous time. Or instead I may state a rule which changes what we produced though it does not incorporate a new sentence.

The rules read like this: If you have a sentence of one particular pattern and a second of another particular pattern, it will be good English if you rewrite them into one according to the formula. Instead of using abstract but more exact symbols like NP for noun phrase or VP for predicate, I have used the words *someone* or *something* for noun phrases, and the words *did something* for predicates in general.

A twelfth grader consolidates 5 sentences into 1, using noun modifiers.

S1 The sailor finally came on deck.
S2 The sailor was tall.
S3 The sailor was rather ugly.
S4 The sailor had a limp.
S5 The sailor had offered them a prize.

Transformation #1

Someone did something + Someone did something else → The someone (who did something else) did something.

Application to S1 and S2:

The sailor who was tall finally came on deck.

Transformation #2

Someone (who was X) did something → Someone X did something (or some X person did something).

Application to what we produced last time:

The tall sailor finally came on deck.

Transformation #1 again

Someone did something + Someone did something else → The someone (who did something else) did something.

Application to S3 plus what we produced last time:

The tall sailor (who was rather ugly) finally came on deck.

Transformation #2 again

Someone (who was X) did something → Someone X did something (or some X person did something).

Application to what we produced last time:

The tall, rather ugly sailor finally came on deck.

Transformation #3

Someone had something → someone with something.

Application to S4 plus what we produced before:

The tall, rather ugly sailor with a limp finally came on deck.

Transformation #1 again

Someone did something + Someone did something else → The someone (who did something else) did something.

Application to S5 plus what we produced before:

The tall, rather ugly sailor with a limp, who had offered them a prize, finally came on deck.

An average fourth grader does not write four modifiers to a single noun. He will write only two or at most three at a time. He would be likely to resort to *and*'s and produce about three sentences.

The sailor was tall and rather ugly and had a limp. He had offered them the prize. Finally he came on deck.

I have just finished talking about noun modifiers, attempting to show that syntactic maturity is the ability to consolidate several sentences by reducing some sentences to modifiers of a single noun.

. . . . .

SUMMARY AND CONCLUSION

This has been an exceedingly rough sketch of g-t grammar. We started out with fairly explicit rules that generated an exceedingly simple sentence and also its structural description. Then we saw that questions, imperatives, and passives bear a certain explicit relationship to those simple active statement sentences, both in form and in meaning.

Then we saw that quite complicated sentences can be consolidated out of a number of exceedingly simple sentences. As children get older, they can consolidate larger and larger numbers of them. Average twelfth graders consolidate half a dozen with moderate frequency. But to find as many as seventeen consolidated into one, one must look to the highbrow magazines such as *Harper's* and *Atlantic*. Only superior adults can keep that many in mind at once and keep them all straight, too.

QUESTIONS FOR STUDY AND DISCUSSION

1. Draw tree diagrams for the following sentences, using the pattern in the example, or any other pattern you have learned.

   Example: The arena will open in June.

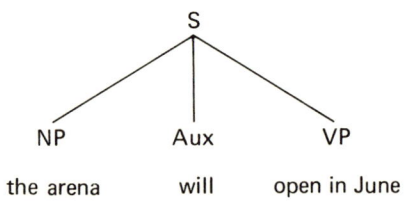

   ```
            S
          / | \
         NP Aux VP
         |   |   |
   the arena will open in June
   ```

   a. The fair will succeed in Chicago.
   b. The airlines may gain power.

How Little Sentences Grow into Big Ones   149

   c. The industrialists will become wealthy.
   d. The poet could praise San Francisco.
   e. The children would enjoy his poems.

2. Which of the following sentences can be generated by the same basic formula, or string, of grammatical components?

   a. This country welcomed dissenters.
   b. These people settled on the land.
   c. The settlers worshiped in their own manner.
   d. The pioneers were energetic.
   e. The farmers migrated to the Midwest.

3. Hunt makes a distinction between a formal subject of a sentence and a semantic subject.
   a. Select the formal subject and the semantic subject in each of the following sentences. The formal subject occupies the position usually filled by the subject. The semantic subject in these sentences names the actor.

      (1) The city has witnessed violence.
      (2) The Indians destroyed Fort Dearborn in 1812.
      (3) The Indians resented the settlements.
      (4) Fort Dearborn was destroyed by the Indians in 1812.
      (5) The Lowrys are difficult to entertain.
      (6) The Lowrys are reluctant to entertain.

   b. Which of these sentences have approximately the same meaning?
4. Structural descriptions make it possible for us to discover the regularities in our language. In mathematics you learned about *sets*, such as 2, 4, 6, 8, which is a set of even numbers. Similarly, form classes, or parts of speech, are sets in grammar.
   a. Substitute as many different words as you can to fill the blanks in the following sentences:

      (1) The boys _____ the lawn.
      (2) The _____ were sitting in the living room.
      (3) The dinner will taste _____.
      (4) He entered the room _____.

b. What name is given to the set of words used to fill the slot in sentence (1)? in sentence (2)? in sentence (3)? in sentence (4)?
5. a. Structural descriptions are also useful because they reveal what can be conjoined, or coordinated. Select from this group the grammatical sentences which show that grammatical structures, rather than words, are conjoined.

   (1) The men and the children were playing ball in the yard.

   (2) The women are preparing dinner and in the kitchen.

   (3) The women are preparing dinner and watching the children.

   (4) The men are playing cards in the living room and on the porch.

   b. Refer to one of the tree diagrams and identify by symbol the grammatical elements that are conjoined in the grammatical sentences.
6. Similar grammatical components may have different grammatical functions. For example, Hunt's tree diagram shows two NP's, one stemming directly from S functioning as subject, the other stemming directly from VP functioning as direct object. Select every NP in the following sentences and explain how it functions in the sentence. Use your general knowledge of grammar.

   a. The people love the land.

   b. The land is productive in good growing seasons.

   c. Their wealth is their land.

   d. They give the land their best efforts.

   e. We Americans and our land have reached a crisis.

7. Transformational rules show how statements, questions, and requests are related, although they have structural differences.
   a. Change these statements to questions.

      (1) Americans have traveled to the moon.

      (2) Space travelers must wear special clothing.

      (3) Astronauts are highly trained specialists.

      (4) They know how to use their equipment.

   What changes in word order did you make in sentences (1), (2), and (3)? What word did you have to introduce in sentence (4)? Try to formulate a grammatical rule to cover these operations. Convert some of your own statements into questions to see whether the rule will work.

b. Supply the statement from which each imperative sentence is formed.

   (1) Be prepared for your examination.
   (2) Read the daily paper.
   (3) Check the sign of the zodiac.
   (4) Get a good night's sleep.

8. a. Transform the following sentences into the passive.

   (1) The Indians raised horses in their well-built villages.
   (2) Someone sent the message.
   (3) The Indians ate corn on the cob in a four-day Green Corn Festival.
   (4) Someone mixed corn with beans and squash to make succotash.
   (5) Someone dried the corn to make a traveler's ration.
   (6) Fish populated the lakes.

   b. When can the *by-phrase* be deleted from the passive version without changing the meaning of the sentence?

9. Hunt points out that two adjoining sentences often have a meaning relationship that can be more precisely expressed in a subordinate clause than in a compound sentence. Transform the following compound sentences by changing one of the statements to a subordinate clause beginning with such subordinators as *when, because, if, after, although*.

   a. *Propaganda* has a negative connotation, and most people associate the word with lies and half-truths.
   b. We conclude a successful mission in war or space, and our reporters call it "news."
   c. Most American homes have a daily newspaper, but some families tend to form their ideas about national and international problems from radio and TV broadcasts.
   d. Some men pick up a newspaper, and they turn immediately to the sports section.

10. a. One important transformation explains the so-called adjective relative clause, one introduced by *who, which*, or *that*. This transformation enables us to embed one sentence in another if certain conditions are present. In the following groups of sentences, embed

the second sentence in each group in the first sentence as a relative clause.

(1) Hawthorne wrote tales.
Hawthorne lived in Concord, Massachusetts.

(2) Melville admired Hawthorne.
Melville wrote *Moby Dick.*

(3) We enjoyed the novels.
We studied the novels.

b. Sometimes a relative clause can be reduced to a word or a phrase modifier of a noun. After you have embedded the second sentence in the first as a relative clause, reduce the relative clause to a word or a phrase.

(1) The gardener looked at the visitor.
The gardener was trimming the roses.

(2) The woman spoke to her guests.
The woman was young.

(3) The audience applauded the senator.
The senator was a forceful speaker.

(4) The book is a new dictionary.
The book is on the desk.

What operations did you perform to produce the reduced structures?

SUGGESTED ACTIVITIES

1. Hunt explains that as children get older they are able to consolidate larger and larger numbers of sentences. Analyze some of your own sentences in a writing assignment and try to discover how many little sentences you have consolidated into one larger sentence.
2. Consolidate this group of little sentences into a single sentence. More than one version is possible, of course. Compare results.

The Nineties represented an era.

The era was transitional.

The era was kind.

The era was cruel.

The era was prosperous.

The era was bleak.

The era was genteel.

The era was crude.

3. Children in the earlier grades coordinate sentences far more often than adults do, Hunt's investigations have shown. Count the number of sentence coordinations in one of your themes. If you think some of the compound sentences could be improved by using other transformations, reconstruct the sentences.

Part Five

USAGE

14
USAGE IS SOMETHING ELSE AGAIN
Harold B. Allen

Recent developments in grammatical investigations emphasize the underlying uniformity of English throughout the world. They show how similar is the "deep grammar" of speakers of English in the United States, Great Britain, Australia, and a number of other countries. But the normal human counter trend toward diversity appears in the surface features of English, in the surface grammar as well as in vocabulary and pronunciation. Because these surface features are easily associated with education and social and economic class as well as with geography, they almost inevitably are the subject of considerable argument. The customary relationships between language features and all these other matters is what is called "usage."

As Allen points out in his historical survey of this branch of linguistics, only recently have linguists specializing in usage studies and teachers of English become aware of the complexity of the environmental factors which affect usage. Here Allen introduces three important concepts about usage. First, there are at least five interacting environmental dimensions of any language item; and second, each dimension must be visualized as a continuum. (The dimension of time has already been considered in the essays on the history of English; the dimension of space, which involves regional dialects, or linguistic geography, will be given more detailed treatment in the next section of this book). In this essay Allen also considers the dimensions of medium, style, and social variation. A third important idea about attitudes toward language evolves from these first two: all statements about language usage must be descriptive in terms of the five dimensions rather than prescriptive in terms of "rules" or personal preference. This third premise is so important that it, too, will be discussed again in the section on lexicography.

Harold B. Allen is emeritus professor of English and linguistics at the University of Minnesota. Since 1957 this lecture on his concepts of

---

Source: Lecture first delivered to the English Teachers Club of Greater Chicago, November 16 1957. Printed by permission of the author.

the dimensions of usage has been given numerous times, with varying changes and applications, most recently at Auburn University, the University of Rhode Island, and the University of Maine.

The exploding popular concern with man's abuse of his environment is curiously relevant to a long-standing concern of our schools, the teaching of "correct English." The language of man, his means of human communication and control, is also part of his environment. This amazingly complex system exists without his doing anything about it. But some men want to do something about it; they want to make changes in it and in how men use it. For whatever reasons, some men have tried to interfere with the system without understanding the complex relationships within it. Some have insisted upon *It is I* in speech and thereby have polluted the language with the unanticipated *between you and I*. Some have insisted upon the pronunciation /ask/ and hence have unwittingly encouraged such odd forms as /hat/ for /hæt/. Some have insisted upon spelling as a guide to pronunciation and hence have helped to produce such forms as /æntarktik/. Today some would like to change the way millions of Americans talk, the so-called culturally different in Appalachia, Harlem, Washington, Chicago, and Detroit, with a possible effect upon their speech and their social attitudes that can hardly be estimated. Then we always have with us such people as those who served as the "Usage Panel" for the *American Heritage Dictionary of the English Language*, people who apparently are not unwilling to have their personal linguistic prejudices and biases considered as guides to language behavior for those whose linguistic insecurity has been fostered by the correctness concept taught in the schools.

I would suggest that a sound attitude must rest upon as much solid support as can be provided rather than upon personal opinion and feeling. Here I would like to propose a pragmatic approach to the problem of developing such an attitude.

Ultimately three kinds of persons are involved in the development of a sound attitude toward language matters. Theoretically, any one person could be all three, but at different times. Practically, it is not very often that any one person has the opportunity or the ability to act in all three capacities.

The first person studies language as language. He is a scientific scholar in the field of language, a linguist. To such a person a language is a system primarily manifested in vocal symbols used for the communication of meaning among human beings. Any given language is such a system. English is such a system. We infer the existence of the system only by perceiving its overt manifestations. Its primary overt manifestation is in human speech; its secondary overt manifestation is in human writing or printing. A possible tertiary manifestation could occur through symbols related to alphabetic letters, such as the Morse code or Braille.

In what he hears or sees this first person finds combinations of sounds or letters that seem to point to things or associations outside the language, that is, that have referential or dictionary meaning—and he so classifies and describes them. He also observes different kinds of signals that show how these lexical symbols are related to each other in a given utterance. These signals he classifies according to shape and tune and volume and position. Statements based upon observations constitute what is known as a grammar. If the statements are confined to the description of the overt manifestations, it is the relatively weak kind of grammar called structural. If it consists of a series of sequential rules, the operation of which accounts for or explains any and all possible acceptable sentences in the language, then it is the much more powerful kind of grammar called generative.

Note that the concern of this first person is simply to describe the working of the system in all its complexity. Whether this approach is that of the structuralist or that of the transformationalist with his generative grammar, he is still dealing with the system itself. He is not concerned with what is outside the system, even though he may limit his concern to the language used by one person (an idiolect) or that used by a community of people (a dialect).

In observing the language forms of some individual, for example, the linguist may record *I did it* and *It was me* and *Me and him did it*. His rules would have to state that in preverbal position and after a certain type of verb both *I* and *me* appear, but that in preverbal position *me* does not occur alone (that is, as in *Me did it*). He might also observe *He saw me* and *between you and I*, and will accordingly have a rule that *me* occurs after a certain type of verb as object and that *I* occurs in this combination after a prepositional function word.

Now there is a second kind of person involved in all this. Unlike the linguist or grammarian, he looks not into the language but away from it. He is concerned not with the internal operation of the language, but with the correlation of linguistic matters with the nonlinguistic environment in which people use language. This person may be a linguistic geographer, or a sociolinguist, or a psycholinguist, or a dictionary editor—or a graduate student writing a dissertation! Such a person would ascertain the situation in which *me* occurs after a form of *be* and the situation in which *me* occurs in a coordination before a verb as in *Me and him did it*. His description of the situation would include details about the speaker's education and social group, the kind of rapport with the listener, the time and nature of the occurrence, and the audience. This relationship between a language feature and the complex nonlinguistic contexts is the usage of the feature. Any description of such a relationship is a statement about that usage. A set of such statements about a number of language features is a description of usage of that language. Such a set may be in expository form, with the support of tables and charts, or it may be in alphabetical or other sequential lists, as in a dictionary of usage.

I do not want to seem to be laboring this point, to be unnecessarily obvious. But I do want to be very clear about this matter that has been seriously misrepresented in many textbooks and classrooms. Grammar is a set of statements about what goes on inside a language. That is one thing. Usage is the relationship between what occurs in a language and the external context of speaker, purpose, time, place, mood, and audience. Usage is something else again.

Now there is a third person involved in all this. He is the teacher, the professor—usually of English, but also of speech. This person has a very special job, one derived from the very nature of our democratic society. As Charles C. Fries wrote in his *American English Grammar* in 1940, the schools and colleges in this country assume the obligation of helping students to gain control of those language matters that correlate with the speech and writing of educated people, that is, of what we call Standard English. At least until recently a high degree of such control has been held essential for the individual citizen with respect to his personal advancement through the utilization of all his personal capabilities and as essential for the individual citizen in a society where full communication is a *sine qua non* in economics and political life.

This third person, then, has an obligation to center attention upon those particular language matters, those particular correlations of language and context, that are peculiar to one or more varieties of Standard English. If he has students who lack control over some of these correlations, that is, who cannot imitate them, then he has the problem of helping them to modify their speech and writing habits. If the students actually have nonstandard dialect quite different in essential features, then he has the problem of helping them to acquire control of a second dialect, almost as if it were a second language, not to replace their original dialect but rather to be added to it. In short, this third person is a teacher of usage.

Clearly this third person is not the first person. But some serious misunderstanding has resulted from confusing these two jobs. The linguist observes, describes, generalizes, and theorizes about language, but he does not prescribe. The teacher, on the other hand, must assume the responsibility of prescribing, of indicating the choice between Standard and Nonstandard English. He is prescriptive in the same way that a foreign-language teacher is prescriptive, for he is teaching control of a different set of language forms. But there are two kinds of prescriptiveness. One has been manifested in certain traditional textbooks often found in high schools and colleges today. This prescriptiveness is often associated with some kind of indefinable mystique called "correctness," a mystique more transcendental than objective, more unreal than real.

There is another kind of prescriptiveness, based upon some awareness of the facts of language. This second kind cannot exist except as the third in a sequence of activities. First, the linguist analyzes a language and describes it in a grammar. Second, the student of usage determines the relationships between language and context and describes those in statements about usage—in general principles as in Martin Joos's little monograph *The Five Clocks* or in various compendiums ranging from Margaret Bryant's *Dictionary of Current American Usage* to *Webster's Third New International*. Third, the teacher of usage chooses those particular correlations characteristic of Standard English and endeavors to teach them. The second person cannot do his job unless the linguist has done his. The third person, the teacher, cannot do his job unless the usage scholar has done his. If he tries to, then he is in grave danger of elevating personal taste and private prejudice to the status of public dogma.

Clearly it is the second person, the student of usage, who is critical in the teaching of usage. It is to him we must now turn as the one to rescue us from the unhappy and untenable position from which can be seen only a right and a wrong, only a correct and an incorrect form. Life—and the language of life—is not quite so simple.

I would suggest that instead of this two-valued split, this dichotomy between two extremes, we should less naively and more realistically look at language correlations in terms of the dimensions provided by the second person.

The first important step in this direction was taken by the late John S. Kenyon. Of course, for two milleniums scholars had had before them the classical Horatian statement that usage is the standard of speaking, *Usus est norma loquendi*, and in the eighteenth century the rhetorician George Campbell had elaborated that simple dictum by declaring that the standard, the *norma*, has three characteristics: contemporary, standard, and reputable. It was not until 1939 that the late Porter Perrin introduced the notion of levels in his book, *Index to Usage*, but Perrin made the mistake of assigning colloquial to one level and Standard English to another. Textbooks adopting this analysis were soon confusing students everywhere by suggesting to them that one can't talk Standard English, one can only write it. Kenyon, in his articles in *College English* and in *The English Journal* in October, 1948, for the first time recognized the important distinction of functional varieties that exist upon one level. He pointed out that colloquial standard and written standard, for example, exist on the same level.

But even Kenyon's analysis retains the concept of level, one I think which is misleading in its implicit analogy to floors in a building or levels in a mine. I would offer instead the term *dimension* as a deliberate attempt to present the idea of a range, a continuum. I would offer specifically the consideration of five dimensions as a frame of reference for English usage. The limitation to five is admittedly an oversimplification, but it is pedagogically workable. Any analysis, even Joos's in *The Five Clocks*, is bound to be an oversimplification, so complex is the language-culture context. But the concept of five dimensions is pragmatically sound.

This concept will also admit easy visual demonstration. Let a line represent the continuum between the primary manifestation of language, speech, and the secondary manifestation of language, writing. Some language matters fall peculiarly at the speech end of the continuum; others occur at the writing end. Some words people scarcely ever write. Such a word is *ficety* or *feisty*, a term widely heard in the South Midland area. Rarely will a speaker admit having written it, and then he is unsure of the spelling. At the other extreme is a word like *tergiversation*. Semantically it would be possible to say, "Some ficety people are subject to tergiversation," but actually it is an impossible combination, for these two terms are at opposite ends of the first dimension. All our words are locatable, then, somewhere along this dimension with respect to the relative frequency with which they occur in speech and in writing, somewhere between the exclusively spoken and exclusively literary.

Grammatical forms also range along this dimension. *If it's true* is at a point different from where we would place *If it be true*. *It's me* is colloquial and *It is I* is uncommonly literary written English. Contractions like *won't, ain't, she's, I'd 've* are clearly spoken forms. *There's some books on the table* is much more likely to be heard than to be read. So many forms are close to this end of the continuum that there actually can be a grammar of spoken English in contrast to that of written English.

Such a grammar would have to include also the differences in syntax, for here too there is a range between speech and writing. Some written English offers the Latinate expressions *to whom, from whom,* and *than whom* at the one extreme end of the continuum. *That's the boy that his father owns a supermarket* is a kind of construction much closer to the other end. A nonrestrictive clause is common in writing; it is rare in speech. Coordination between clauses is common in the speech of most persons; it is much less common in writing. In short, we simply do not write precisely as we speak and we do not speak precisely as we write. Some language forms may be typically found in speech; other language forms may be typically found in writing. All language forms can be placed somewhere along this dimension.

But as you consider these sample forms I just cited you notice, of course, that they differ in other ways. In reading aloud his sermon, a minister may say, "It is not I who thus admonish you. These are not my words, but Paul's." Yet an hour later he may answer the telephone with, "Yes, it's me. Oh, no, I wasn't really trying to scold you, Norman." The difference here between *It's me* and *It's I*, and between *scold* and *admonish*, points to a second dimension, a second range of relative frequencies of occurrence—the range between formality and informality. This dimension extends from all points on the first dimension, so that to illustrate it you now need a two-dimensional figure, a square. Any language matter is identifiable in terms of its position somewhere in that square.

Some written matters vary between formal and informal. Punctuation features do, for instance. The dash is much more informal than the colon or semicolon. Certain abbreviations are more informal than the full words they represent. Even numerals are sometimes more informal than written words. Notice the style, for example, on a formal wedding invitation with

June Fourth carefully spelled out in elegant type. Likewise, some exclusively speech matters range from formality to informality. In formal public address a speaker will use much more precise articulation than in intimate conversation; he may even use spelling pronunciations such as "pumpkin" and "antarctic" for "punkin" or "antartic."

At the same time, language matters that occur in both speech and writing still exhibit contrasts of formality and informality. Take, for example, the whole body of terms comprised under the headings of slang, cant, jargon, and the like. These tend to bunch up toward the informal end of this dimension. But some technical cant or jargon may bunch up at the other end. None of us will have any difficulty in placing these two quotations:

Man, you just play it real cool and quit puttin' us on.

This maximal, nondiscrete sphere of social relationships has no corporate organization and is not segmented into lineages, age-sets, secret societies, territorial districts, political factions, and the like.

Many occupations, of course, have two sets of terms in their special jargons—one set for formal communications such as top-level reports and committee sessions and descriptive literature, and another set, colorful, slangy, even obscene, used by the working force, such as the men on the machines. Similar contrasts occur in the language of teen-agers who like to make over old automobiles and in the language of music fans and hi-fi enthusiasts.

Martin Joos's analysis in *The Five Clocks* would break this dimension into these sections, these five kinds of style: (1) intimate (the language of people emotionally close to each other and not concerned at the moment with communication as much as empathy.) (2) casual (the style of a social group with common understandings.) Its speech is marked by ellipsis:

Nice day. Been pretty warm, though. Thanks. OK.

(3) consultative (the style of ordinary communication, usually with some kind of feedback from the audience, if only an occasional "Mmh, mmh.") (4) formal (a style not characterized by feedback. It is the style of the formal public address, of the magazine article, and essay. It is marked, says Joos, by detachment and by cohesion.) (5) frozen (the style of formal edited English, ranging from the rewritten textbook to the rewritten sermon, whether rewritten by the writer or by an editor. At its extreme the frozen style may be the language of ritual.)

Now we add lines to suggest a three-dimensional figure, a cube, in order to allow for the third dimension, the one uppermost in the concerns of many teachers of English. This is the range or scale of variations between Standard English and Nonstandard English. Remember that these are designations undefinable in terms of absolutes. They can be defined only in terms of correlation with nonlinguistic features of our cultures. Professor Fries, back in 1927, defined Standard English, Good English, as that used habitually by men and women who carry on the affairs of the English-speaking world. This is surely a matter of relativity, of frequency of occurrence.

A college graduate in a given community is vice-president of a bank, a director on the local hospital board, chairman of the Community Chest campaign, and past commander of the American Legion post. He goes on a hunting trip with three friends. That night they relax with a little game of poker. And a tape recording of the conversation would reveal that at one time he said, "Say, I'm doing all right, ain't I?" This single occurrence in the speech of even a community leader does not make *ain't I?* Standard English.

An unskilled laborer in the same community left school when he finished the fourth grade. He has no social life except that of his home and the beer tavern. He has accepted no community responsibilities. But he has a television set. By sheer chance some dramatic program impresses him with the statement, "And if he were here now, I'd shoot him." The next night in the tavern he comes out with this: "And if he were here now, I'd slug him." This single occurrence in such a context does not make *If he were* Nonstandard English.

On the contrary, determination of what is and is not Standard English must necessarily be a matter of judgment based upon the accumulation of evidence. The vast majority of linguistic matters—of pronunciation, vocabulary, grammar, and syntax—occur in the standard part of the continuum as well as in the nonstandard. They are common in the language of all users of English. Other matters, like much of the vocabulary, occur only in the writing of educated persons. In either case judgment is automatic. But a small minority of language matters can cause trouble, some because they are borderline cases and hence induce dogmatic judgments not always justified, and others because they are so indubitably nonstandard that they handicap the user socially, educationally, and occupationally.

Here is where the growing body of evidence now available helps to underlie a reasonable judgment. Let's take some speech items for example. Throughout the country many teachers for years have tried to get children to pronounce the adverb *just* as it is spelled. Indeed, that is their criterion— the spelling. But evidence from the Linguistic Atlas projects is clear; the usual pronunciation is /jɨst/* as in *Just a minute.* Actually four words contrast in this sentence: "The just judge said that he just couldn't get the gist of the jest." Spelling is also the criterion with another shibboleth—*government.* The presence of the medial *n* is used as an argument that it should be pronounced. Again, evidence collected by *Webster's* reveals that in ordinary use educated people do not pronounce the *n*. Some teachers and others have

---

* The symbol /ɨ/ represents a vowel not identified in English spelling. It is a sound made with the tongue higher than for the vowel in *bun* and farther back than the position in *bit*. Northern and Southern speakers usually have it in the second syllable of *horses*.

tried to promote the British forms /ask/, /dants/, etc., instead of /æsk/ and /dænts/. Again, evidence is clear that on all levels the /æ/ vowel is normal in most of the United States.

Should I mention *It's me*? There are still people who object to it; yet studies show that this is the normal conversational use all over the United States. How about *like* as a joiner of clauses, in such a construction as *It looks like it'll rain*? One of my Ph.D. students several years ago found that 66 per cent of 155 school textbooks flatly said that *like* cannot be used as a conjunction; and 48 college freshman texts took the same position. But the New England Atlas shows that *like* is so used by 46 percent of the college graduates; and in the Midwest 47 percent so use it. Clearly, with the third dimension of usage as with the first and second, we have a continuum, a range, from one extreme to the other rather than a dichotomy of right and wrong, correct and incorrect. With respect to all three dimensions, then, an attempt to locate any given language item will be inadequate unless the attempt is made with awareness of the relation of the language item to other items and to the correlated nonlinguistic features.

But there is a fourth dimension as well—and to illustrate it we move our imaginary cube from one place to another. It is the dimension of space, from here to there or anywhere. And as we move the cube we find that what is

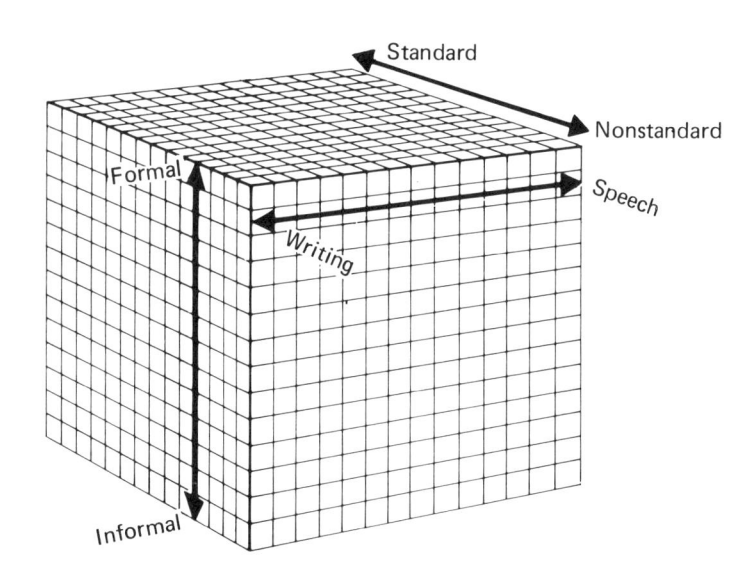

The Five Dimensions of English Usage.

Any given language element may undergo a change of position within the cube, or disappear completely, as the cube is moved into the fourth and fifth dimensions, space and time.

nonstandard or nonexistent in one area may be standard and common in another; what is formal written in one may be informal spoken in another, and standard, or perhaps nonstandard, in both places.

Schools in the northern part of the country have long insisted upon /ruwf/ as the correct pronunciation of *roof*, that is, with the vowel of *loose*. This is of course the common form in the South, but in the Upper Midwest 68 percent of the informants for the *Linguistic Atlas* have my normal pronunciation, /ruf/, with the vowel of *put*. Schools also, and likewise on the basis of spelling, insist upon /kriyk/ for *creek*. This too is normal standard in the South; but in my region 79 percent of the people actually say what I say, /krik/, riming with *pick*. Take *due*. My pronunciation /duw/ is considered pretty lowbrow by some teachers of speech—and it may sound pretty bad to you—but in the Upper Midwest it is, by 83 percent, the majority form.

Until I began teaching in southern Illinois many years ago, I had never heard anyone say *I'd like for you to do this*. I dutifully tried to correct my students but gave up when I discovered that my colleagues said it too. Now I realize that this is standard spoken informal English in a very large section of the country, even though it simply doesn't exist in my own Northern dialect.

When several centuries ago the plural *you* displaced the singular *thou*, there still was some felt need for a distinctive plural. In the United States this need was met in the North by *youse*, in the Midland area by *you ones*, usually as *you'uns*, and in the South by *you all*, usually *y'all*. But the first two have never gained social respectability, and are nonstandard. Southern *y'all*, however, is standard spoken English in the South. As a matter of fact, sometimes there is no possible term except a regional term. There is no national word, for example, for the strip of grass between sidewalk and street. In the Upper Midwest two dozen names for it have been recorded— from *boulevard, parking, parking strip, terrace, tree lawn, curbing, curb strip*, and *devil strip* to the curious word *berm*. They are all regional, and all standard!

Finally, let's move our imaginary cube slowly, ever so slowly—and now we represent the passage of time. As we move it back to 1900, back to 1600, back to 1400, many language matters will shift their relative positions and perhaps disappear, while new ones will take their place. Even in our own lifetime we can experience this shift. The change is slow with syntactic forms, as when over the centuries the wandering adjective settled firmly into place before the noun; it may be more rapid, as with the swift acceptance of the progressive *-ing* verb phrase in the eighteenth century; it may be almost overnight, as with such words as *beatnik* and *hippie*. We who teach need to keep this fact in mind as we ourselves grow older, for otherwise we'll find ourselves trying to make our students use our own sometimes old-fashioned forms. My own pronunciations, *isolate* with the vowel of *fit*, *economic* with the vowel of *bet*, *cigaret* with the stress on the final syllable, and *juvenile* with the last syllable rhyming with *pill*, are different from those used by my students—and probably by you.

Usage, we see, is not a simple black-and-white contrast. To assume that it is, and to criticize others accordingly, is the easy way out. It is easy to follow the dictates of a given textbook without questioning by what right the author makes his judgments. It is easy for the teacher to correct by the book and to drill accordingly. But that is not real teaching. Real teaching is educating, not drilling. And education is the process of developing discriminative reactions. That calls for sensitivity. With respect to language it means that we seek to have not correct-incorrect distinctions but rather active awareness of what is appropriate for the speaker and the occasion and the audience.

I have suggested a point of view that rests squarely upon observation of language in use and upon recognition of the fact that language is a social phenomenon integral with the complex fabric of our social structure. This point of view rejects the presentation of personal whim, preconceptions, and unsupported generalizations as guidelines for others to follow. It is, I submit, a point of view that makes sense—and for better control of our language as we use it day by day.

QUESTIONS FOR STUDY AND DISCUSSION

1. In what ways is the work of a linguistic geographer or an editor of a dictionary different from the work of a linguist?
2. Describe the working relationship which should exist between a linguist, a student of usage, and a teacher of English.
3. George Campbell (1709-96) was a Scottish minister, educational administrator, and rhetorician. His *Philosophy of Rhetoric* is one of the most comprehensive treatments of the art of eloquence since classical times. What important idea did Campbell contribute to the understanding of usage? How has Allen extended the concept of usage?
4. What was wrong with usage studies that considered all usage problems under the one main heading, "levels of usage"? Why, for example, is it unsound to categorize language items as *standard, nonstandard*, and *colloquial*?
5. When writers of fiction attempt to capture the characteristics of the speech of their characters in writing, they suggest the vocabulary, grammatical structures, and pronunciations by selecting a few representative forms. *Catcher in the Rye* and *The Adventures of Huckleberry Finn* have been acclaimed as artistic successes in this respect. Do you consider the following samples of speech in writing also successful? Where would you place them on Joos's style continuum? Locate the stop you select on a chart like this:

| Frozen | 1 | 2 | 3 | 4 | 5 | Intimate |

a. I was getting along fine with Mama, Papa-Daddy and Uncle Rondo until my sister Stella-Rondo just separated from her husband and came back home again. Mr. Whitaker! Of course, I went with Mr. Whitaker first, when he first appeared here in China Grove, taking "Pose Yourself" photos, and Stella-Rondo broke us up. Told him I was one-sided. Bigger on one side than the other, which is a deliberate, calculated falsehood; I'm the same. Stella-Rondo is exactly twelve months to the day younger than I am and for that reason she's spoiled.
—Eudora Welty, "Why I Live at the P.O.", in *A Curtain of Green and Other Stories* (Harcourt, Brace, 1941)

b. In consequence, I'm inclined to reserve all judgments, a habit that has opened up many curious natures to me and also made me the victim of not a few veteran bores. The abnormal mind is quick to detect and attach itself to this quality when it appears in a normal person, and so it came about that in college I was unjustly accused of being a politician, because I was privy to the secret griefs of wild, unknown men.
—F. Scott Fitzgerald, *The Great Gatsby* (Scribner's, 1925)

6. Locate each of the following selections on the frozen-intimate and standard-nonstandard continuums.

Frozen	1	2	3	4	5	Intimate
Standard	1	2	3	4	5	Nonstandard

a. When lilacs last in the dooryard bloom'd,
And the great star early droop'd in the western sky in the night,
I mourn'd, and yet shall mourn with ever-returning spring.
—Walt Whitman, "When Lilacs Last in the Dooryard Bloom'd"

b. " 'Why looky-here,' he says, 'ain't that Buck Miller's place, over yander in that bend?' "
—Mark Twain, *Life on the Mississippi*

c. One of the most noteworthy phenomena of this literary revival was the opulence, power, and popularity of poetry and drama.
—Sculley Bradley, *et al.*, eds., *The American Tradition in Literature*, vol. 2 (Norton, 1967) p. 1030

d. *Amen* with the broad *a* seems to be making progress. E. W. Howe tells a story of a little girl in Kansas whose mother, on acquiring social aspirations, entered the Protestant Episcopal Church from the Methodist Church. The father remaining behind, the little girl had to learn to say *amen* with the *a* of *rake* when she went to church with her father and *amen* with the *a* of *car* when she went to church with her mother.
—H. L. Mencken, *The American Language*, ed. Raven I. McDavid, Jr. (Knopf, 1963)

7. Study the definitions of *jargon* in your dictionary. In which sense is Allen using the term? Locate the jargon in each of the following selections and show how it reveals the occupations of the people using it.

   a. With their twangy, rubbery Pogo stick beat—produced, mind you, with an authentic folk instrument called the electric wah-wah pedal—The Band is ideal for the adult bubble gum market.
   —*The Milwaukee Journal*, February 8, 1970, Sect. 1, p. 16

   b. If the poison has been inhaled, insufficient oxygen, carbon monoxide, and toxic gases will cause asphyxia.
   —*Medical Emergencies* (a handbook)

   c. ... industrial production continued to decline, to 170.9 in December, the most recent reading of the Federal Reserve index.
   —*Fortune Magazine*, February, 1970, p. 29

   d. What is hurting now—more than a productivity upturn can be helping—is the sharpening of competition (and the rise of fixed costs) resulting from the drop in utilization of capacity.
   —*Ibid.*

   e. One hundred social studies educators have been selected to participate in a three-day Guided Self-Analysis Research Training Program (GSA-RTP), which will utilize Parsons' Guided Self-Analysis techniques, interaction analysis and anthropological research techniques.
   —A program of the National Council for the Social Studies

   f. Encapsulated in the novellas of Tolstoy, Dostoyevsky, and Kafka are motifs and attitudes which generate and shape fiction today.
   —*The English Journal*, January, 1970, p. 52

8. Listen for examples of code-switching in your own speech and in that of other people, including speakers on TV and radio. Note changes in pronunciation, in word choice, and in grammatical forms and structures that produce shifts on the formal-informal, the standard-nonstandard, or the regional continuums. Was there any reason for the shift? What was the effect?

9. Spelling is the device regularly used in writing to represent nonstandard pronunciations. Some misspellings successfully record such pronunciations. Others more nearly represent the usual standard pronunciations. Which does the misspelled word in each of these sentences do?

   a. I took this pitcher of my father with my new camera.

   b. Tom wuz wrong that time.

   c. Why didn't you lissen to me?

d. I felt sorry for the poor critter.

e. Dese boys are pals.

f. You must of changed your mind.

g. He's agin everything.

h. Jim has a new suit of clo'es.

i. Mrs. Pruitt is deef.

j. I wuns won a prize.

k. This is strikly off the record.

10. The following misspellings frequently occur in student writing. What pronunciations do they suggest? Do you hear these pronunciations? If so, where would you place each one on the standard-nonstandard continuum?

    pronounciation, atheletics, prespiration, mischievious, rememberance

11. A technique of the comic journalists of the nineteenth century was to burlesque what they considered nonstandard provincial pronunciations by altering the spelling of words. But sometimes their misspellings merely indicated standard pronunciations. (Maybe they were also burlesquing the spelling of poorly educated Americans.) In the selections that follow, which of the misspelled words seem to represent nonstandard pronunciations? Which seem to accomplish nothing except to reveal nonstandard spelling? Read the selections aloud.

    a. The muel is haf hoss and haf Jackass, and then kums tu a full stop, natur diskovering her mistake.
    —Josh Billings, *Essay on the Muel* (1865)

    b. My perlitercal sentiments agree with yourn exactly. I know they do, becawz I never saw a man whoos didn't.
    —Artemus Ward, *Artemus Ward: His Book* (1862)

    c. "I'm the boy," continued he; "perhaps a leetle, jist a leetle, of the best man at a horse-swap that ever trod shoe-leather."
    —Augustus Baldwin Longstreet, *"The Horse-Swap"* (1835)

    d. "It's a painful duty, Lewtenant! a very painful duty, Lewtenant Snipes; and very distressin'. But the rules of war is very strict, you know!"
    —Johnson Jones Hooper, *Adventures of Captain Simon Suggs* (1845)

    e. "I tell yu now, I minds my fust big skeer jis' es well as rich boys minds that fust boots, ur seein the fust spotted hoss sirkis."
    —George Washington Harris, *Rare Ripe Garden-Seed* (1867)

SUGGESTED ACTIVITIES

1. In writing fiction, an author attempts to make dialogue represent conversation. Yet the aimless conversation of most people would not make effective dialogue for a drama or story. Test the truth of this assertion by recording on tape a normal conversation between friends or members of a family. Replay it. Then rewrite some segments of the conversation to create readable dialogue. What differences between speech and "written speech" are apparent?
2. Allen says we reject language that represents a mixture of the extremes of the speech-writing continuum. Similarly we reject as inappropriate a choice on the informal-formal continuum unsuited to the occasion, or else we find the incongruity humorous. The comedy of the late W. C. Fields, who is often imitated, is a good example of this kind of verbal humor. Write a monologue using pompous or overprecise language. For example, pretend that you are selling a soft drink in a television commercial.
3. Allen says that *ficety* rarely occurs in writing, though it is common in southern Midland speech. Its unstable spelling is proof that it is used primarily in speech, for *fice* (a tough small mongrel dog) also occurs in novels as *feist* and *fyce*. (Recent dictionaries have found the form *feisty* now common enough to be used as the main entry.) Are there any words or expressions that your family uses but which you have never seen in print? Think of expressions relating to food, feelings of fatigue or well-being, traits of personality. Write a familiar essay on this topic.
4. In the sixties it became fashionable to use "shock" language. In this context, journalists often referred to the "rhetoric" of certain "movements" as if the language were not to be taken at face value. What is your position on the use of obscenities and invective (name-calling)? Write an essay giving examples of invective and stating your opinion on the use of invective and obscenities.
5. In contrast to excessively blunt language is the euphemism, the substitution of a pleasant term for a harsher one. Familiar euphemisms run the range from coy phrases, such as "powder room," to government gobbledygook, such as "culturally deprived area" or "economically disadvantaged" for "poor." Some euphemisms are merely amusing (farfetched substitutions for the term "burying ground," for example), but others blunt realistic thinking. Write a humorous essay on euphemisms in which you comment on their use in some sector of American society (which substitutes "blemishes" for "pimples," for example) or a serious essay on the effects of euphemisms in some field, such as education, economics, sociology, journalism, or government

(which substitutes "casualties" for "dead" or "wounded," and "underachiever" for "lazy student").*

6. Sometimes a word or phrase from the technical jargon of a profession or trade is picked up by journalists and others and so widely used that it soon loses definite meaning. Such words and phrases are called "vogue words." A recent example is *charisma*. Other popularized technical expressions are *genocide, concept, differential, liquidate, shibboleth, seminal, implement* (v), *racism, imperialism*. For one week make a list of vogue words, collecting them from newspapers and popular magazines, as well as television and radio. Try to place them in categories and summarize your findings in an essay.

7. The cliché, a trite or hackneyed expression, has one value: it is readily understood—so much so that the reader or listener doesn't even think about it. If you can find some of Frank Sullivan's skits, "The Cliché Expert Takes the Stand," published in *The New Yorker* (beginning August 31, 1935, and continuing into the fifties), you will be surprised to discover that most of the clichés of the thirties are still around in the seventies. Write a skit in which you bring the cliché expert up to date.

8. Subcultures develop a jargon to describe distinguishing features of their life-style. If you have access to any publications of the so-called "underground" press, collect words and phrases characteristic of the "hippie" communities. Write a summary report or create a dialogue which reveals the meaning of the jargon.

9. Sometimes words used in a special jargon have meanings different from those usually found in a dictionary. Compare common meanings of these words with meanings assigned them in black English vernacular. (See next article by Labov.) Such meanings are given below in the key.

   (1) Honky   (a) Hungarian, (b) white boy, (c) loud horn, (d) bar.

   (2) The nap   (a) police, (b) run, (c) swinger, (d) a downy surface.

   (3) Old lady   (a) wife, (b) mother, (c) girl friend, (d) teacher.

   (4) Crib   (a) baby bed, (b) garage, (c) house, (d) cheating.

   (5) Tough   (a) bully, (b) good athlete, (c) nice, (d) pigheaded.

   Key: 1b, 2a, 3c, 4c, 5c.

10. a. Select one of the following usage items for investigation as suggested by the questions that follow and be prepared to present your findings in a panel discussion. Check general dictionaries, usage dictionaries, and handbooks.

---

* H. L. Mencken in *The American Language,* edited by Raven I. McDavid, Jr., has an excellent discussion of euphemisms in American life, pp. 339–55.

(1) (It is I; It's me.)
(2) (Me and Sally, Sally and I) will give the report.
(3) Please wait for Mary and (me, I).
(4) They invited Bill and (me, myself) to the party.
(5) (Whom, Who) do you know in Toronto?
(6) (This, This here) book is mine.
(7) Joyce acts (as, like) a senior should.
(8) You (were, was) right, John.
(9) Jeff didn't give (any, no) reason for staying at home.
(10) Carl (saw, seen) his mistake right away.
(11) Jim (did, done) his best.
(12) Jill has (gone, went) home.
(13) He (dived, dove) off the pier.
(14) He (doesn't, don't) read detective stories.
(15) I'd like (to have you do it, for you to do it).
(16) (Am I not, Ain't I) right?
(I'm not, I ain't) going.
He (isn't, ain't) here.
He (hasn't, ain't) come home.

b. During the next week keep a record of the alternate forms of the usage item every time you hear them used and note

(1) the situation in which the conversation occurs (Joos's five styles). Is the speaker using the form unconsciously or consciously for effect? Does he shift forms?
(2) other language forms that the speaker uses (for example, if he says "It's me," does he also say "he don't"?)
(3) the apparent educational background of the speaker.

If you have seen examples of the speaker's writing, does he use the form in both speech and writing?

c. Where would you place the item on the continuums of Allen's movable cube? Diagrams would be helpful.
d. Check the usage item in *Webster's Third New International Dictionary*, the *Standard College Dictionary*, and, if possible, in Margaret Bryant's *Current American Usage* and Bergen and Cornelia Evans's *A Dictionary of Contemporary American Usage*. Compare your observations on the usage item with the status labels in these sources.

15
THE STUDY OF NONSTANDARD ENGLISH
William Labov

In the following excerpt from his monograph, Labov gives special attention to the dialect of uneducated black people, which he calls "nonstandard Negro English." In a more recent book he prefers to designate this dialect as the "black English vernacular," which he defines as "the relatively uniform dialect spoken by the majority of black youth in most parts of the United States today," especially in the inner-city areas of the North, where he has done extensive research. He asserts, however, that "it is also spoken in most rural areas and used in the casual, intimate speech of many adults."* The broad term *black English*, frequently used for nonstandard Negro English, is a misnomer, for the English of both black and white people represents a broad spectrum covering Allen's five dimensions of usage.

Labov disagrees with those who maintain that nonstandard black English is essentially the same as nonstandard Southern white English. Though there is overlapping, he finds enough differences to classify nonstandard black English as a separate dialect.

Historically, many characteristics of nonstandard black English, like other nonstandard forms, can be traced back to earlier English structures. Nonstandard black English may also reflect in some ways the influence of Creole languages, the mixed languages that the West African slaves brought to America. But Labov is concerned with nonstandard black English as it exists today.

William Labov is professor of linguistics at the University of Pennsylvania.

---

* William Labov. *Language in the Inner City* (Philadelphia: University of Pennsylvania Press, 1972), p. xiii.

Source: *The Study of Nonstandard English* (Champaign, Ill.: The National Council of Teachers of English, 1970), pp. 11–14; 40–42. Reprinted by permission of the publisher and the author.

The traditional view of nonstandard speech as a set of isolated deviations from standard English is often countered by the opposite view: that nonstandard dialect should be studied as an isolated system in its own right, without any reference to standard English. It is argued that the system of grammatical forms of a dialect can only be understood through their internal relations. For example, nonstandard Negro English has one distinction which standard English does not have: there is an invariant form *be* in *He always be foolin' around* which marks habitual, general conditions, as opposed to the unmarked *is, am, are*, etc., which do not have any such special sense. It can be argued that the existence of this distinction changes the value of all other members of the grammatical system and that the entire paradigm of this dialect is therefore different from that of standard English. It is indeed important to find such relations within the meaningful set of grammatical distinctions, if they exist, because we can then *explain* rather than merely describe behavior. There are many co-occurrence rules which are purely descriptive—the particular dialect just happens to have X' *and* Y' where another has X and Y. We would like to know if a special nonstandard form X' *requires* an equally nonstandard Y' because of the way in which the nonstandard form cuts up the entire field of meaning. This would be a tremendous help in teaching, since we would be able to show what sets of standard rules have to be taught together to avoid confusing the student with a mixed, incoherent grammatical system.

The difficulty here is that linguistics has not made very much progress in the analysis of semantic systems. There is no method or procedure which leads to reliable or reproducible results—not even among those who agree on certain principles of grammatical theory. No one has yet written a complete grammar of a language—or even come close to accounting for all the morphological and syntactic rules of a language. And the situation is much more primitive in semantics; for example, the verbal system of standard English has been studied now for many centuries, yet there is no agreement at all on the meaning of the auxiliaries *have . . . ed* and *be . . . ing*. The meaning of *I have lived here*, as opposed to *I lived here*, has been explained as (a) relevant to the present, (b) past *in* the present, (c) perfective, (d) indefinite, (e) causative, and so on. It is not only that there are many views; it is that in any given discussion no linguist has really found a method by which he can reasonably hope to persuade others that he is right. If this situation prevails where most of the investigators have complete access to the data, since they are native speakers of standard English, we must be more than cautious in claiming to understand the meaning of *I be here* as opposed to *I am here* in nonstandard Negro English, and even more cautious in claiming that the meaning of nonstandard *I'm here* therefore differs from standard *I'm here* because of the existence of the other form. Most teachers have learned to be cautious in accepting a grammarian's statement about the meaning of their own native forms, but they have no way of judging statements made about a dialect which they do not speak, and they are naturally prone to accept such statements on the authority of the writer.

There is, however, a great deal that we can do to show the internal relations in the nonstandard dialect as a system. There are a great many forms which seem different on the surface but can be explained as expressions of a single rule, or the absence of a single rule. We observe that in nonstandard Negro English it is common to say *a apple* rather than *an apple*. This is a grammatical fault from the point of view of standard speakers, and the school must teach *an apple* as the written, standard form. There is also a rather low-level, unimportant feature of pronunciation which is common to southern dialects: in *the apple*, the word *the* has the same pronunciation as in *the book* and does not rhyme with *be*. Finally, we can note that, in the South, educated white speakers keep the vocalic schwa which represents *r* in *four*, but nonstandard speakers tend to drop it (registered in dialect writing as *fo' o'clock*). When all these facts are put together, we can begin to explain the nonstandard *a apple* as part of a much broader pattern. There is a general rule of English which states that we do not pronounce two (phonetic) vowels in succession. Some kind of semi-consonantal glide or consonant comes in between: an *n* as in *an apple*, a "*y*" as in *the apple*, an *r* as in *four apples*. In each of these cases, this rule is not followed for nonstandard Negro English. A teacher may have more success in getting students to write *an apple* if he presents this general rule and connects up all of these things into a single rational pattern, even if some are not important in themselves. It will "make sense" to Negro speakers, since they do not drop *l* before a vowel, and many rules of their sound system show the effect of a following vowel.

There are many ways in which an understanding of the fundamental rules of the dialect will help to explain the surface facts. Some of the rules cited above are also important in explaining why nonstandard Negro speakers sometimes delete *is*, in *He is ready*, but almost always delete *are*, in *You are ready*; or why they say *they book* and *you book* but not *we book*. It does not always follow, though, that a grammatical explanation reveals the best method for teaching standard English.

Systematic analysis may also be helpful in connecting up the nonstandard form with the corresponding standard form and in this sense understanding the meaning of the nonstandard form. For example, nonstandard speakers say *Ain't nobody see it*. What is the nearest standard equivalent? We can connect this up with the standard negative "foregrounding" of *Scarcely did anybody see it* or, even more clearly, the literary expression *Nor did anybody see it*. This foregrounding fits in with the general colloquial southern pattern with indefinite subjects: *Didn't anybody see it*, nonstandard *Didn't nobody see it*. In these cases, the auxiliary *didn't* is brought to the front of the sentence, like the *ain't* in the nonstandard sentence. But there is another possibility. We could connect up *Ain't nobody see it* with the sentence *It ain't nobody see it*, that is, "There isn't anybody who sees it"; the dummy *it* of nonstandard Negro English corresponds to standard *there*, and, like *there*, it can be dropped in casual speech. Such an explanation is the only one possible in the case of such nonstandard sentences as *Ain't nothin' went down*. This could not be derived from *Nothin' ain't went down*, a sentence type which never occurs. If someone uses one of these forms, it is important for the teacher to know what was intended, so that he can supply the standard equivalent. To do so, one must know a great deal about many underlying rules of the nonstandard dialect, and also a great deal about the rules of English in general.

Differences between standard and nonstandard English are not as sharp as our first impressions would lead us to think. Consider, for example, the socially stratified marker of "pronominal apposition"—the use of a dependent pronoun in such sentences as

My oldest sister she worked at the bank.

Though most of us recognize this as a nonstandard pattern, it is not always realized that the "nonstandard" aspect is merely a slight difference in intonation. A standard speaker frequently says the same thing, with a slight break after the subject: *My oldest sister—she works at the bank, and she finds it very profitable*. There are many ways in which a greater awareness of the standard colloquial forms would help teachers interpret the nonstandard forms. Not only do standard speakers use pronominal apposition with the break noted above, but in casual speech they can also bring object noun phrases to the front, "foregrounding" them. For example, one can say

My oldest sister—she worked at the Citizens
Bank in Passaic last year.

The Citizens Bank, in Passaic—my oldest sister
worked there last year.

Passaic—my oldest sister worked at the Citizens
Bank there last year.

Note that if the foregrounded noun phrase represents a locative—the "place where"—then its position is held by *there*, just as the persons are represented by pronouns. If we are dealing with a time element, it can be foregrounded without replacement in any dialect: *Last year, my oldest sister worked at the Citizens Bank in Passaic*.

. . . . .

Not many years ago, linguists tended to emphasize the differences among the languages of the world and to assert that there was almost no limit to the ways in which languages could differ from each other. Dialectologists concentrated upon the features which differentiated their dialects—naturally, for these are the features which define their object of study.

However, the opposing trend is strong in linguistics today—there is a greater interest in the ways in which languages resemble each other and how they carry out the same functions with similar rules. When we look at English dialects from this point of view, the differences do not appear very great. They are largely confined to superficial, rather low-level processes which have little effect upon meaning. Sometimes the dialect forms seem very different on the surface. In the general discussion we saw how the most common white nonstandard dialects differ from standard English on fine points of rule-ordering. We find in nonstandard Negro English such forms as *Didn't nobody see it, Didn't nobody hear it*. These appear to be question forms used as declaratives, which would be a truly radical difference from standard English. But closer investigation shows that this is merely an extension of the standard rule of literary English which gives us *Never did he see it*, or *Nor did anybody see it*: the negative is placed at the beginning of the sentence along with the first member of the verb phrase, which contains the tense marker. This inversion of the tense marker and the subject shows the same order as in questions, but it does not indicate a question with *Never did he see it* any more than with *Didn't nobody see it*.

Dialects differ of course in their sound patterns; such differences can produce a great deal of misunderstanding, but they do not register differences in the underlying semantic structure of the language. Dialects differ in foregrounding and rearranging transformations and in the order of their rules such as that noted above. They also differ in their selection of redundant elements. Where standard English has two elements to signal a certain meaning, nonstandard English often has one. For example, to signal the progressive we use both *be* and *-ing* as in *He is going home*; the first element is normally dropped in nonstandard Negro English: *He goin' home*. We also have two signals for the present perfect, *have* and *-ed* in *I have lived here*. Either the first or the second of these is usually deleted in the nonstandard Negro form. The Negro vernacular does not have a possessive *-s* in attributive position: *This is John mother* in place of *This is John's mother*. But here the order of the two nouns shows the relations involved. When the second noun is deleted, the possessive *'s* is always present. *This is John's* is the regular form, and *This is John* means something altogether different.

Conversely, the nonstandard dialect often uses two elements where standard English uses one. Nonstandard Negro English usually shows *or either* where the standard uses *either*, and *and plus* where the standard uses only *and*. Negative concord shows a reduplication of the negative where the standard uses only one negative element: *He didn't hear anything* can correspond to *He didn't hardly not hear nothing*.

These are not logical or semantic differences but rather different formal selections from a common repertoire of forms. There are a few cases where the nonstandard language makes a grammatical distinction missing in the standard. The most noteworthy of these is the invariant *be* of nonstandard Negro English which signals habitual or general state; this dialect can distinguish *He be with us* (meaning "he is generally with us") from *He is with us* or *He with us* which can mean either general state or momentary conditions. On the other hand, several of the finer points of the standard tense system, such as the future perfect, may be missing in some nonstandard dialects. But the main body of dialect differences do not affect the semantic or "deep structure" level. Furthermore, it seems increasingly plausible to write pan-dialectal grammars in which the differences between the various dialects will appear as stages in the evolution of the language as a whole—to some extent in a linear series, but also as a set of parallel and competing lines of development. Nonstandard Negro English represents some radical departures from standard English, in that certain general rules of English are extended far beyond the environments and frequencies at which they operate in other dialects. Some of these extensions may be motivated by an underlying Creolized grammar common to Gullah, Trinidad, Jamaica and other dialects which are the product of complex contact situations. Or we may explain some of them by a process of "creolization" in the simplification of morphological forms and the development of a more analytic syntax. But no matter what historical explanation we give for some of these directions of development, we are plainly dealing with a dialect of English which is not, in the larger view, very different from other developments within the language.

QUESTIONS FOR STUDY AND DISCUSSION

1. Dialects are frequently classified as social (reflecting the language usage of a social class) and regional. Into which category does nonstandard Negro dialect fall? Explain.
2. Consult a standard dictionary for the various meanings of the noun *vernacular*. Which meaning seems best suited to Labov's use of the term in Negro *vernacular*? Why?
3. Allen refers to the dimension of Standard-Nonstandard English as a continuum. What does *continuum* suggest about the relationship of the two dialects? Compare Labov's point of view with Allen's.
4. The following exercise is designed to help you understand what Labov means by co-occurrence rules. Supply the appropriate form of the omitted member of the following constructions. Then be ready to explain the term *co-occurrence* and to show how co-occurrence rules illustrate the systematic nature of language.

Standard English

	X		Y	
	Neither	Justin	_____	Halbert came.
	Both	Sarah	_____	Karen objected.
I	have		_____ (wait)	an hour.
	She		_____ (be)	usually here on Monday.
	He	is	_____ (a, an)	honest man.
	Tony		_____ (be)	playing tennis now.
	The debaters	have prepared	_____ (they)	arguments.
This is	_____ (Janet)		room.	

Nonstandard Black English

	X'		Y'	
	She		_____ (be)	usually here on Monday.
I	have		_____ (wait)	a long time.
	He		_____ (be, play)	tennis now.
This is	_____ (Janet)		room.	
He is	_____ (a, an)		honest	man.
	The debaters	have prepared	_____ (they)	arguments.

5. It is often said that Nonstandard English is ungrammatical. Would Labov agree? Review the definitions of grammar in Wilson and Allen.
6. Labov mentions the difficulty in explaining the meaning of the auxiliaries in *have* . . . *-ed* and *be* . . . *-ing*.
   a. In your speech do you distinguish the present perfect aspect of the verb from the simple past tense: "I *lived* here when I was a child" but "I *have lived* here five years"? What difference in meaning do the two forms provide?

b. Which of the meanings of "I *have lived* here" suggested by Labov is most apparent in each of these sentences?

(1) I have lived here all my life.

(2) I have lived here ever since I finished high school.

(3) I have lived here off and on most of my life.

(4) I have lived here until today. Now I am moving away.

c. What time does *be* plus *-ing* signify in each of the following sentences?

(1) Charles is driving fifty-five miles an hour.

(2) Charles is driving to Albany tomorrow.

(3) Charles is driving a truck while he attends college.

7. How does Labov account for the fact that New Englanders, whose speech normally does not include an /r/ following a vowel at the end of a word or a syllable, frequently retain or intrude an /r/ in such structures as "the four eggs in the basket," "the idear is absurd," "Africar is a large continent," etc.?

8. How would Labov proceed in teaching someone to substitute *an* for *a* in *a ant, a elevator, a ounce, a hour*, etc.? Do you approve of his method? Draw upon your own experience or that of others.

9. Review Mrs. Sargon's discussion of *juncture* to explain the distinction between "My oldest sister she worked at the bank" and "My oldest sister—she worked at the Citizens Bank in Passaic last year."

10. Find an example of what Labov calls pronominal apposition in the Twenty-third Psalm as translated in either the King James version of the Bible or in the Revised Standard Version. Is this an example of Standard or of Nonstandard English? What happens to the rhythm if the pronoun is omitted?

11. According to Labov, what is the relationship to the standard English forms of "Ain't nobody see it" and "Didn't nobody see it"?

12. Show that you understand foregrounding by foregrounding the element designated for the following sentence:

My two best friends—they enrolled at the University of Minnesota this year.

Adverbial of place:

Adverbial of time:

13. Since one dialect is not intrinsically superior to another, there are those who argue that students who have learned a nonstandard dialect at home

should not be required to learn Standard English in school. Evaluate this point of view.
14. Is it possible for a person to shift from Standard to Nonstandard English to suit the occasion? Draw upon your own experience and/or that of others.

SUGGESTED ACTIVITIES

1. The speech of Huck and of Jim in *Huckleberry Finn* offers a contrast between the nonstandard speech of a white boy and that of a black man. Analyze the differences in their usage in a selected portion of the novel.
2. Numerous short stories by black writers are available in anthologies of black literature and in short story collections. Read a story containing nonstandard black dialect and select two or three pages from which you list the nonstandard usages. What is the approximate age of each speaker, and what seems to be his level of education? Does the speech of the black characters reveal any differences? Record your findings in a short paper. (You may prefer to choose a selection from a play or a novel: *A Raisin in the Sun* by Lorraine Hansberry, *Simply Heavenly* by Langston Hughes, *His Own Where* by June Jordan, *The Autobiography of Miss Jane Pitman* by Ernest Gaines, and so forth.)

    Among the many fiction writers who frequently use nonstandard black dialect are Arna Bontemps, Junius Edwards, Ernest J. Gaines, Rudolph Fisher, C. H. Fuller, and Langston Hughes.
3. The following structures are frequently listed as characteristic of nonstandard black English. Record each sentence by letter, list the nonstandard item(s) and label each item NB (nonstandard black English) if you have not heard it in the nonstandard speech of white people or NW (nonstandard white English) if you have heard it in the nonstandard speech of white people. Rewrite the sentence in Standard English.

    a. I don' got no book.
    b. I ate a orange.
    c. This is he bicycle.
    d. She be here every day.
    e. My cousin he live in Baltimore.
    f. My sister comin' home tomorrow.
    g. Us got to clean this house.
    h. I wonder did Jason tell the truth.

i. Last week I work thirty hours.

j. I ain't did my homework.

k. Joe ain't here now.

l. I been in Chicago a week.

m. I don't know who done it.

n. We was singin'—and we dancin' too.

o. You done took the candy.

p. Ain' nobody gon' boss me.

q. What this thing for?

r. I'm a fight you tomorrow.

s. Gloria ain' go to school yesterday.

t. Clark workin' at the supermarket today.

u. Clark be workin' at the supermarket all summer.

v. Clarice have a new hairdo.

w. Which one you want?

x. I found them books on the steps.

y. You mean you goin' to quit?

4. If you have a tape recorder, record some black nonstandard conversation and play it in class. Then read the same conversation in Standard English.
5. If you can speak nonstandard black English, recount an incident in this dialect either in speech or in writing and then in Standard English.
6. Use nonstandard black English to rewrite part of a scene in a play. **Example:** the balcony scene from *Romeo and Juliet*; a conversation between Happy and Biff in *Death of a Salesman*.
7. The reprint from Labov emphasizes the structure of nonstandard black English. Many articles stress vocabulary; others show nonstandard black speech as performance, often accompanied by such paralinguistic features as singing or dancing to draw the audience into participation. "Hip" language, or "jive," has an in-group vocabulary, used primarily by urban blacks to identify their own life-style. It is sometimes also used by others in contact with urban blacks who accept or admire this culture. What do the following terms mean currently? Add to the list.

momma	fox	rip off	split
baby	tripping	kicks	scene
soul brother	dig	rags	hog

8. "Hip" language often has a colorful metaphorical base. What do these expressions mean currently? Add to the list.

   a. You blew, baby!
   b. That ain't no sweat.
   c. Lighten up, baby.
   d. He's in a world of hurt.
   e. Don't sham on me, baby.
   f. Where's that taste?
   g. Baby, work your show.
   h. You're sweet as bear meat.

9. Listen to a conversation of black students and then one of white students. What differences, if any, do you notice in intonation patterns, gestures, other body movements, and so forth?

16
THE DREAM WORLD OF ENGLISH GRAMMAR
James C. Bostain

"Any fool can make a rule
And every fool will mind it."
—Thoreau

"The dream world of English grammar" is just that—an unreal world that has little to do with the grammar (the system) of English but instead is concerned with what many people imagine grammar to be: rules of language etiquette. The point is, there are rules and there are rules. Some are discovered, while others are legislated. The linguist tries to discover and describe the rules (specifications) that generate the sentences of a language; but the self-appointed language legislators Bostain is talking about often state their preferences about language usage as if these were, indeed, immutable laws.

Even when these man-made rules were formulated, many of them did not represent the usage of educated people. Rather, they reflected what Allen calls "an indefinable mystique called 'correctness'." It is this right-wrong doctrine which Bostain deplores.

As a social phenomenon, language calls for choices appropriate to the situation. Because educated people use and prefer certain language patterns, students, too, should be able to handle these patterns as the occasion demands. If some students think nonstandard usage fits other situations better, the choice is theirs.

For those who are socially anxious about their speech, "The Dream World of English Grammar" and "Usage Is Something Else Again" should be reassuring. Many of the forms that have been labeled "incorrect" are thoroughly acceptable in speech and even in informal writing. Because there are relatively few nonstandard forms, learning to use Standard English should pose no great problem for most people.

James C. Bostain is a scientific linguist with the Foreign Service Institute, U.S. Department of State.

Source: *NEA Journal* 55 (September 1966): 20–22. Copyright © 1966 by James C. Bostain. Reprinted by permission of the publisher and the author.

Almost anyone who has survived the educational system in this or most other countries is certain to be confused about one language—his own. The grammatical tradition of Western Europe is based on an assumption so unsound that it seems ridiculous if stated aloud—namely, that language has nothing to do with people.

Most of the language teaching in our schools is based on the theory that to find out what goes on in a language you look in a textbook, or look to logic, or look to some other language, like Latin—in fact, look anywhere except at what people do. (Languages are pure; people are corrupt.) The truth of the matter is that language not only does have to do with people, it doesn't have to do with anything else.

About nine-tenths of the statements about language in the textbooks disregard what people say. Textbooks tell you, for example, that double negative means positive, but this is a statement about logic, not about language. If a child says, "I didn't eat nothing," who but an idiot would ask, "Was it good?"

English has two special kinds of double negative that do mean positive. One of them involves a negative particle, like *not*, and a negative prefix, like *un*: This is *not un*common, *never im*possible. The other involves putting a special emphasis on the second negative. The man on a diet says "I didn't eat *nothing*," and you know he had at least a piece of lettuce. But most double negatives mean negative.

Textbooks are full of dream-world statements about what things might be like if only English-speaking people would shape up—if they would quit using English the way they do and start using it some other way.

The textbook rules apply to what I label "otherworld" English: They describe the speech and writing habits of some other (and perhaps finer) world than this.

The textbooks' *shall-will* rule is a prime specimen of otherworld English. *I shall, you will, he will* for simple futurity (whatever that may be), and *I will, you shall, he shall* for volition. That's the rule, but when Douglas MacArthur left the Philippines in 1942 and said, "I shall return," he meant volition. There was no doubt in anybody's mind that he meant volition, that it was one of the strongest statements of volition anybody ever made in English.

Shall turns up in writing according to the *shall-will* rule sometimes. But most often it signifies a strong, emphatic form of *will*. "This operation will be performed" is merely a command. "This operation shall be performed" is a legal command, the kind the Internal Revenue Service regulations contain.

Just where did this sacred cow come from? The rule came from a man named Johannis Wallis, who made it up back in 1674, apparently because he thought it inefficient to have two words meaning the same thing. But as far as anyone has ever been able to determine, the *shall-will* rule never—before, during, or since Johannis Wallis' time—has represented an accurate statement about the spontaneous linguistic behavior of any sizable group of English-speaking people.

Just as otherworldly is the notion that *can* means ability and *may* means permission. As far as I can tell, *can* means either ability or permission. You indicate which you mean by a second clause: You can do that *if you want to* (permission); you can do that *if you're big enough* (ability).

May, in my speech, means probability in statements. "It may be raining" is not permission for the sky to do anything; it is a middle-range probability. In questions, *may* is permission: "May I help you?" "May I have another apple?" But in statements, it is probability; it goes with *must* and *might*: "It must be raining" (very high probability); "It may be raining" (middle probability); "It might be raining" (very low probability).

People worry about the mistakes children make when they use language, and rightly so. In the schools, teachers have to try to get them to stop making mistakes. But there are three kinds of mistakes people make when they use language, and I think the mistakes the kids make are almost never language mistakes.

Suppose a child says, "Chicago is 300 miles due west of St. Louis." He's made a *factual* mistake, but his grammar is impeccable. If he says, "Chicago ain't 300 miles due west of St. Louis," his statement is factually sound, but most people would say he had made a grammatical mistake. I'd like to get rid of that term "grammatical" in this sense because it begets misunderstanding. It *is* indeed a mistake (in polite company) to say, "Chicago ain't 300 miles due west of St. Louis," but presently I'll characterize that kind of mistake with a different label.

Here is what I would call a grammatical mistake: "Chicago 300 west St. Louis due miles of isn't." You see, the view I am advocating is that language does have to do with people, that it is a human activity, that it is best understood as a special kind of organized noise—organized down to the smallest details. (There is also, for English and many other languages, a set of organized marks—a writing system; but that's a separate study, because the organization of the writing system is not quite the same as the organization of our speech.)

The organization of the noises is the grammar of the language. A "grammatical" mistake in this view is an *organizational* mistake. The speaker produces nonnative noises and arrangements, like "I am here since six months." People often make factual errors in their native tongue, but they almost never make organizational mistakes. Foreigners do, though, because they tend to use the word arrangements and sentence patterns of their own language instead of ours.

In English, one of the grammar patterns we like puts *always* in front of a verb (except the verb *to be*; we like to put *always* after *to be*). So I would say, "We always drink tea," "I always smoke a pipe," but "I'm always there." You *can* put *always* in front of the verb *to be* and it's not too bad—"I always am there"—but if you put it after any other verb, it really sounds un-American.

A German is likely to say, "I smoke always a pipe." When you tell him, "We don't say that," he comes back with, "Ach, I forget always your crazy grammar!" He's making a grammatical mistake.

Some people have suggested that we ought to use elementary school primers as texts for foreign language courses. But the trouble is that the elementary primer presupposes the one thing the foreigner doesn't have—perfect control over the little grammatical elements, the lightly regarded part of the language, the prepositions, conjunctions, and endings. The nouns, verbs, and adjectives are the last things to learn in any language. All of us are still learning them in English. Yet the first thing most people do when they're assigned to a language course is rush out and buy a dictionary, which is the last thing they need. What they've got to do is to get the grammatical (that is, the *organizational*) features of the language under perfect automatic control, then start learning vocabulary.

Almost everybody gets control of the grammar of his native language by the time he's six. A six-year-old can give you a sentence that will drive an English teacher of the old school, with his warmed-over Latin analysis, to drink—as one little boy said to his sister, "What did you bring that book I didn't want to be read to out of up for?"

Now let's take another look at "Chicago ain't 300 miles due west of St. Louis" in terms of the third kind of mistake. Just what kind of mistake is it? The error lies in choosing the wrong alternative. When you choose *ain't* you haven't made a grammatical mistake, for the sentence is organized perfectly. But you chose that kind of a negative particle that has unfortunate social consequences in polite company. You've made a *social* mistake.

The essential difference between *isn't* and *ain't* is that *isn't* people run the schools (and the rest of society). It is a social blunder to use *ain't* around these people. It is like the person who insists on wearing blue jeans every time he goes out of the house. No one will arrest him for indecent exposure, but certain doors will be closed to him.

Language is a social phenomenon. We have to make choices as we go: isn't/ain't, like I did/as I did, he doesn't/he don't. It is crucial to an understanding of the nature of language to realize that we do not make these choices on the basis of reason, but on the basis of the social consequences we anticipate. In short: *No statement about correctness in language is complete if it does not contain information about the company and the occasion.*

School textbooks represent the prejudices and fantasies of the power class. They don't represent the *facts* of the language very well at all. Most of the statements of the textbooks are advice, but this advice is usually presented as if it were fact.

For example, we have an imitation Latin pattern in English that some people are very fond of—*It is I; that is he.* Sometimes, however, a speaker would be regarded with suspicion if he used it. Can you imagine what would happen if a teen-age boy in a football game asked a teammate, "Who's got the ball?" and the teammate answered, "I think that is he"? For a teen-age boy to say "That is he" in the heat of a football game would be social suicide. It is just as bad as it would be for an elementary teacher to use swear words in front of a PTA meeting.

The judgments we pass on other people's linguistic behavior can be—and have been—infinitely refined, but there are three primary evaluations: *stilted*, *OK*, and *uncouth*. To be sure, we do not always agree on the classification of a given linguistic act: Is *OK* OK or uncouth? Is *That is he* stilted or OK? (Whichever you decide, *This is him* is one notch lower—either OK or uncouth.)

Nevertheless, though the status of some patterns is uncertain, there is general agreement that certain patterns are stilted ("If that be so . . . "), others are OK ("I haven't seen any"), and others are uncouth ("I ain't seen none").

These evaluations have tremendous social significance, but it is of the first importance to realize that statements about these evaluations *are not statements about the English language*; they are statements about people's linguistic prejudices. That information about these prejudices has value and belongs in the curriculum is obvious; the point I am anxious to establish is that it is not *linguistic* information.

Every time we speak, we must decide which language patterns to use, but when we decide, we're making social choices, not grammatical ones. Kids in school need to learn that it is a mistake to use *ain't* in some circles and learning this they're learning about the power structure of our society, not about the grammatical structure of English.

To sum up: Language is a social phenomenon, an activity that people engage in. We pass judgment on each other's language behavior, just as we pass judgment on each other's eating and dressing and dancing and so on. The occasion and the company are factors in determining the correctness or propriety of any linguistic act; what is right one time may be wrong another time. This picture of language makes some people very nervous; nevertheless, until we find out who owns the English language, it's the only possible objective answer.

Where does this leave the teacher? What should he teach? Are there no rules?

Yes, of course, there are rules. But they are the kind of rules we are familiar with in books of etiquette—that is, proper behavior. We are here concerned with one sub-branch of that study—proper language behavior.

There is a large body of language patterns which educated people have been trained (at home or in school) to prefer. A student who does not have these patterns under control when he comes to school must be made competent to handle them. If he comes in saying, "I seen him," he must be equipped to say, "I saw him," whenever and wherever "I saw him" is appropriate.

Notice that he need *not* give up saying, "I seen him," when it is appropriate; you need not insist that he replace "I seen him" with "I saw him" if this produces crises of divided loyalty. All you really have to do is add "I saw him" to his grammatical repertory. .

The one thing to be shunned and avoided is the attempt to justify the preference of the power system. Haranguing the poor kid about the wickedness of "I seen him" will either depress him or antagonize him.

If the time and effort wasted in this rationalizing process were devoted to equipping him to say, "I saw him," the teaching of English would be both more efficient and more humane.

QUESTIONS FOR STUDY AND DISCUSSION

1. Bostain asserts that "the organization of the noises is the grammar of the language." Show that this statement is in harmony with Wilson's definition of *the grammar* of a language and with Allen's definition of grammar. Are these definitions consistent with the discussions of the nature of language by Chafe and Moulton?
2. Write five original illustrations of different kinds of organizational mistakes, or grammatical errors.
3. If you have studied a foreign language, do you agree with Bostain that the organizational features (the grammar) are more difficult to learn than the vocabulary? Explain.
4. Test Bostain's statement about the position of *always* in a sentence by using the word in five sentences, each containing a different verb, and then in five sentences containing a form of *be* (*am, are, is, was, were*).
5. Note the meanings listed for *can* and *may* in a recent standard dictionary and construct a sentence to illustrate each meaning. Do you agree with Bostain that *may* suggests higher probability than *might*? Construct a few sentences using each word and try them out on your classmates.
6. The double negative, freely used by Chaucer, appeared in literature as late as the eighteenth century. In 1762 the grammarian Lowth condemned its use in his grammar by applying the law of logic—that two negatives make a positive—and the model of Latin grammar, in which the double negative did not occur. Were you ever told that two negatives make a positive, that "I don't have no pencil" means "I have a pencil"? If so, what was your reaction? If the double negative is perfectly clear, why not use it?
7. Occasionally the use of a double negative is an effective means of achieving understatement. Restate each of the following double negatives as affirmatives. What is the difference in meaning? How are these double negatives different from the kind in "I don't have no pencil"?

The Dream World of English Grammar 191

a. I am not unwilling to run for the office.

b. This is a not unusual excuse.

c. My remark was not irrelevant.

d. The senator is not indifferent to public opinion.

e. Jan is not unattractive.

f. It is not improbable that he will vote for the motion.

g. Carol is not unlikely to change her mind at the last minute.

8. Bostain says there are three primary evaluations that we make about other people's linguistic behavior: *stilted*, *OK*, and *uncouth*. How many of Allen's five dimensions do these three terms involve? Consider each term separately and place it in its approximate position on the appropriate dimension.

9. Do you use Standard English in some groups and at least some forms of Nonstandard English in other groups? If so, with what groups do you use each kind of English and why? What are some of your nonstandard usages?

10. Compare the points of view of Bostain and Allen on the teaching of Standard English in the schools. What is your point of view?

11. Dialogue often employs Nonstandard English effectively. In the following illustrations select what you consider to be the nonstandard usage. (Ignore spelling.) If you haven't checked the items in a dictionary, do so now. What do even these brief quotations reveal about the speaker?

a. We was playin' just as fast as we could, because we seen we couldn't hold him much longer.—Ring Lardner, "Alibi Ike"

b. "I come pretty near goin' to Syracuse," I says, "only they wasn't no railroads runnin' through there in them days."—*Ibid.*

c. It all begun when we dropped down to C'lumbus, Ohio, from Pittsburgh to play a exhibition game on our way to St. Louis.—Ring Lardner, "You Could Look It Up"

d. Captain Kozak interrupted, "Let the jackroller tell us how he done it hisself."
"I ain't no jackroller."—Nelson Algren, "A Bottle of Milk for Mother"

e. "Lady," Slick said defensively, ... "Look at that there stove. It is a Heat Master and they cost. Them coffee urns, now. Money can't buy no better. And this here lot, lady, the diner sets on."—Robert Penn Warren, "The Patented Gate and the Mean Hamburger"

SUGGESTED ACTIVITIES

1. Select one of the short stories from which the quotations in question 11 are taken or another short story that contains Nonstandard English. Record five to ten recurring nonstandard usages every time they occur and the character who uses them. Are they charactcristic of the speech of a single character or of the speech of several characters? Show that the nonstandard usages are in keeping with other information that the author reveals about the character or characters.

    Some other good sources for nonstandard usages are "The Bear" and "Wash" by William Faulkner, "Mrs. Ripley's Trip" by Hamlin Garland, and "The Celebrated Jumping Frog of Calaveras County" and parts of *The Adventures of Huckleberry Finn* by Mark Twain.
2. The rules that Wallis made up for the use of *shall* and *will* in the seventeenth century were repeated in handbooks and in composition and rhetoric texts for many years. If you have access to one of these books (dated earlier than 1930), you might be interested in finding out what the rules were. Compare these rules with Bostain's discussion and with statements in current dictionaries.
3. Check the rules for *can* and *may* in a source mentioned in number 2. Compare the rules with Bostain's treatment of the two words and with statements in current dictionaries.
4. Write a short paper in which you explain clearly to an uninformed reader the difference between a grammatical mistake and a social mistake in language. Draw upon both the Allen and the Bostain essays. Supply your own illustrations.

17
TRIALS OF A WORD-WATCHER
Charlton Ogburn, Jr.

Purism in language is the insistence upon what is supposed to be "correctness." Purism not only dominates the prescriptive grammars referred to by Aiken and Allen and the textbook rules overridden by Bostain but also characterizes the attitudes of many people toward language. Indoctrinated with purism in early childhood, Ogburn describes himself as an addict forced to go through life suffering—from government jargon, from the speech of his associates, and finally from the speech and questions of his own children.

As a personal reminiscent essay, "Trials of a Word-watcher" is written in a style quite different from that of an informative article. Since the tone of the essay provides much of its delightful quality, the reader will want to discover Ogburn's real attitude toward purism and toward himself as a self-styled purist.

Charlton Ogburn, Jr., a former State Department official, is the author of numerous nonfiction books, among them *The Marauders* (1959), *The Winter Beach* (1966), *Forging of Our Continent* (1968), *The Continent in Our Hands* (1971); and of two novels, *The White Falcon* (1955) and *The Gold of the River Sea* (1965).

Recently I was at a party at which one of the guests spoke of a collision of airplanes in mid air. "Mid air," another of the guests—a magazine editor—repeated with a smile. "Airplanes always collide in *mid* air. One wonders where else in the air they could collide." His manner was amused, off-hand.*
But I did not miss the working of his jaw-muscles, the clenching of his fists. Here, confronted by a pet abomination, was a fellow-martyr to that condition known by the inadequate and not very descriptive term of *purism*,

---

* The author's system of hyphenation has been followed faithfully throughout this article.
Source: *Harper's Magazine* 230 (April 1965): 88–93. Copyright © 1965 by Charlton Ogburn, Jr. Appeared originally in *Harper's Magazine*. Reprinted by permission of McIntosh and Otis, Inc.

defined by the *Oxford English Dictionary* as "scrupulous or exaggerated observance of, or insistence upon, purity or correctness, esp. in language or style."

Until that moment I had employed the expression *mid air* with contentment and assurance. I now felt that all my life my intelligence had been insulted by it. I experienced the exhilaration of an obsessive collector who unexpectedly acquires a prize. At the same time, my heart sank as I recognized that I had taken on another distraction, an increment to a burden under which I was already staggering. A sultan who has added a notable beauty to a harem already ruinous in its demands upon him would know what I mean.

Purism is like alcoholism or drug-addiction. Once it takes hold, the victim's most heroic efforts of will to combat it are likely to prove inadequate. I had found this out during the years I spent in the government. I was supposed to be an official charged (in government terminology) with substantive responsibilities. Yet all the while, possibly because of the kind of thing I had to spend my time reading, I found myself falling ever more deeply under the sway of an ever-proliferating array of bugaboos of syntax and vocabulary and becoming a mere compulsive proof-reader. "Cannot help but believe new regime certain grow disenchanted its present internatl assocs," I would read in a telegram from an overseas post, but instead of considering whether my superiors should not be "alerted" (ugh!) to the opportunities such a development would open for the U.S., I would be sent off on a tangent by the reporting officer's English. "It is not enough that he cannot but believe," I would mutter. "It is not enough that he cannot help believing. Nothing will do but that he *cannot help but* believe!"

One does not, of course, have to be a fetishist about words to be put off by the flatulent jargon endemic in bureaucracies. ("Prior to implementation of approved directives, all concerned agencies will consult as to appropriate instrumentalities.") But worse than that, to one who suffers from morbid inflammation of the word-consciousness, are the affronts to grammar habitually employed in the government with an air of professionalism—such as, for example, "hopefully" used to mean "I hope" or "it is to be hoped." You read, "Hopefully, the government of X will see the error of its present course in time," and your morning is ruined. You start imagining where the precedent could lead: "Fearfully, the government of X will not see its error in time. . . . Expectfully, the U.S. will have to bail it out."

Then there is that "effective immediately" routine, with which notices begin. I used to have a day-dream in which I got back at my superiors who, among their other trying ways, permitted this travesty of English. In it, I would appear before them to reply to the charge of having failed to comply with an order stating, for example, *Effective immediately, all chairmen of inter-agency committees will keep this office informed of all meetings held and of the action taken.* "I am not," I would say with devastating trenchancy, "an immediately effective chairman."

While my colleagues were striving to forge new links with our partners in the Free World (working out "agreed positions" to be set forth in "agreed texts"—as if you *could* agree a position or a text!) I was fighting the battle of "presently." The government had been swept by a vogue for this word. "Now" was becoming almost as rare in official disseminations as "eftsoons." In a carefully controlled voice, I would explain in a drafting committee, as if I had not done so in a score of others, that "presently" did not mean "at present." It meant "in the immediate future." Not only were the results of my efforts disappointing, to say the least, but one of my associates whom I *had* impressed came to me one day with an aggrieved air and a tale of having lost a dollar by betting that "presently" had just the sense I had said only to find that "at present" loomed as large as any other among the meanings given in his dictionary. He had, if you please, looked it up in *Webster's*! I had patiently to explain that *Webster's* would accept any usage if enough word-slingers gave it currency.

PRESERVED FROM VAINGLORY

The pathological word-watcher, it should be made clear, is no more apt to rejoice in his fixation than is the book-keeper who cannot see a row of figures on a license-plate or railroad-car without adding them up. He can hardly help realizing that just as a philatelist who devotes his life to Mauritian issues is likely to become fairly expert in his field, so is a person who gives the better part of his attention to the pitfalls of English—even if his family goes in want, as it is apt to. Actually, if he is like me—I being one who as a child was sent to progressive schools, where I was taught no formal grammar—he may be unable to parse "The cat sat on the mat" or guess what is being talked about when hanging participles or gerunds are brought up. He may, like me, be unable to spell and have to depend upon his wife to catch mistakes in what he writes, usually the same ones over and over again. (Says mine, "Absense isn't going to make *my* heart grow fonder until you learn that it ends with an 's-e,' not a 'c-e.' "*) The word-watcher is also preserved from vainglory by the lack of conspicuous popular demand for what he has to offer.

"Will I type this up in triplicate?" my secretary used to ask. She was an Irish-American lass from New Hampshire. "I don't know," I would reply. "Shall you?" Her eyes would travel to the bronze paper-cutter on my desk. Before she came finally to sink it in my neck, however, she married a military attaché on home leave from Helsinki and that was the last I saw of her.

It is difficult to administer correctives in such a way as to make them appreciated; that is the point. I have heard purists resort to the device of

---

* She says I have got it wrong again. It seems only honest for me to leave it as it is, however. —C. O., Jr.

repeating the offender's erring statement in correct form, reflectively, as if unaware that they had altered the expression but trusting him to benefit from the example. Thus, when he hears the sentence, "If the information would leak out we'd be in trouble," the purist will, after thinking it over, muse, "Umm. Yes. If it should leak out, that would be too bad." But possibly because a slight stress on the *should* is almost unavoidable, this may provoke the testy retort, "What's the matter, did I say something wrong again?"

An alternative method is for the purist to pretend to be a partner of the offender's in fallibility and interestedly speculate upon the unseemly locution as upon one he himself might well have employed. "Whether we go or not depends upon the weather," he repeats with a faint smile at the ceiling, weighing the words. "Curious, isn't it, how we put in that 'or not' after 'whether' even when it is subsumed under the word 'whether' itself; that is to say [*chuckle*], regardless of *whether or not* it is needed." I have never heard anyone get away with this.

I do not mean to imply that the purist is motivated primarily by the desire for gratitude in setting others to rights. In the case of a reiterated corruption of the language it is a matter of self-preservation. I discovered the limits of what one can take in connection with the policy papers put out by the National Security Council, the nation's supreme policy-making body in foreign affairs. For years I steeled myself to the notation at the head of these papers. It read, "The President approves NSC 168 [or whatever] and directs its implementation." But human nerves can bear just so much. In a meeting with the Secretary of the Council something inside me finally snapped. "The President directs its implementation, you say? He does nothing of the kind!" I cried. "His subordinates do that!" My voice was shrill. "What you mean is, 'The President directs that it be implemented.' Good God, man! What . . . what . . . " I threw up my hands. It was held that the prolonged crisis in Southeast Asia had been too much for me.

Why does anyone fall into this "exaggerated observance of . . . correctness, esp. in language or style"? Psychologists tell us that excessive concern with detail is a form of escapism originating in a basic sense of insecurity. They are no doubt right. So are most human pursuits—coin-collecting, cigarette-smoking, reading, drinking, big-game-hunting, girl-chasing, money-making, probably even psychology-studying. Anyone who has not got a basic sense of insecurity and an over-riding desire to escape has fewer brains than a rabbit. As for why the compulsion leads in some persons to purism instead of to some less generally irritating and more socially acceptable extravagance, my guess is that it is a matter of the influences one comes under in one's formative years.

One of my early memories is of my grandfather's refusing to attend the local Methodist church any longer because of the minister's abuse of English. " '*That* much,' '*that* important,' " he scoffed. "Are we to have 'that' foisted upon us as an adverb? Is the minister's time *that* important that he cannot say 'as important as that'?" To have moved my grandparent—otherwise the gentlest, most forbearing of men—to such impatience, the offense, I judged, must have been heinous. Indeed, I conceived the notion at an early age that violations of the canons of English were almost as reprehensible as violations of the moral code, and that there were canons to right of us, canons to left of us, canons in front of us.

That does not mean I learned easily. I can still hear my father saying, time after time, "Not different *than*. Different *from*." And, "Not *in back of*. *Back of*, or *behind*." It must have taken years of such delinquencies to be extirpated from my juvenile prattle, with my mother working at it as conscientiously as my father. I remember from boyhood the astonishment in the face of a friend of mine when, upon my asking if I had to "stay home," my mother replied that I could not stay home now or ever. "Home is not an adverb. You stay *at* home." Her condemnation of the use of "place" for "where" in "eat some place" or "going some place" was (and still is) so unsparing—how can you eat a place or go a place?—that I cannot meet with the usage without a sense of imminent disaster, and I can never speak of church-goers or theater-goers without a twinge of conscience. Can you go a church? Should there not be a "to" in there somewhere? To-church-goers? Go-to-churchers?

I must be at least as hard on my children as my parents were on me. I sometimes wonder that they have not given up talking altogether, for they seldom get three sentences out consecutively without being brought up short by their mother or father. (They catch it from both sides, for the wife of a purist is either another purist or a good prospect for a divorce-lawyer.)

"Not 'I did it already.' Say, 'I've already done it.' "

"Not '*Robin* Hood.' 'Robin *Hood*.' You wouldn't say '*John* Smith.' "

"Not 'They're both alike.' 'They're alike.' It wouldn't be possible for just one of them to be alike."

"Not 'The Matthews.' 'The Matthewses.' . . . Yes, I know they've got 'The Matthews' on their mailbox. It's still wrong. One Matthews, two Matthewses."

"Not 'I feel badly.' That would mean that your sense of feeling is impaired. Say, 'I feel bad.' "

" 'Escapers,' not 'escapees.' . . . I don't care what they say in school or in the newspapers. 'Employees' are persons who are employed. 'Payees' are persons who are paid. 'Escapees' would be persons who are escaped—the guards, that is."

I JUST KNOW IT—THAT'S ALL

The two girls get their own back, however. Not only do I hear them correcting their friends, but they correct me.

"Why do you say 'idear' and 'Canader'?" one of the sprites asks.

"Well, it's this way," I explain. "New Englanders and Southerners, like

President Kennedy and your father—and like the English—don't sound *r*'s except when they precede vowels. We say . . . let's see. . . . We say 'Baltimoah, Maryland,' but 'Baltimo*rr r*and Ohio.' We separate the vowel sounds by sounding the *r*. So when we get two vowel sounds in succession, one at the end of one word, one at the beginning of the next, we tend to put in an *r* from force of habit, even when it doesn't belong there. We say 'the ide*ah* wasn't mine,' but then we're apt to say 'the ide*arr* is a good one.' Same with Canada. 'Canad*ah* goose' but 'Canad*arr* ale.'"

"But it's wrong, isn't it?"

"You could say it's colloquial."

"Wrong."

"Well, yes."

The girls are just beginning to learn that relying on my authority has its risks. For example, I know that "Do you have?" means "Do you ordinarily have?" or "Do you make a practice of having?" whereas "Have you?" or "Have you got?" means "Are you in possession of the object at present?" I know it is incorrect to say, "Do you have a pencil with you?" It is just as incorrect as it would be to say, "Have you [or have you got] a good time in the country?" But I cannot cite any rules of syntax that make this so. I just know it, that's all. I know by the way it sounds and because I've had it on good authority. To insist upon what you know is right, tolerating no divergent opinion, when you cannot say why it is right, takes character. But it does not always win arguments.

There is the further complicating fact that, like any confirmed word-watcher, I supplement the accepted rules of English with others of my own devising. Or, as I prefer to think of it, I discover hitherto unformulated principles. One of these is my law of A-or-An-Before-H. This law states that "a" shall be used before a word beginning with "h" if the accent is on the first syllable of that word (provided the "h" is sounded) but that if the accent is on a subsequent syllable, "an" shall be used. Thus we are to speak of *a* history but *an* historical novel, *a* hexagon, but *an* hexagonal figure. Neat, isn't it? I should add that the law permits no exception. True, "an hotel" may sound a little affected or precious, but a people which has the Saviour in the Sermon on the Mount speaking of "an hill" (the translator of the King James Bible having of course lacked the benefit of my law) should certainly have the resolution to say "an hotel" in a clear, unfaltering voice. I demand nothing less from my offspring—who, by the way, regard the word "hotel" as a queer derivative of "motel"—and the fact that nobody but me recognizes my law does not move me.

THE HYPHEN, ALAS!

It is the misfortune of the purist to appear arrogant when all he is doing is being right. Perhaps much may be forgiven him in recognition of his being committed to a losing cause. Poor sod, as the British would say, he is driven on the one hand to pursue a perfection perhaps unattainable this side of the grave (at least the ugly suspicion insinuates itself that the only purity of speech is to be found in total silence, of which language is in its entirety a corruption) and on the other to cling to positions that irresistibly are eroded away beneath him; for, like the noblest headlands, destined to be undermined by the remorseless seas, it is the fate of language to deteriorate. (I am aware that some would say evolve.) I, for example, have given the best years of my life to the hyphen—and to what end?

The hyphen is being done away with—indefensibly, ruthlessly, as if a conspiracy had been formed against it. And we must understand that if the hyphen goes, so does the very conception of the structure of English.

The hyphen permits us to shorten "a railroad operated by the state" to "a state-operated railroad." But in National Intelligence Estimates costing tens of thousands of dollars each we may read "a state operated railroad" or even "a state owned and operated railroad"—a phrase in which the parts of speech are impossible to identify and one devoid of meaning. We may read of "Western oriented regimes," which can mean only Western regimes facing east, and of "white collar workers," which could mean either workers with white collars or white men who work on collars.

Writers who should know better do not show it. John Hersey gives us *The Child Buyer*, apparently believing that a child buyer is one who buys children, whereas in fact it is a child who buys. And Joseph W. Alsop in his book *From the Silent Earth* (his exciting book, I must admit) may think he is describing a helmet encrusted with boar's tusks in his phrase "a boar's tusk-encrusted helmet" but what he is actually describing is a tusk-encrusted helmet belonging to a boar. (He did use one hyphen, though.)

Where is this leading? It has already led, as I can report from my own observation, to a headline reading "Child Chasing Fox Found Rabid" and to an advertisement suggesting "For the pet lover on your Christmas list, a perfect little four-poster bed for the corner of the living room."

One would expect the nation to draw back from the brink while there is time, but I am pessimistic. The hyphen is disappearing, and neither the purist's outrage nor his lamentations will save it, I fear, or retard the degeneration of the English language into mouthfuls of words indiscriminately spewed forth. He pounds the table till his wattles shake, and it does no good.

And yet the purist—even such as I—has his vindications. Do you know why Mariner I, the "probe" aimed at Mars, went off course into oblivion? I ask you, do you know? Because, in all the complicated instructions fed into its guidance system, one hyphen was inadvertently omitted. One tiny hyphen that requires you only to extend your little finger to the upper right-hand corner of the keyboard. It cost the American people two million bucks.

And if you ask me, it served them damned well right.

QUESTIONS FOR STUDY AND DISCUSSION

1. What analogy does *word-watcher* suggest to you?
2. Is Ogburn an "obsessive purist"? Consider the tone of the essay and the author's attitude toward his subject and toward himself.
3. Do the illustrations of "government terminology" (jargon) and the usage which Ogburn's parents objected to belong in the same category? Explain.
4. What is the basis for Ogburn's objection to "he cannot help but believe"?
5. What is meant by "the flatulent jargon endemic in bureaucracies"? Show that the illustration, "Prior to implementation of approved directives, all concerned agencies will consult as to appropriate instrumentalities," fits the definition. Which of Bostain's three primary evaluations of other people's linguistic behavior would you apply to this sentence? Restate the sentence more simply. Look for another example of "flatulent jargon" in your reading.
6. What is the structural problem in these sentences: "Hopefully, the government . . . will see the error of its present course in time" and "Effective immediately, all chairmen . . . will keep this office informed. . . ."? Restate the sentences. Contrast the sentences as quoted by Ogburn with these: "Hopefully, the candidate began his campaign" and "Effective immediately, a new city ordinance prohibits overnight parking on the streets."
7. "Will I type this up in triplicate?" the Irish-American secretary asked. What meaning does *will* suggest? What modal would you use in this question? What meaning does it convey? Would you use the same modal in the statement," I ——— type this up in triplicate"?
8. Why does the use of *would* in this *if* clause seem out of place: "If the information would leak out, we might be in trouble"? Check the various meanings of *would* in a recent standard dictionary. Does the use of *would* in the illustration fit any of them? In the following conditional clause, what does *would* mean? "If Paul would work harder, he might get better grades." Can an objection be raised to this use of *would*?
9. How does Ogburn account for his so-called purism? Have you or any of your friends been similarly indoctrinated with purism? If so, explain the circumstances and discuss the language taboos.
10. In referring to "the canons of English," Ogburn assumes that the reader will enjoy the pun because of his familiarity with Tennyson's *The Charge of the Light Brigade*. In that poem Tennyson describes the heroic attack of the British Light Brigade against greatly superior forces of Russians in the Crimean War.

Cannon to right of them,
Cannon to left of them,
Cannon in front of them
    Volley'd and thunder'd;

*Storm'd at with shot and shell,
Boldly they rode and well,
Into the jaws of Death,
Into the mouth of Hell
    Rode the six hundred.*

What are canons of English? In drawing the analogy between canons of English and cannon, what similarities does Ogburn suggest?
11. Compare Ogburn's rule for the choice of *a* or *an* with the explanation in a recent standard dictionary. Do you say or write *an historical*? Do you know people who do? Account historically for the use of *an* before *hotel*. (See *Standard College Dictionary*.)
12. What do you think Ogburn is really saying in this sentence: "To insist upon what you know is right, tolerating no divergent opinion, when you cannot say why it is right, takes character. But it does not always win arguments"? What is your reaction to people who show such character?
13. Do the preceding essays on language in this book indicate that language deteriorates or evolves? What is Ogburn's point of view?
14. Why was it important for the publisher to follow faithfully the author's system of hyphenation?
15. Where would you place this essay on Allen's informal-formal continuum? Consider the point of view from which it is written, the vocabulary, the sentence structure, and the general tone of the essay.

SUGGESTED ACTIVITIES

1. The purist objects to the following usage items, Ogburn says. Do you hear them used? Do you find them in writing? Where would you place them on Allen's continuums? What status label is attached to them in a recent standard dictionary?

   in back of

   different than

   feel badly

   stay home

   eat some place

   It isn't *that* important.

   Question: Are *home, some place,* and *that* adverbials?

2. Is Ogburn correct in saying that the hyphen is disappearing? Check a newspaper for the use or absence of a hyphen in these combinations and others?
   a. Compound nouns: *vice-president* or *vice president*?
   b. Adjective-noun: *natural-gas pipeline* or *natural gas pipeline*? *a small city police force* or *a small-city police force*? (Does there seem to be a difference in meaning?)
   c. Adjective-participle-noun: *a low-priced car* or *a low priced car*?
   d. Amassing of nouns in headlines and in names of organizations and government agencies: *Failure Effect Analysis Report, The Electronic Ground Automatic Destruct Sequencer Button, Community Action Program Residents' Council.*

   If any of the illustrations you collect are ambiguous, explain the ambiguity.
3. Nearly everyone has language prejudices. Make note of those you hear during the next few days. Then write an informal essay incorporating these prejudices.

— or —

Write an informal reminiscent essay on one of the following subjects:

My Encounter with a Purist

Some Purists I Have Known

My Indoctrination with Purism

Untouched by Purism

My Own Language Prejudices

18
NOW EVERYONE IS HIP ABOUT SLANG

Bergen Evans

Slang is not new—it seems to have been a part of all languages in all periods. The term *slang*, however, is fairly recent. When it first appeared in England in the eighteenth century, it was applied to the special vocabulary of the underworld of thieves, previously known as *cant*. Somewhat later *slang* came to be used interchangeably with the French word *argot*, a term used among London thieves to designate their secret vocabulary. At about the beginning of the nineteenth century, *slang* began to take on its broader present meaning.

Today *cant*, *argot*, and *jargon* are generally used to designate the vocabulary of a special group, trade, or profession, either in the underworld or in the upperworld. *Slang* has remained a more inclusive term, though there are varieties of slang for individual groups—high school and college students, for example.

Slang tends to "bunch up toward the informal end" of the informal-formal dimension, as Allen points out, and is more characteristic of speech than of writing. A slang term may be a new word, or it may be an old word with a new, often figurative meaning. It does not replace an existing word in the vocabulary but exists side by side with it. Since slang strives for novelty and for striking expression, it is ironic that it soon loses its shock value.

Evans illustrates the long history of slang in the English language. He shows that a slang term may follow one of three courses: it may drop out of use, remain slang, or cease to be slang and pass into general use. It is the third route that slang tends to take today, Evans thinks.

Bergen Evans is professor of English at Northwestern University.

Source: *The New York Times Magazine*, March 22, 1964, p. 22 ff. Copyright © 1964 by the New York Times Company. Reprinted by permission of the publisher and the author.

One of the most interesting changes taking place in our language today is the acceptance of an enormous amount of slang into standard English. Formerly it often took centuries for a piece of slang to gain such acceptance, if it ever gained it. Dr. Johnson, in 1755, insisted that words such as *frisky*, *gambler* and *conundrum* "ought not to be admitted to the language." But times have changed. So rapid, indeed, has the process of absorption become that there is a possibility that slang, as a clearly delimitable form of language in America, may be on the way out.

Square, for instance, in its slang meaning, has lost almost all of its original sting of irreverence (a characteristic of slang). It is no longer "secret" talk and its use certainly doesn't mark the user as one who is "in." It seems highly likely that it will soon be regarded as standard.

Hip, to choose another example from the beatnik talk which only yesterday seemed so wild and strange, is listed in Merriam-Webster's *Third International* merely as a variation of *hep*, and *hep* (though I would disagree) is not labeled slang. (That Merriam-Webster chose to define *hep*, as the dominant form, illustrates the unavoidable lag of dictionaries; *hep* has been "out," decidedly unhip, for years!) Also not marked as slang is *gig*—a job, especially a jazzman's job. *Dig, cool, chick, bug, bag* and *hung up* are labeled slang but it is not unreasonable to assume that these will either have disappeared from use, or will have been accepted as standard, within a decade or two. (A good deal of British slang has apparently already been accepted. A new edition of *The Concise Oxford Dictionary*, published last month, contains a number of "slang" expressions without indication in the text that they differ from standard English.)

Those who get disturbed about slang as something "modern" that is "corrupting" the language ought to know that it is as old as language itself. Indeed, it *is* language, and one of the minor pleasures of reading is to come across it in the literature of the past. Chaucer, for instance, uses *gab* exactly as we use it today. A desirable woman was a *piece* in the fourteenth century, and a *broad* or a *frail* in the sixteenth. Bishop Latimer, in a sermon before Edward VI (1547), said that those who had defrauded the King of money ought to "make restitution . . . cough up." John Adams, in a morning-after letter (1774) said, "We drank sentiments until 11 o'clock. Lee and Harrison were very high." Charlotte Brontë referred to a foolish person as a sap—as others had been doing for 200 years before her.

From the difference between certain standard words in Latin and in the Romance languages, we know that even the Romans used slang. Thus, although the formal Latin word for head was *caput*, the French is *la tête* and the Italian *la testa*—which obviously derive from the Latin *testa*, an earthen pot. And where the formal Latin word for leg was *crus*, the French is *la jambe* and the Italian *la gamba* (whence "gams" and "gamboling"), derived from the Latin *gamba*, hoof. The Romans wrote formally about the head and the leg, but they apparently spoke of "the pot" and "the hoof."

One of the purposes of using slang, as with thieves' cant, from which much of it has sprung, is to make it possible for certain groups *not* to be understood by the uninitiated. Its use marks the user as one of the knowing, a member of a prestigious in-group. (And when the word is no longer good slang, its user is no longer "in.") It is also used to shock and, if possible, irritate. Thus *neat* is a term of approval with the younger set even though a labored defiance of neatness is obligatory among them. Even more useful, or more used, are expressions of contempt—*drip, clod, creep, dope, jerk* and *fink*—which reinforce status by rejecting the unworthy.

A large element in the creation of slang is sheer playfulness, an extension of the impulse that leads to such duplications of sound as *hotsy-totsy, heebie-jeebies* and *okeydoke*. The word *slang* is itself slang and embodies much of what it designates: it is breezy, catchy, eminently suitable, yet intriguing; we feel that we know its meaning but we find it hard to define and difficult to trace. It is probably language that is being slung about instead of being handled with stately consideration. In an early fifteenth-century poem we are told of one who "bold words did sling" and there *is* a boldness and a sling in slang. It risks daring metaphors and audacious allusions; it impudently defies propriety and dissolves with triumphant laughter into meaninglessness when solemnity indignantly demands that it explain itself.

Pomposity is slang's natural enemy, which may account for the fact that there are probably more slang words that describe drunkenness—the antithesis of dignity—than any other state or activity. Solemnity meets the condition with the plain *drunk*, the disapproving *drunken*, the scientific *intoxicated* and highfalutin *inebriated*. The Quakers, with gentle evasion, called it *tired*. But slang riots in every degree of its indignity, from the mild *lit*, through the hilarious *plastered* to the terminal *stiff*.

Benjamin Franklin once compiled a "Drinker's Dictionary" containing 228 terms, but *The American Thesaurus of Slang* found it necessary 200 years later to list four times that number. And it is interesting, and perhaps significant, that modern slang seems to represent drunkenness less as a disreputable escapade, a breaking away from dull routing (as in *spree, toot, jag, bender, binge*) than as a sodden stasis (*loaded, pie-eyed, stewed, blotto*).

Much slang is humorously euphemistic. There are some situations so ghastly that one must ignore them or laugh at them. Airsickness, for example, is so outrageous an assault on our dignity (coupled, as it usually is, with humiliating fear) that it has come to be "one of those things we just don't talk about." The airlines—who can't ignore it—refer with ludicrous delicacy, to the equipment provided in the seat backs as "discomfort containers." But college students—who, at least in retrospect, seem to find the business amusing—call them "barff bags."

At one end of the gamut of slang's humor is the inane—what Oliver Wendell Holmes called "the blank checks of a bankrupt mind"—such fatuities as "Sez you!", "Banana oil!", and "So's your old man!" But at the other are such concepts as "to join the majority" (to die), which goes back to ancient Rome, or the eighteenth century's "scandal broth," for tea, or the

British lower classes' late nineteenth-century "nobby" (also "with knobs on") for smart, elegant or fashionable—a shrewder appraisal of Victorian design and decor than the upper classes were capable of making.

Grose, in his *Classical Dictionary of the Vulgar Tongue* (1796),* tells us that "a forward girl, ready to oblige every man that shall ask her" was called an "Athanasian wench"—and is so flattering to his reader as not even to explain why. The explanation is that the first two words of the Athanasian creed are: "Whosoever desires...."

If such allusiveness seems too recondite for anyone but dwellers in the groves of Academe, one must consider rhyming slang, which originated in the underworld, was developed by London Cockneys in the nineteenth century, enjoyed a vogue for several generations and is now disappearing.

Here the meaning lies in a word which is not spoken at all but which rhymes with the last of two or more words in a phrase. At first, similarity of sound was the sole connection—as *cherry ripe* for pipe or *apples and pears* for stairs. But Cockney wit and humor and linguistic imaginativeness (what ignorant nonsense in Shaw to assume that Professor Higgins's English was better, as speech, than was Eliza Doolittle's—Eliza's class danced linguistic circles around the gentry!) soon wove an implication of meaning into the allusion of sound. So a liar became a *holy friar*; a church, *chicken perch*; a lodger, an *artful dodger*; a gal, *rob my pal*; kids, *God forbids*, and so on—in one of the giddiest whirls language has ever been swept into.

And then, as though this were not involved and clever enough, the rhyming word itself was sometimes merely implied as a part of a well-known phrase. Thus *china* came to mean mate because "plate" rhymes with "mate"; and *Oliver* to mean fist because the unspoken "Twist" rhymes with "fist."

Now all of this surely marks slang, not as a degeneration of language, but rather as a sort of spume or spindrift of language riding its forward-surging wave; but, even so, language—as much a part of it as law or liturgy and shaped and controlled by the same forces that shape and control standard speech.

This is illustrated by the thousands of instances in which slang repeats the etymology of a standard word. Thus *to impose* is, literally, "to put something over on," *to excoriate* "to take the hide off," *to apprehend* "to catch on," *to converse* "to go round with" and *to exaggerate* "to pile it on." He who is *ecstatic* is "beside himself"; he has been driven out of himself, or "sent." He who is *replete* is "fed up" and that which is *superlative* has been "laid on thick." *Handsome* originally meant "pleasant to handle" or, as the young now say, "smooth." To be *recalcitrant* is to "kick" backwards (from Latin *calx, calvis*, heel).

To be *dependent* is to be a "hanger-on" and to be *enraptured* is to be "carried away"—gone, man, gone! Where the meticulous speaker of standard

---

* The first edition appeared in 1785.—Eds.

English might ask, "What's fretting you?", a slangy speaker might ask, "What's eating you?" And where the standard speaker might stiffly aver that he was "not prone to accept" a certain imposition, the other might more vividly insist that he "would not take it lying down." Yet both have said the same thing: for *fretting* means voracious or gnawing eating, and *prone* means lying face downwards.

Many slang words pass into standard use and once they do, of course, they don't sound slangy at all. Among such now-sturdy-respectables are *club* (social), *dwindle, flout, foppish, freshman, fretful, glib, hubbub, nice, ribaldry, scoundrel, simper, swagger, tidy, tantrums, tarpaulin* and *trip* (journey).

Even more interesting is that many slang words stay in the language for centuries, but remain slang. *Booze*, once standard, became dialectal and then slang and has remained slang for centuries, spawning recently, in British slang, *boozer* (a pub). *Brass* (impudence) is also centuries old. So is to *chisel* (to use trickery), and so are *frisk* (to search a person for weapons), *corporation* (large belly), *leery, pad* (bed), *mum, blab, gag* (joke), *pigeon* (dupe), *hick* (rustic), *grub* (food) and hundreds of others.

A word can remain slang and undergo a semantic change just as if it were standard. Forty years ago a *nut* was a ludicrous eccentric; today he is one who is dangerously deranged. Like so many other things in the world, the word has acquired a menace.

Still other words pass from slang to standard within a few years of their creation. *Cello*, a nineteenth-century clipping of *violoncello*, and printed as *'cello* up until a few years ago, is now standard. *Bleachers* was slang in 1904, but fully standard within two decades. *Sweater* was slang in 1880, but standard by 1914. These last two words, by the way, illustrate the way in which a slang word can lose its metaphorical vitality in the process of becoming a standard verbal symbol. We have to stop to think of the idea of bleaching in the *bleachers* and, offhand, would see nothing contradictory in a reference to a woman's wearing a dainty cashmere *sweater*.

Except through the caprice of usage, there's no accounting for the status of words. *Bored* (wearied by dullness), for instance, was listed as slang in 1722, but is now standard. But *flabbergast*, which was included in the same list, remains slang. The modern slang use of *dizzy* to mean foolish in a featherheaded way ("dizzy dame") recaptures the word's original standard meaning: a ninth-century West Saxon version of Matthew 25:1-3 says of the 10 virgins who went forth to meet the bridegroom, "Five of them were dizzy . . . and took lamps but they didn't take no oil with them."

It is, in fact, becoming increasingly difficult to draw a hard and fast line between slang and colloquial, and colloquial and standard,* and thus to establish that this or that word is definitely not acceptable in dignified

---

* Evans seems to be using the term *colloquial* in a restricted sense to mean dignified speech. *Colloquial* is, of course, a broad term meaning simply *conversational*, which may be either standard or nonstandard.—Eds.

speech or writing. *Blues*, for instance, is still slang if it means low spirits. But if it means a genre of song expressing low spirits, it is standard.

Jazz in its meaning of sexual intercourse is still low slang, very close to the underworld cant it originally was. As a description of a kind of music, however, it is standard. But in its recently acquired vogue meaning of fussy routine or nonsense ("and all that jazz") it is slang again.

Kid meaning a child was cant in the late sixteenth century, but had become slang by the mid-eighteenth century, and is now colloquial. The verb *to kid* (to tease by jesting, as with a child), remains slang. But *kidnap* has been standard for almost 300 years. *Gal* is slang only when a deliberate mispronunciation of *girl*; if it is the speaker's natural pronunciation, it is simply a social or regional variant. In 1748 Swift singled out *mob* (a clipping of *mobile vulgus*, the moving or fickle populace) for particular detestation as a corruption of the language. But despite the Dean's disapproval the word stuck and is now standard when it means a riotous assemblage.

A striking illustration of the extent to which even experts disagree in this matter of labeling is furnished by comparison of Wentworth and Flexner's *Dictionary of American Slang* (1960) with the Merriam-Webster *Third International* (1961). Of 2,355 words which Wentworth and Flexner list as slang, and with the meanings of which the *Third International* agrees, the *Third International* lists only 549 as slang.

In the face of such a divergence one must wonder if slang is not losing its identity. The increasing frankness of all expression has weakened its euphemistic value. The disappearance of fixed social classes has removed one of the chief motivations for its impertinence. And its universal use has destroyed its secrecy and reduced its value as an expression of in-group superiority.

There is also just too much of it around for it to be in any way esoteric. *The American Thesaurus of Slang* lists over 100,000 terms and the *Dictionary of American Slang* estimates that slang makes up perhaps one-fifth of the words we use. A single issue of *Time*—that of January 10, 1964—contains 266 words and phrases that in the days of *The Literary Digest* would have been considered sub-standard and unfit for serious writing. *The Washington Post* of the same date contains 152.

Very little contemporary slang has enough shock value left to tickle our fancy. The beatnik and teen-age jargon, of which so much has been made, is pretty unimaginative stuff when compared with, say, rhyming slang or the eighteenth-century slang in Grose's *Classical Dictionary of the Vulgar Tongue*. Impudence, impiety and indecency are now in the public domain and rarely startle. Greed, brutality and what passes for religion can still shock, but the mark of the in-group today is more the capacity to *be* shocked than the ability to shock.

American slang had a period of vigor and we were proud of it. "When Americans are through with the English language," Mr. Dooley boasted, "it will look as if it had been run over by a musical comedy." Perhaps our delight in slang was part of our traditional defiance of the British; after all, it was the *King's* English that we were tying in knots. But now that we are the senior partner, and it is the *President's* English, some of the fun may have gone out of twisting its tale. And perhaps there will be a renaissance of slang in British English—to mock and startle *us*.

QUESTIONS FOR STUDY AND DISCUSSION

1. Explain what Evans means by saying that slang "may be on the way out." Select any five terms that you think are slang and find out whether they are labeled *slang* in a recent standard dictionary. If possible, check two dictionaries: a Merriam-Webster dictionary and the *Standard College Dictionary*.
2. Why do you use slang? Are your reasons similar to those listed by Evans?
3. List some current slang terms which show that "pomposity is slang's natural enemy."
4. Show that some slang is inane, "the blank checks of a bankrupt mind."
5. Some rather formal words in English are derived from Latin words that were not necessarily formal in that language, for conversational Latin offered many picturesque expressions not present in classical Latin. The etymological meaning in Latin of such words can frequently be best translated into English by a slang word or phrase. The following words, listed in *English Words and Their Background* by George H. McKnight (Appleton, 1923), illustrate this point. Record the etymology of each word as it is given in a recent standard dictionary.

assault	diatribe	fool	interrupt	polite
delirious	effrontery	impose	inveigh	precocious
depraved	excoriate	insult	perplexed	supercilious

6. Here are some slang terms from earlier periods. With how many of them are you familiar? Are they included in a recent standard dictionary? If so, record any status label that is attached to them. If possible, compare the entries in a Merriam-Webster dictionary and the *Standard College Dictionary*.
   a. Words listed as slang in *Modern English: Its Growth and Present Use* by George Philip Krapp (Scribner's, 1909):

bamboozle	cahoots		hocus pocus
biff, n.	chump		plunk, n.
bogus	flub, n. (a heavy or stupid person)		mosey

b. Words listed as slang in *English Words and Their Background* by George H. McKnight (Gordian, 1923):

Terms designating a dull and stupid person

bonehead, duffer, dumb-bell, poor fish, wall-eyed shrimp, bats in belfry

Terms applied to a young woman

jane, dame, flapper, skirt, peach, bird, priss, lemon, drag, gloom, hairpin, pippin, sweet patootie

Terms applied to a young man

candy-leg, gold mine, nifty guy, tightwad, lounge lizard, parlor leech

c. Expressions listed by McKnight as still current in student language in the early 1920s. (Are they used today?):

Ain't it the truth?	You bet your neck.
I should worry.	You bet your bottom dollar.
Go way back and sit down.	Come off your perch (or horse).
You know me, Al.	What's eating you?
I'll say.	Nobody home.
I'll tell the world.	

Evaluate the effectiveness of the words or expressions listed above. Why do you think many of them have gone out of use?

7. Which of the current popular slang terms do you think are most likely to be in use twenty-five years from now? Why? File your forecast and check it in twenty-five years. Your guesses might provide amusing entertainment at a class reunion.
8. Evaluate the usefulness of slang: its contributions to the language and its dangers.

SUGGESTED ACTIVITIES

1. As a cooperative class enterprise, prepare a dictionary of slang used in your school.
2. If there are students in the class who have recently transferred from a high school in another section of the country, they might write a short paper comparing the slang terms of the two schools.
3. Leaf through a dictionary of slang and select some words or expressions that interest you. When did they enter the language? Were they new

words or old words used in new ways? Note any changes in meaning that they have undergone. Write a report on your findings.

If these dictionaries are available, consult them: *Dictionary of American Slang* by Harold Wentworth and Stuart Flexner (Crowell, 1960); *The American Thesaurus of Slang* by Lester V. Berrey and Melvin Van Den Bark, 2d ed. (Crowell, 1953). If you are interested in British slang, use *A Dictionary of Slang and Unconventional English*, 5th ed., by Eric Partridge (Macmillan, 1967).

4. Young foreigners are always interested in learning American slang. Write a paragraph addressed to such readers using current slang terms and then rewrite it in conventional English.
5. Interview several people in each of these approximate age groups, 30–50 and 55–75, to find out what slang terms were current when they were in high school or college. Which of the terms have gone out of use, which have survived as slang, which have become part of the general vocabulary? Write a report of your findings.
6. The late Ring Lardner was one of the real masters of written slang. Read one of his short stories, *Fables in Slang* by George Ade, or a short story by O. Henry. Note the date of publication. List some of the terms which you think are slang and check them in a recent standard dictionary to find their present status. Do you consider the use of slang effective in the story you read? Why or why not? Write a paper in which you report your findings and your evaluation.
7. *Catcher in the Rye* by J. D. Salinger represents the vernacular of teen-agers in the 1950s, including slang. Read the novel and list some of the slang terms. Consider what has happened to each one. Do you think the best ones have survived? Explain. (*Note:* The language of *Catcher in the Rye* has been analyzed by numerous critics. Their critical analyses, used in conjunction with the novel itself, provide excellent material for a research paper. Consult the *Book Review Digest* for reviews.)
8. Create some new slang terms by using the rhyming technique of the nineteenth-century London Cockneys.

Part Six

REGIONAL DIALECTS

19
AMERICAN DIALECTS
Jean Malmstrom

"He talks funny" is a frequent response when a speaker from one section of the United States hears a speaker from another for the first time. Since it is the other person's speech that is funny rather than one's own, it follows that everybody is going to sound funny to somebody. And so it is, for everybody speaks a regional dialect of American English.

Dialectology is a branch of linguistics concerned with both regional and social aspects of language, as illustrated by Allen's space and standard-nonstandard continuums. Every language comprises regional and social dialects which are ordinarily mutually intelligible but which are distinguished by certain differences in pronunciation, vocabulary, and grammatical forms.

The systematic study of American regional dialects began when a project for a Linguistic Atlas of the United States and Canada was established in 1930 to be carried out by linguistically trained field workers. Although this project was not realized, the results of a pilot study in New England were published in *The Linguistic Atlas of New England* (1939–43). From this study and from the unpublished data of other independent regional atlas investigations, dialectologists have described three large dialect areas, corresponding, in great part, to the westward migrations: Northern, Midland, and Southern. (See map on p. 217.)

In these selections from her book, *Language in Society*, Malmstrom draws upon linguistic atlas data and other research of linguistic geographers to present a concise discussion of American regional dialects for the popular reader. She points out certain differences between the major regional dialects, describes the procedures of fieldworkers in securing data for the atlas, and shows the historical reasons for dialect differences. Each region has its own standard-nonstandard continuum, and the speech of no one section is superior

Source: *Language in Society* (New York: Hayden, 1965), pp. 40–46; 54–55. Copyright © 1965 by Hayden Book Company, Inc. Reprinted by permission of the Hayden Book Company, Inc., and the author.

to that of another. But significant and interesting as the distinctive features of regional dialects are, it is important to remember that similarities in these dialects far outweigh differences: We all speak English.

Since this chapter was written, a second regional atlas project has reached publication. The first volume of *The Linguistic Atlas of the Upper Midwest*, by Harold B. Allen, was published in 1973 by the University of Minnesota Press. The Linguistic Atlas of the Middle and South Atlantic States is expected to begin to appear in 1975, under the imprint of the University of Chicago Press. No other projects are close to immediate publication.

Jean Malmstrom is professor of English at Western Michigan University.

By interviewing native speakers of American English in many parts of our country, linguistic geographers have discovered that three main dialect areas exist in the United States: Northern, Midland, and Southern, as shown on the map[1] on page 217. They are clearest on the Atlantic Coast, but they blend and fuse the farther west they go, reflecting the westward movement of the pioneers. As our ancestors moved west, they carried their dialects with them.

These three areas are defined by dialect boundaries based on consistent differences in pronunciation, vocabulary, and grammar occurring throughout large areas. The word lists in this chapter show many names for things and ideas, but many of these variants are only local uses: that is, they do not occur throughout an entire main dialect area, but only in certain localities within the area. The linguistic geographer records every variant he hears, but only regional variants are widespread enough to establish main dialect boundaries. The local variants shown in the word lists are fascinating because there are so many of them. Indeed, the linguistic geographer knows that however many variants he hears, he may discover another new one the very next day. The consistent differences that define the main dialect areas concern us here.[2]

For example, Northern speakers regularly pronounce these pairs of words with different vowel sounds: *mourning* (as in moan) and *morning* (as in taught); *hoarse* and *horse*. Northern speakers also customarily say the verb *grease* and

---

[1] Adapted from page 43, *Dialects—U.S.A.*, by Jean Malmstrom and Annabel Ashley (Champaign, Illinois: National Council of Teachers of English, 1963). By permission of the National Council of Teachers of English.

[2] The examples of differences in pronunciation, word choice, and grammar given in the following pages came from the regional linguistic atlases and from other original materials of various linguistic geographers.

MAJOR DIALECT BOUNDARIES

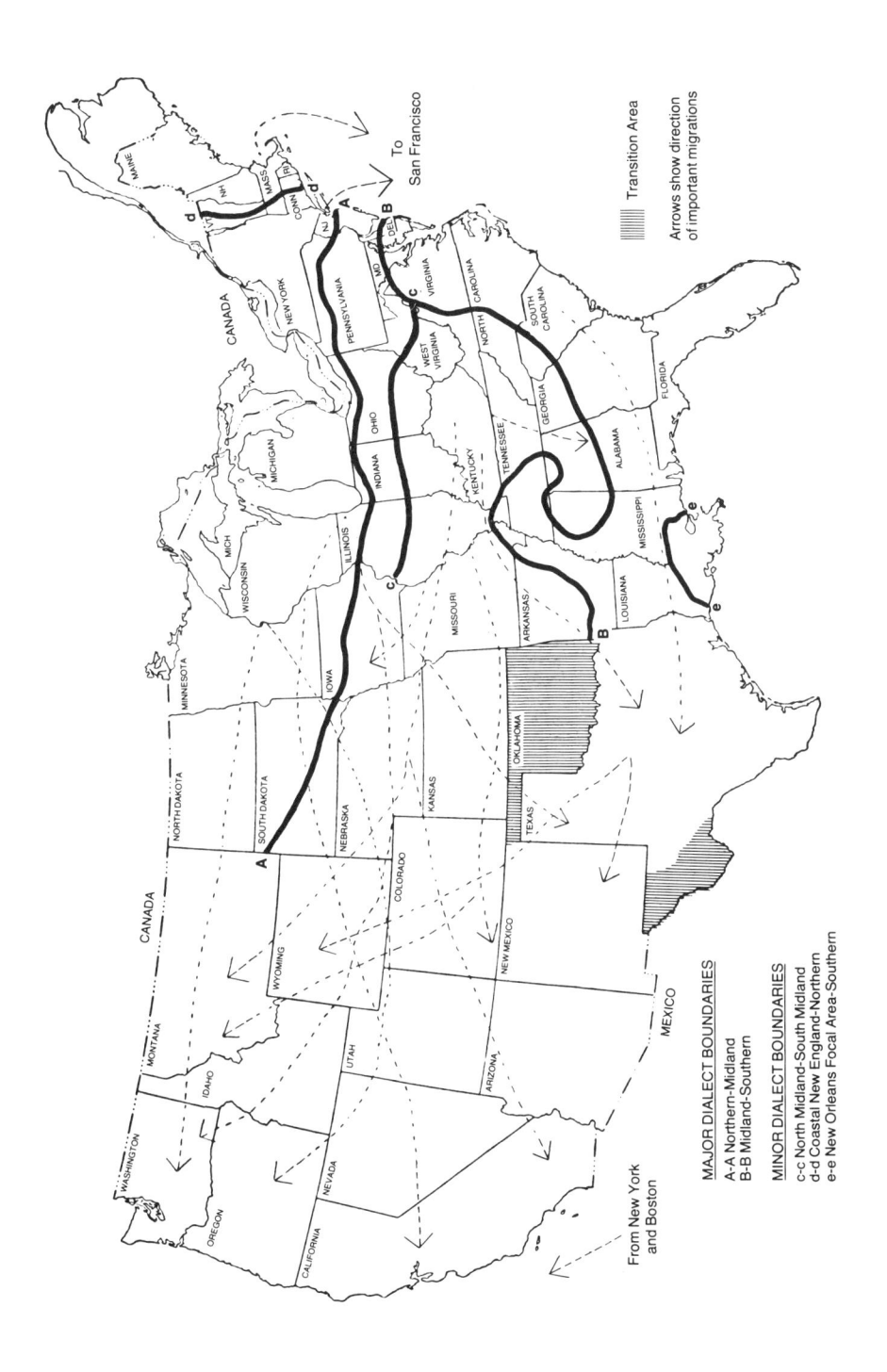

A-A Northern-Midland
B-B Midland-Southern

MINOR DIALECT BOUNDARIES

c-c North Midland–South Midland
d-d Coastal New England–Northern
e-e New Orleans Focal Area–Southern

Transition Area

Arrows show direction of important migrations

the adjective *greasy* with an "s" sound (instead of a "z" sound). They also regularly end the word *with* by the last sound of *breathe*, not that of *breath*. Midland speakers regularly use the last sound of *breath* instead. Midland speakers also characteristically keep the "r" sound after vowels and even insert an "r" sound into *wash* and *Washington*. They seem to be speaking a very "r-y" dialect. Southern speakers are quite different in this respect; their "r" sounds are consistently nonexistent except before vowels. Moreover, they pronounce the verb *grease* and the adjective *greasy* with a "z" sound instead of the "s" sound that Northern speakers use.

Differences in word choice are clear and interesting too. Northern speakers call the siding on their houses *clapboards*. Midland and Southern speakers use the words *weatherboarding* or *weatherboards*. The Northern speaker's *pail* is the Midland or Southern speaker's *bucket*. The Northern name for *earthworm* is *angleworm*, a *small stream* is a *brook*, *cornbread* is *johnnycake*, the *seed* of a cherry is a cherry *pit*, a *gutter* on the roof is an *eavestrough*, and a *frying pan* is a *spider*. In the Midland dialect area a *frying pan* is a *skillet* and *eavestroughs* are *spouts* or *spouting*, *window shades* are *blinds*, a *paper sack* is a *poke*, a *dragon fly* is a *snake feeder*, and *string beans* are *green-beans*. In Southern speech, *string beans* are *snap beans* or *snaps*, a boy *carries* a girl to a dance instead of *escorting* or *taking* her, and cows *low* instead of *moo*.

Each of the three main dialect areas has its characteristic grammatical structures too. Northern speakers prefer *dove* as the past tense of *dive*, whereas in the Southern area the majority prefers *dived*; in the Midland, both forms occur, although the more educated and modern speakers prefer *dove*. In the Midland *all the farther* is widely used for *as far as*, the preferred Northern form.

In addition to these geographical differences, the linguistic geographers have discovered some interesting facts about the relation of education to dialect. Three types of persons are regularly interviewed for the Linguistic Atlas: a typical college graduate, a typical high school graduate, and a typical person with less than a high school education. Each of these types speaks distinctively. On the basis of these observed distinctions, we can name three types of American speech. By "Standard English" we mean the typical language of the college graduate. "Popular English" is a name for the typical speech of the high school graduate. "Folk English" refers to the characteristic speech of the person who has not graduated from high school, and who has roughly an eighth-grade education or less. These are not, of course, hard and fast distinctions, but simply useful guidelines.

The typical college graduate in the Northern dialect area, for example, does not normally use the following forms that are quite frequent in the speech of less educated Northerners: *he isn't to home* for *he isn't at home*, *hadn't ought* for *oughtn't*, and *scairt* for *scared*. The typical Midland college graduate does not regularly use these forms, which occur often in less educated Midland speech: *I'll wait on you* for *I'll wait for you*, *I want off* for *I want to get off*, or *a quarter to the hour* for either *a quarter of the hour* or *a quarter till the hour*. Southern college graduates do not normally use these common expressions of the less educated members of their communities: *he belongs to be careful* for *he should be careful*, *all two* or *all both* for *both*, or *on account of* for *because*.

To draw out the typical speech of each informant, the linguistic geographer uses a long questionnaire written on work sheets bound into a notebook. On the following pages is a sample of a work sheet[3] that might be used to draw out the words and expressions people use in talking about the times of day and weather conditions. It contains suggestions and questions, enclosed between slant lines, to remind the interviewer of important details. In this list, the items in the right-hand column are *known variants*. That is, they are words and phrases that are known to be used by speakers of American English.

The interviewer, carefully steering the conversation, tries to catch his informant's natural relaxed usage as they chat together casually. On matters of time and weather, for instance, the interviewer hopes to get information on the expressions in the left-hand column of the work sheet shown. The center column reminds him of contexts and details that may be helpful, informative, or interesting. The informant may very likely use one of the known variants that are suggested in the right-hand column. For example, in some parts of the United States, evening begins at noon, while in other parts, evening begins at sunset. Therefore some people's *evening* is other people's *afternoon*. The interviewer uses a special code called a *phonetic alphabet* to write down in his notebook exactly what his informant says. He is always alert to catch unexpected new variants. He tries to avoid direct questions that might make his informant self-conscious. However, an occasional question such as the one on the work sheet—"Do you say 'good night' at meeting?"—is the best way to find out the desired information. Thus, work sheets are guides to interviewers for carrying out interviews that will produce accurate information about how we use our language.

WHY AMERICAN DIALECTS DIFFER

Languages change differently in different parts of the world, even though they originally came from the same parent language. If these changes are reinforced by geographic separation, political differences, or economic rivalry, they accumulate to produce first, different dialects, and finally, different languages.

The Romans carried their Latin language with them to the provinces of the Roman Empire. When the Roman Empire fell because of the Germanic

---

[3] Selected from "Compilation of Work Sheets of the Linguistic Atlas of the United States and Canada and Associated Projects," compiled by Raven I. McDavid, Jr., and Virginia McDavid (Ann Arbor, Michigan: The Linguistic Atlas of the United States and Canada, December 1951), mimeographed.

Expressions	Helpful Details	Known Variants
good morning!	/until what time/	
afternoon	/the part of the day before supper; when does it end?/	evening
good day!	/in meeting? in parting?/	
evening	/the part of the day after supper/	night
Do you say "good night" at meeting?		
we start to work before sunrise		sunup
the sun rose at six	/when did the sun rise?/	riz, raised, came up
we work until sunset		sundown
he came Sunday a week?	/record equivalents/	
is he coming Sunday a week?	/record equivalents/	
what time is it?		what time have you? what time are you? what o'clock is it?
half past seven	/7:30/	half after seven
quarter of eleven	/10:45/	to, till
it's a gloomy day		smurry, dreary, glummerin'

American Dialects

Expressions	Helpful Details	Known Variants
it's a nice day		pretty, fine
it's clearing up		clearing, fairing up, fairing off
the weather is changing	/when rain or snow is expected/	breaking, gathering, turning
		threatening (a storm)
thunder storm		thunder shower, tempest, storm, electric storm, electrical storm
it blew		blowed
it's drizzling		splitting, spitting
the wind is picking up		breezing on, breezing up fresh, getting stronger, raising, rising, gusting, coming up, blowing higher
it's letting up	/strong wind? light wind?/	laying, going down, dying down, easing up, lulling, abating
it's rather snappy this morning		sharp, edgy, keen, fresh, airish
the lake froze over last night	/thick ice or thin?/	friz, skimmed, skum, skummed, scaled over

invasions, the provinces were separated from each other and from Rome. Because of this separation, different dialects developed, and changes multiplied until today we have separate languages: French, Spanish, Italian, Portuguese, and Rumanian. These are all called Romance languages because they came from the Roman language, but today they are separate and distinct languages.

If we examine the settlement history of the United States, we see enough distinctive differences to produce different dialects, but other forces prevented the development of different languages. Thus today all of us speak some regional dialect of American English instead of different languages.

The earliest settlers in our country spoke many dialects of Elizabethan English because they came from many parts of England. Many of the dialect differences on the Atlantic Seaboard can be explained by the English origin of the earliest settlers and also by the closeness of contact between England and the colonies during the Colonial Period. Moreover, contacts among the colonies themselves were difficult. Therefore the colonists tended to maintain their original dialects. These dialects were still preserved after 1750 when contacts among the colonies became easier.

In addition to these settlers from England, other nationalities also came to our country. The Ulster Scots, the Palatinate Germans, the Dutch, the French, and the Spanish all added important elements to American English in the regions where they settled. In the nineteenth and twentieth centuries immigrants from Mexico, Germany, Italy, and many other countries added their share of words. Today American English truly reflects the fact that the United States has been "the great melting pot."

The westward movement caused other dialect differences in our country. The pioneers carried words from Georgia to Texas, from Kentucky to Nebraska, and from Wisconsin to Washington. The map on page 217 shows the directions of the important migrations from east to west.

Other dialect differences stem from the prestige and influence of great cities. New York, Philadelphia, Denver, St. Louis, Chicago, San Francisco, and Dallas, for instance, are centers of culture and wealth. Their influence spreads out around them in all directions. Their dialects are copied by their neighbors.

In addition, the geography of our country has influenced our American dialects. Sometimes, canyons and rivers have blocked the spread of certain words and expressions. At other times, new geographic features have forced new words into the language. Examples are the words *butte* and *prairie*, which reflect the geography of the western United States. These words were not needed in the dialects of the Atlantic Coast because these land features are not found there.

In countries where social classes are strictly separated and where people cannot move freely from class to class, each class speaks its own dialect. For example, in Charles Dickens' *Great Expectations*, George Eliot's *Silas Marner*, and other English novels, lower-class characters and upper-class characters do not speak in the same way. The differences are often greatest when a villager or farmer is depicted in the story. His dialect means not only lack of education but also geographic isolation from the great cities.

Social dialect differences are less apparent in the United States than in England. The structure of our society permits a person to better his social position more easily. Our people have always moved around the country more freely than Englishmen have moved around England. For many years we have had free compulsory education for all our young people until they are at least sixteen years old. Education erases dialect differences, and travel is one kind of education.

QUESTIONS FOR STUDY AND DISCUSSION

1. Assume that you are a fieldworker for a linguistic geographer. Using this work sheet, interview three native residents in your area; an older person with less than a high school education, a middle-aged person with a high school education, and a young college graduate. In the course of your informal conversation, include the following questions and record the responses. Compare your data with those of your classmates. Locate your area on the map of dialect boundaries.

Suggested Question	Some Variants
a. In what room are callers entertained at your house?	living room, sitting room, parlor
b. What do you call the window covering on rollers?	blinds, curtains, shades
c. What is the unfurnished area at the top of a house?	attic, loft, garret
d. What is the name of the yard adjoining a barn?	barnyard, barn lot, corral
e. What is the paper container for groceries?	bag, poke, sack
f. What do you call a harmonica?	breath harp, mouth organ
g. What is a swampy land with a stream running through it?	marsh, bayou, swamp, slough
h. What is the name for "quick" bread made with cornmeal?	corn bread, corn pone, dorn dodger, johnny cake
i. What is the part of the day immediately after supper?	evening, night

	Suggested Question	*Some Variants*
j.	What is the grass strip between sidewalk and street?	berm, boulevard, parkway, sidewalk plot, terrace
k.	With what kind of worm does a fisherman bait his hook?	angledog, angleworm, baitworm, fishworm, earthworm
l.	If Jim plunged headfirst from the springboard yesterday, what did he do?	dived, dove
m.	What do you say to let someone know you'll wait until he arrives?	I'll wait for you; I'll wait on you.
n.	What do you say to a motorman to let him know you want to leave the bus at Oak Street?	I want to get off at . . . ; I want off at . . .
o.	How else would you say that it is 10:45?	a quarter to 11; a quarter of 11; a quarter till 11

2. Although variations in vocabulary are the easiest to notice, regional differences in grammar and pronunciation also account for dialects in the United States. What variations in vocabulary, grammar, or pronunciation have you observed from your travels in the United States, from listening to classmates or teachers from other sections of the country, or from listening to television or radio? (Newscasts featuring public officials from many states reveal interesting variations in speech.)
3. Pronunciations of the following words vary from region to region.
    a. Copy this chart, listen for pronunciations of these words for a week, and put a check mark for each pronunciation each time you hear it.

(1)	grease, greasy	*s* as in *cease*	*z* as in *seize*
(2)	which, while, where, when, why, whether (any word spelled wh-)	*hw* as in *Whig* when distinguished from *wig*	*w* as in *wig*
(3)	barn, bird, four, mother	*r* retained	*r* lost (except before vowels)
(4)	The idea(r) is . . .	no intrusive *r* between vowels	intrusive *r* between vowels
(5)	ask, dance, glass, bath, path	*a* as in *map*	*ä* as in *father*
(6)	cot, fog, frog, hog, coffee	*ä* as in *father*	*ȯ* as in *saw*

(7) root, roof, soot   *ü* as in *boot*   *u̇* as in *book*

(8) coffee *with* milk   *th* as in *thin*   *th* as in *this*

(9) due, new, Tuesday   *ü* as in *do*   *yü* as in *few*

    b. Compare your data with those of your classmates and check the pronunciations recorded in a recent standard dictionary.

4. What words of non-English-speaking immigrants are now a regular part of your dialect area? What is the ethnic origin of these words? What do they tell you about the history of the region? Think especially of food names (*stollen, smorgasbord*); geographical terms (*sault, savanna, sierra, chaparral*); names of animals (*caribou, alligator*).

5. What did you learn about the Westward Movement in your American history courses? How did it affect the development of American dialects? What is your dialect? Does it tell something about your family history?

6. Many linguists agree that standardization rather than differentiation has become the dominant force in American English. What characteristics of our society tend to break down barriers between regional dialects? Between social dialects (Standard-Nonstandard English)?

SUGGESTED ACTIVITIES

1. George Bernard Shaw's *Pygmalion* (now famous as *My Fair Lady*) is a classic contrast in upper- and lower-class dialects spoken in London. Read the play and summarize the characteristics of Eliza Doolittle's Cockney dialect, which Professor Higgins tried to make conform with his own Received Standard English.

2. Eugene O'Neill's *The Hairy Ape* contrasts the standard American English of Mildred Douglas and her aunt with that of Yank, who speaks a very nonstandard Brooklynese. What aspects of Yank's dialect contrast with Mildred's?

3. American literature is rich in examples of regional dialect. Examine the dialectal variations in Holmes's *The Deacon's Masterpiece* and *The Bigelow Papers*. How do they contrast with your dialect? Write a summary essay.

4. Jesse Stuart writes about the mountain region of Kentucky and its people. Select what you think is regional dialect in one of his short stories or in part of one of his novels and write a report on it.

5. Elizabeth Maddox Roberts writes about the pioneers and the "poor whites" of Kentucky and the Virginias. Select what you think is regional dialect in one of her short stories or in part of one of her novels and write a report on it. *The Great Meadow* deals with the settlement of Kentucky by the pioneers. *The Time of Man* depicts the life of the migrant Kentucky farmer in the early twentieth century.

6. "Americans Speaking" by John T. Muri and Raven I. McDavid, Jr., is a long-playing recording of a set passage and free discourse read by speakers from six dialect areas in the United States. It can be secured from the National Council of Teachers of English (#24315), if it is not available in your school. See whether you can isolate differences in pronunciation, word choice, and grammatical structures.
7. Educated people are frequently much more interested in and tolerant of speech variations than the uneducated and the untraveled, who tend to think of the other fellow's speech as barbaric or clownish. Write a paper in which you discuss the popular exploitation of the dialect of some ethnic group for entertainment.

20
THE ENGLISH LANGUAGE IN THE SOUTH

Cleanth Brooks, Jr.

Mention "dialect" to someone from the North or West, and his first response will be "Southern." Even before the Civil War, travelers from the North missed the *r* from Southern speech, were struck by *you-all*, and enjoyed and even adopted such words as *fix* for *arrange* and *mosey* for *move along*.

Yankees often developed strange theories about the origin of the Southern dialect. One of the notions, perpetuated no doubt by Hollywood, was that Southern whites learned their speech from black nursemaids. No one seemed to ask where the blacks learned their English in the first place. The understanding of the origin and nature of the Southern dialect has, at the moment, great social relevance, for large migrations of Southern blacks to Northern cities have called attention to problems of communication.

Although recent dialect research in the United States and Great Britain has provided much new information about the relationship between American English and its British origins, this article by Cleanth Brooks is still worth reading for its general overview. He reiterates in greater detail Malmstrom's statement that regional differences in the speech of American colonists merely reflected the speech of the section of England from which they had come. He also infers the cultural reasons why Southerners preferred to go on using older forms of British while other Americans accepted newer forms prescribed in textbooks and promoted by formal education.

Cleanth Brooks, now professor of English at Yale University, is a Kentuckian by birth, though he spent most of his childhood in Tennessee. He was an undergraduate at Vanderbilt University in Nashville and a graduate student at Tulane, in New Orleans. Although he is best known as a literary critic, he also directed his early scholarship to the origins of Southern speech patterns.

Source: Stark Young, ed., *A Southern Treasury of Life and Literature* (New York: Charles Scribner's Sons, 1937): 350–58. Copyright 1937 by Charles Scribner's Sons. Reprinted by permission of the author.

One of the prices of democracy and democratic education is that you want to speak like everybody else. And one of the ills of isolation, one, if you like, of the limitations of the provincial, is that you are nervous, or may become so, as to what is done in the great world outside. It follows, therefore, with regard to the South and Southern people, that sometimes they are not sure of themselves, that they abandon too readily their own guns, and are apt to be defenseless before accusations that are mainly limited, if not even ignorant. It is not necessary to speak a language that is archaic and out of tone with our present world. But, on the other hand, we are not obliged to be exactly like the general mass spread over the entire United States; nor must we, on a lower plane, seek that generalization of speech that represents everybody who is not anybody. Within limits, it is a good thing to speak your own way, the way of your own part of the world. It follows, therefore, that it is not a bad idea to look into the background of your inherited speech, with the mingled purposes of justification, defense, and, if need be, compromise. Tone of voice is one thing and so is rhythm. The present article is about the language spoken.

A Southern pronunciation—lumping it all together, despite the fact that in the South there are many different ways of speaking—is usually thought to have emanated from the Negro; on the lips of a Virginia girl, pleasantly quaint, like other relics of the influence of the Negro mammy, but corrupt English after all. This popular belief has from time to time acquired the dignity of publication. Dr. Embree, for example, in his *Brown America* unhesitatingly attributes the Virginia lady's accent to the influence of the Negro. The origins of Southern speech, however, cannot be accounted for under a theory of Negro influence. Moreover, Southern English is not a corrupt form of "standard English." To make this point is to raise a number of questions with regard to the criterion of correct English—questions which divers people with their dogmatic assumptions on the subject never take into account.

In the first place, the speech of the Southern states represents an older form of English than that which is found in standard British English today. Indeed, it conforms rather closely to the description which A. J. Ellis gave in the last century of the behavior of the speech of a colony. The speech of a colony is conservative. It is in the language of the mother country that innovations are made. For example; few people other than professional students of the language know that the so-called broad *a*, heard in the British pronunciation of words like *path, staff, last,* and *dance,* is a later form than the vowel that is usually met with in these words in America. The broad *a*, most scholars agree, did not become fashionable in England until late in the eighteenth century. The settlement of America by Englishmen began early in the seventeenth. Obviously, the form used by Englishmen today could not have been the pronunciation carried over by the seventeenth century colonists.

It can be said that a large part of the United States is capable of making criticisms of Southern speech that are merely refined criticism; for the speech of other sections of this country is in its origins also seventeenth-century English. Such criticisms are usually based on a hazy assumption that present "standard British" (the speech of the educated classes in London) is "correct," and that the nearer American speech approximates this, the more nearly correct it is. The assumption is not necessarily true, and only ignorance and fear can make us think so. What we can say, however, is that if American English is based originally on seventeenth-century English, the South has clung more tenaciously to these original forms than have other parts of the country. Indeed, many of the pronunciations which are usually regarded as specifically "Negro" represent nothing more than older native English forms. The pronunciation, for example, of *get* as "git," so widespread in America and certainly not confined to the Negro, was the standard English form in the eighteenth century; and the pronunciation of *yellow* as "yal-uh" was also the polite eighteenth century pronunciation. Examples could be multiplied. To give only a few: *boil* pronounced as "bile"; *oblige* as "obleege"; *china* as "chainy." One remembers that Boswell remarks on Dr. Johnson's pronunciation of *heard* with the vowel of *hear*, and that Noah Webster prefers the pronunciation *hierd*, taking *heard* as merely an affectation that he has heard since the Revolution. In Anglo-Saxon it was *hierde* and often enough in Middle English. The so-called dropping of the *g* in final *-ing* as in "darlin'" for *darling* was perfectly correct in England itself in the eighteenth century, not to mention its practice nowadays by the British upper classes. Many a lord says "it don't." Matthew Arnold said "fascinatin'," not *fascinating*.

You will hear pronunciations in the South, however, which do not go back to any pronunciation in earlier *standard* English. This does not mean that they originated on our side of the Atlantic. They represent forms from the provincial dialects—pronunciations which occurred in the dialects of certain parts of England but which did not, as such dialectal forms occasionally did, obtain a footing in the standard language. These dialect forms are of great importance because they offer a possible means for determining the regions in England from which came the colonists who set the speech pattern of the South. Joel Chandler Harris has Uncle Remus pronounce *until*, *unsettle*, etc., as "awn-til," "awn-settle," etc. *Un-* is still pronounced "awn" by dialect speakers in Devon. Uncle Remus pronounces *corner* as "cawnduh," inserting a *d* in it. The living dialects of Somerset and Devon give the same form. When Uncle Remus pronounces *whether*, he leaves out the *th*, but so do the dialects of Wiltshire, Dorset, Somerset, and Devon. Again, the word *seven* is frequently heard in the South as "sebn," but the same form occurs in a number of dialects of England, including those of the southwest. In the southwest of England, "gwine" occurs for *going*. Even the dropping of a final *d* as in *told*, "tole," or in *hand*, "han'," or of a final *t* as in *last*, "las'," is not a corruption. If it is a corruption at all, it is one which probably came into this country by passage across the Atlantic. Such forms are the regular developments in many of the living dialects of Great Britain.

As a matter of fact, a number of words in the South, which appear to be new words entirely, represent in their origin merely dialectal forms of standard English: *roil* is a purely literary word, but "rile," which is related to it in the same way as "bile" to *boil*, is common. "Ingun" is a variant of *onion*, still to be found in many of the counties of England and Scotland. The word "frail," used in the South in the sense of a severe beating ("I'm going to *frail* the life out of him") has no relation to *frail* in the sense of "fragile." It is a development of *flail* which has occurred in many of the provincial dialects of Great Britain. The word "rare" as used in the phrase "rarin' to go" is related to the word *rear* in the same way that "quare" is related to *queer*. Both "rare" and "quare" are widely distributed through the dialects of Great Britain. "Peart" is a development of *pert* and must have been brought across the Atlantic by the early settlers, for it still exists in a number of English counties.

In this connection one may point out that the Southern *r* is connected with the south of England as well as with the Southern states of America. In this part of England the consonant *r* was lost very early, before consonants and at the end of words. From the seventeenth century onward this development had penetrated the standard language, and this treatment of *r*, far from being a slurring or a corruption, is the treatment standard in British English today. It is the normal treatment also in some other parts of America—eastern New England, for example. On the western edges of the Southern states, Midwestern influence has come in bringing the *r* with it; in the mountain regions of the South also (under Scotch-Irish influence?) the *r* is preserved.

As one instance after another of Southern speech traces itself back to England, either to earlier standard English or to provincialisms of the south and southwest counties, it rapidly becomes apparent that any theory of Negro influence must be abandoned. The Negro learned his speech from the colonists, who must have come predominantly from the English southwest. The Negro has then preserved many of these original forms, even after most of the whites have discarded them. This is not to state, of course, that Uncle Remus speaks the dialect of Hardy's peasants. But the fact that his dialect, wherever it deviates from modern British English, differs together along *with* the dialects of the southwest counties indicates that Southern speech has been colored by the English southwest.

The only alternative to this theory is to accept what amounts to a staggering coincidence. The magnitude of the coincidence will be made more vivid by consideration of a few more specific cases. Take the Southern variants of *muskmelon*, for instance. *Melon* is often heard as "million" in the South, especially among Negroes; and *muskmelon* is frequently, even among whites, pronounced "mushmelon." The form "mushmillion," which Harris has Uncle Remus use, and which may still be heard among old people in the South in country districts, would accordingly be considered by most people as about as thoroughly "Negro" as a word could be. The form seems obviously to be a corruption. But one holding such a view will be disconcerted to find in the Oxford Dictionary precisely this form occurring in a passage written by one Jerome Horsey in 1591. . . .

The interpretation of the origin of Southern speech given above raises questions with regard to the origin of the speech used in other parts of the country. If the speech of the Southern states shows forms from seventeenth and eighteenth century standards and from the provincial dialects of England, why do not such forms appear in the states of the North? The answer, of course, is that they do. In James Russell Lowell's *Biglow Papers*, written in the New England rustic dialect, occur many spellings which indicate such pronunciations. We find even more parallelisms with Southern forms when we consult early New England records with their occasional spellings which indicate dialectal pronunciations, or else the remarks on pronunciation made by the early grammarians of this section. To take only a few examples collected by the late George Phillip Krapp in his *English Language in America*, "skase" for *scarce* must have occurred frequently in the earlier speech of this country, in the North as well as in the South. It probably derives from the southern part of England, where the *r* was lost early before consonants and at the end of words. *Itch* is pronounced "each" by Uncle Remus, but formerly it was so pronounced in parts of the North. "Drap" for *drop* and "crap" for *crop* are still frequently heard in the South, but such forms were once found in New England also; and in the case of both sections, their ultimate origin was probably in the dialects of the southwest of England.

Most scholars who have worked on the subject believe that the New England coast was predominantly influenced by the south and east counties of England. Pronunciations from the eastern counties, Norfolk, Suffolk, and Essex, are to be found there: for example, the pronunciation of *whole* as something resembling "hull," *stone* resembling "stun," etc. The evidence would seem to indicate, however, in my opinion, considerable influence from the counties of the southwest as well. The influence of the southwest, as has been pointed out, seems dominant in the South, though some forms occurring in Virginia seem to point back to the eastern counties, and other influences may be present in other parts of the South. At any rate, the language of both New England and the South—whatever differences existed between them— in the eighteenth century must have differed very considerably from the British English of today. The marked difference between eastern New England and the South did not exist at this period. These differences came later, and came, not with laziness and corruption in the South, but with innovation in New England through the influence of spelling, the elocution book, and the diligence of the New England schoolma'am. Probably no other part of the English-speaking world in any one period has produced so many spelling books and dictionaries as New England produced in the early nineteenth century.

There is also evidence to indicate that New England has consciously imitated British pronunciation by taking over from it later developments of the qualities of certain vowel sounds, and imposing them in whole classes of words like *corn, morning, short, thorn,* etc., which were distinguished in pronunciation from words like *divorce, store, pork, fort,* etc. The first group had an *aw* vowel, the second a long *o*. Today in British pronunciation, both groups have *aw*, but this development did not take place in England until the nineteenth century. Consequently, the appearance of examples of the present-day British pronunciation in New England (or elsewhere in America) suggests a late imitation of British English.

This difference in attitude toward speech in New England on the one hand and the South on the other is an indication of more fundamental cultural differences. The desire to cultivate "correctness" of speech, the reliance on spelling, the diligence of the New England schoolma'am, may, if you choose to do so, be interpreted as marks of the cultural continuity existing between the New England and the Old. They are susceptible, however, of another account, not quite so favorable, perhaps; they may be interpreted as symptoms of a feeling of cultural inferiority—of anxiety, that is, as to status. But it might be more graceful to let a New Englander speak in this matter of New England's dependence on the mother land. Henry Adams, writing of the mid-nineteenth century, says: "The tone of Boston society was colonial. The true Bostonian always knelt in self-abasement before the majesty of English standards; far from concealing it as a weakness, he was proud of it as his strength."

The attitude of the South (again speaking in relative terms) was quite different. The South never had quite the reverence for the written word which prevailed in New England. Like England itself, especially among country families and the aristocracy in general, it was content to rest the criterion of speech on a living oral tradition. Unconsciously at least and by its very lack of extreme self-consciousness, the South ceased to be a colony. Whatever general conclusion one may wish to draw, it would be hard to deny that the attitude toward speech in the South exhibits a culture in a very healthy state. The continuity between class and class and even between race and race was not severed by that artificial and irritating barrier, a *class* dialect.

The influence of spelling has, of course, exerted itself on Southern speech, but less than it has on that of most other sections of the country. Otherwise, there has been little or no attempt to keep up with the later developments of British English. Many Southerners, educated persons as well as the uneducated, consistently pronounce *better* as "bedduh," *bottle* as "boddle," etc., thus carrying on regularly in their speech a development largely to be found in the dialects of the English southwest. "Taripin" is the almost universal pronunciation of *terrapin,* for few allow themselves to be browbeaten by the spelling. As a matter of fact, *terrapin* is in origin an Algonquin Indian word, and the earliest form seems to have had an *a* rather than an *e.*

The student of language is supposed to be completely objective—to describe conditions rather than to prescribe standards. But perhaps he may be allowed to affect standards, at least in one regard; by giving a true description when a false description is being made the basis for prescriptions. On one fact, scholars are agreed: that the standard of speech for a country is that of the "best" speakers, the educated speakers, of that country. British English is undoubtedly correct for the modern Englishman. It is not correct, by virtue of that reason at least, for the Virginian or Tennessean. Moreover, in trying to find a standard for modern America, the best authorities are agreed that there is no virtue in trying to impose an artificial and synthetic criterion. If the Virginian is not to be forced into imitation of the Oxford don, there is logically no reason for him to be forced into imitation of Boston—or, for that matter, of Chicago or Hollywood.

If the South—or, for that matter, any other sections of the country—under the influence of the radio, the talking pictures, or other "cultural" forces, cares to abandon its characteristic speech, the pronunciation then adopted by the educated speakers of the region will, of course, then be the standard. But that adoption need not be made under the delusion that something poor is being abandoned for something "better." Certainly the heritage the South possesses is not one to be ashamed of—neither the seventeenth century standard forms, nor the coloring of Devon, Somerset, and Dorset. The men of the west country were active in the conquest and settlement of America. One of the most prominent of them, Sir Walter Raleigh, was not ashamed of his provincial accent, even at Elizabeth's court. John Aubrey, the gossipy biographer of the seventeenth century, tells us that he heard one of Raleigh's contemporaries say that "notwithstanding his so great mastership in style and his conversation with the learnedest and politest persons, yet he spake broad Devonshire to dying day." It would be odd, indeed, if Raleigh's fellow countrymen, mariners, adventurers, and colonists, not courtiers at all, had not bequeathed forms of their sturdy speech to their descendants in the New World.

"*Gy* pronounced *gy* in such a word as *garden,* found in Virginia and sometimes in other eastern parts of the South, is traced back to Leicester, northwest Oxford, Hereford, north Derby; *ky* pronounced *ky* in *card—* found also in Maine as well as the South—goes back to west Somerset, Aberdeen, and north Derby.

"Through the South and New England, in the colloquial speech of educated and cultivated people the suffix *-ing* as in *going* commonly *-in'.* . . . This characteristic of eighteenth century speech is not quite so evident in the South generally as it is on the Eastern Shore of Virginia and on the New England coast, where the syllable containing -in' has a stronger stress. For example, *pudding*, which generally becomes 'pudn' colloquially, is on the Eastern Shore and in New England 'pudin.' In *going* ('goin') the second syllable is not obscured. In the South generally, this 'loss of g' may seem slovenly; on the Eastern Shore and in New England the *g* is lost precisely ('pudin,' for example, instead of the Southern 'pudn').

"No one should feel ashamed of this ancient and honorable pronunciation."
—William Cabell Greet, "Southern Speech," in *Culture in the South*, p. 609

QUESTIONS FOR STUDY AND DISCUSSION

1. Brooks states that the language of a colony is likely to be more conservative—that is, older—than that of the mother country, where innovations occur. Why does this happen? Consider environmental factors, both geographic and cultural, which Malmstrom mentions.
2. Brooks traces the origin of some Southern pronunciations to standard British forms characteristic of the seventeenth century. Refer to the section on the historical background of the English language and see whether you can add to his evidence. (For example, how did Pope probably pronounce *join*?)
3. Some of the Southern pronunciations are traced to British dialects of Somerset, Devon, Dorset, and Wiltshire. Locate these provinces on a map of England. List some of the characteristic pronunciations which living dialects of these provinces share with the speech created for Uncle Remus by Joel Chandler Harris. What does this evidence tell you about the origin of so-called Negro dialects?
4. Why did the colonists of New England tend to imitate the innovations in British speech that took place during the eighteenth century? Do you know whether some Americans still believe that the speech of the educated classes of London is in some way prestigious? What factors contributed to the divergence between New England and Southern speech?
5. The interaction between spelling and pronunciation has been discussed in the sections on the historical background of the English language and on spelling. Brooks theorizes that in the North pronunciations were made to conform to spelling. What cultural developments support his theory?
6. Allen discusses the social dimension of language, which he identifies as the standard-nonstandard continuum. According to Brooks, what would be a reasonable definition of the term *standard dialect*? Is "Standard English" the same for speakers from New England, the Northern states, the Midland, and the South?
7. How should a speaker view his own regional dialect?

SUGGESTED ACTIVITIES

1. In "America Talking: A Guide to the Lore and Color of Our Language," Bergen Evans informally describes some of the less widespread subregional dialects, such as those of Charleston, Brooklyn, and the area around Lancaster, Pennsylvania. (See *Holiday*, July, 1961, 30:92 ff.) Read the essay and prepare an oral report.
2. In the American literary tradition the term "regional literature" refers to fiction and poetry that records realistically the details of everyday life among various cultural groups. Mark Twain, the giant among regionalists, was preceded by writers for the popular press who had been recording American folklore in regional dialect, including frontier tall tales and ballads, since the time of Jackson. Library research will yield interesting information on such topics as Negro songs (*Frankie and Johnny*, *John Henry*), cowboy ballads (*The Old Chisholm Trail*, *Git Along Little Dogies*), and comic journalism by Josh Billings and others. Study samples in one of these categories, commenting on the use of dialect.
3. George Washington Cable (1844–1925) in *Old Creole Days* (1879) shows the influence of French on the speech in some sections of New Orleans. If you have studied French, you will enjoy reading a story from the collection *Jean-Ah-Poquelin* and reporting on the dialogue.
4. Mary Wilkins Freeman (1862–1930) records the social history of rural New England in *A New England Nun and Other Stories*. Read "The Village Singer" from this collection and analyze the provincialisms. (Brooks says that New England dialects reveal some of the same provincialisms as Southern speech.)
5. Joel Chandler Harris (1848–1908), to whom Brooks refers, made the only lasting record of folk tales of American Indian and Negro origin in which animals reflect the lot of mankind. He also made the first dependable representation of the speech of Negroes. *Uncle Remus: His Songs and His Sayings* (1881) remains an American classic for both reasons. Read one of the stories, for example, "The Story of the Deluge, and How It Came About," and see whether you can find other examples of the pronunciations analyzed by Brooks. (Brooks's conclusions about the location of Uncle Remus have been modified by recent dialect research.) Write a report.
6. Today Southern writers are so numerous and respected that critics often speak of the Southern renaissance. Well-known authors are Faulkner, Wolfe, Glasgow, Welty, McCullers, Capote. Study the dialogue in a story by one of these writers (you will find them included in many anthologies) and report on the use of dialectal variations.
7. Thomas Hardy (1840–1928) was a British novelist brought up in Dorset (the Wessex of his novels). Read a Hardy novel (*Tess of the D'Urbervilles*, *The Mayor of Casterbridge*, or *The Return of the Native*) and record language

items which differ from your own. Then reread Brooks's essay and see whether he mentions any of these items as comparable to Southern use. Prepare an oral or a written report.
8. Compare the opinions of Brooks and Labov with respect to the position of so-called black English. Some scholars recently have given great prominence to the theory that some of its features derive from an early Creole and hence from West African languages. If you or your teacher can get it, see Walt Wolfram and Ralph W. Fasold, *The Study of Social Dialects in American English* (Prentice-Hall, 1974).

Part Seven

WORDS AND DICTIONARIES

21
THE DICTIONARY'S FUNCTION

Philip B. Gove

If you are in the habit of checking best-seller lists, you may have been surprised in recent years to find dictionaries among the nonfiction books. In the stormy decade of the sixties, three major dictionaries of American English were published, each revealing distinct theories and practices of lexicography, the art of compiling word lists.

Historically, the first such book for English was Robert Cawdrey's *A Table Alphabeticall . . . of hard usual English Wordes*, published in 1604. Nathaniel Bailey's *Universal Etymological English Dictionary*, which ran into thirty editions between 1721 and 1802, was the first attempt to include all the words of the language, not merely the *hard* ones. But the real landmark in English lexicography is 1755, when Dr. Samuel Johnson published his *Dictionary*. Although he started out to *fix* the language, he discovered the irregularities inherent in language and was forced to admit that any living language changes.

The single most important resource for investigating the English language is *The Oxford English Dictionary* (OED). In the *OED* meanings of words are traced historically, with quotations illustrating how words have been used and spelled since they first appeared in print. More than eighty years of continuous research are represented in the completed volumes, dating from 1884 to 1928. A supplement appeared in 1933 and another in 1974.

In America, for a long time *Webster* and *dictionary* have seemed like synonymous terms. Noah Webster (1775–1843)—the compiler of the famous spelling work—published his first dictionary of 28,000 words in 1806; *Webster's Third New International Dictionary*, published in 1961 by the Merriam-Webster Company, lists more than 450,000 words. The editors of this dictionary consider its function to be that of a record of current American usage. In 1966 *The Random House Dictionary of the English Language*, with about 260,000 entries, was published. In the

---

Source: *Dartmouth Alumni Magazine* (May 1962): 10–11. Copyright © 1962 by *Dartmouth Alumni Magazine*. Reprinted by permission of the publisher and the author.

preface, the editor, Jess Stein, writes: "We have been guided by the premise that a dictionary editor must not only record; he must teach." A desk dictionary, *The American Heritage Dictionary*, appearing in 1969, offers "sensible guidance toward grace and precision," as its editor, William Morris, states in the introduction. Its usage labels are based on the judgments of one hundred respected users of the language—the AHD usage panel, composed of authors, editors, and public figures but not language specialists.

So Americans have dictionaries in plenty now, varying not only in size but in function. Most careful writers consult at least two before making a decision about an item of disputed usage.

In the following short statement, the late Philip B. Gove, who was editor-in-chief of *Webster's Third New International Dictionary*, describes, as he understands them, the functions of an unabridged monolingual dictionary.

The function of a dictionary is to serve the person who consults it. Publishers know something about why a person buys a dictionary. Why and when he later consults it is another matter. A thousand people who open a dictionary could be motivated by a thousand different stimuli. Clearly, there must be some rules which a consulter is rather strictly required to follow.

The consulter of a dictionary should not open it to find out who won the Ivy League football championship two years ago or how to make 500 gallons of New England rum. He would not find out how many pheasants a licensed hunter can shoot in South Dakota during the open season or what towns in Kansas have local option. He would not discover how many sonnets Wordsworth wrote or how many grandfather clocks made by Joseph Gooding of Dighton, Mass., are still ticking. If he were to look expectantly for such information, he would at best merely be revealing his utter unfamiliarity with dictionaries; more seriously he could be disqualifying himself for a merit scholarship.

If, however, a consulter wants to know what possible use Eleazar Wheelock might have had for a *Gradus ad Parnassum*, he might conceivably find the answer in a dictionary. He might be able to find out the population of South Dakota—humans, not pheasants—and the area of Kansas. Even these questions, however, lie in a special area not strictly lexical. If a dictionary restricts itself by design to the generic vocabulary, a consulter who looks in it for nongeneric information is asking it to perform a service for which it was not built. I will restrict my consideration of the function of a dictionary to an unabridged monolingual dictionary of our generic English vocabulary.

An ideal dictionary would seem to me to be one in which a genuine consulter can find right off a satisfactory answer to a proper question. The matter of a proper question should concern spelling, pronunciation, etymology, meaning, function, or status, for these are the six kinds of information generally given explicitly or implicitly for each word. By far the most important of these is meaning, which for most words is the chief concern of a lexicographer.

A genuine consulter is one who wants or needs to know something about a word he has heard or read or who wants to know how to use a word in speaking or writing. Since readers in our civilization outnumber writers several thousand to one, the most important function of a dictionary is to enable a reader to find out what a word means so that a passage read can be understood, so that what its author intended can be figured out. A consulter of a dictionary who does not have a context into which to fit a meaning he looks up is not a genuine consulter. He may be motivated by a desire to criticize or to find out how a dictionary treats a word or by several other secondary or tertiary desiderations. He is not looking in a dictionary for a key to open a door to understanding. His findings, though sometimes made articulate, if not vociferous, are relatively trivial.

If a consulter is a writer, a dictionary is chiefly concerned with letting him know what meaning his readers are likely to put on a particular word in a particular context. A dictionary does not undertake to tell him what someone thinks his readers ought to understand. There is no point in telling anybody that the word *arrival* ought to be reserved for a "coming to shore by water" if no one understands or uses it that way. A dictionary is not concerned with telling a writer how he should write. That's his business, in which he must serve as his own arbiter.

The difficulties of using a dictionary are often attributed to the dictionary maker, as if he were responsible for all the complications in the language. The English language is infinitely complex and extremely difficult. No one person can ever master it. There is no formula for making it easy and simple and no panacea for those who stumble around in it in a daze. The reducing of this complexity to some kind of ordered presentation which can most of the time give a consulter the guidance he seeks is one of the lexicographer's chief accomplishments. When a dictionary fails a consulter, it is often either the consulter or the language which is responsible.

For whom is an unabridged dictionary made? Not for foreigners and not for children. The definitions in it are not written under an assumption that the consulter is totally unacquainted with the word being defined nor under any unwieldy or fantastic idea that the word he is looking up belongs on a scale at some vague point above which he cannot rise. Outside of contests, quizzes, or bets words do not exist by themselves; they are surrounded by other words and live in a context of associated and related ideas, from which a consulter takes to the dictionary some little bit of understanding. The definition he finds helps him to fit a word into a frame, which is his objective in consulting a dictionary. If it fails to help him, because the subject is difficult or unfamiliar, he may give up, for lack of genuine and compelling interest, lack of time, or lack of ability or background. Not all words are for everybody. Definitions in an unabridged dictionary are written for adults of all kinds and degrees of interest and intelligence. Yet every user of the language is continually getting into semantic problems over his depth.

For the majority of situations in which a dictionary is consulted for meaning, words may be roughly divided into three groups: (1) Hard words which circumstances make immediately important: "The doctor prescribed synthesized *cortisone*." "*Recidivism* is a serious criminal problem in some urban communities." "*Existentialism* is a subjective philosophy." (2) Words frequently seen, usually understood loosely, but suddenly or recurrently unstable (for the individual): *synthesize, urban,* and *subjective* in the preceding sentences. (3) Common familiar words which unexpectedly need to be differentiated, such as *break* vs. *tear, shrub* vs. *bush,* or specifically clarified, such as *fable, adventure, shake, door, remainder, evil.* Most people get by without having to clarify these common words in the third group until an issue arises to require clarification. Without such an issue definitions of these common words are frequently jumped on because the words look easy to the uninitiated, although in practice they are usually more difficult than hard words to define.

Although a dictionary can be misused and misinterpreted, a lexicographer keeps his mind on the words rather than on people and tries with all his diligence and percipience to tell the truth about them. The only area in which the truth may be found is actual usage. In fine, the function of a dictionary is to reflect the facts of usage as they exist.

QUESTIONS FOR STUDY AND DISCUSSION

1. What type of reference book would tell you who won the Ivy League football championship two years ago? What would be the best reference to consult to find the area of Kansas? What point about the primary function of a dictionary is Gove making here?
2. Explain what Gove means by "an *unabridged monolingual* dictionary of our *generic* English vocabulary." Pay particular attention to the italicized terms. (Italics are the editors'.)
3. List the six different kinds of information that dictionaries give about words. Which of these does Gove consider the most important? Why? Find dictionary examples of each kind.
4. Gove emphasizes the importance of contexts in defining the meaning of a word. Meanings are never in the words themselves but in the meanings assigned to them by the people who use them. Develop this basic premise of word defining by giving examples. Try to provide contexts (sentences) that will make clear different areas of meaning for words such as *power, strike, court, society, chair, cat.*

5. Why would anyone think *arrival* "ought to be reserved for 'coming to shore by water' "? This is the fallacy of assigning meaning on the basis of word origin. Supply other examples. (Refer to the essays on the historical background of English and on etymology.)
6. Why are familiar words more difficult to define than *hard* words? How many meanings for *put* does your dictionary record?

SUGGESTED ACTIVITIES

1. Write an autobiographical essay in which you describe your earliest encounters with dictionaries. Do you know people who refer to "the dictionary"? Which one do they usually mean? Were you taught that the first of two or more entries is better? Is this true? Did you have any knowledge about the way dictionaries were made?
2. The problems of defining, which Gove discusses, are well illustrated by definitions in Dr. Johnson's dictionary. His definition of *network* is famous because it proves that *easy* words are sometimes harder to define than *hard* words. His definition of *oats* is likewise often referred to because it supposedly illustrates the prejudice of an Englishman against the Scots. You can find these and other definitions in an abridged edition of Johnson's work. Compare them with definitions in a recent dictionary. Summarize your findings in an essay entitled "On Defining."
3. Draw up your own word list with definitions of terms used with special reference in your school or college, such as *admit slip, P.A. system, modular scheduling, commons, dean, registration, student government.*
4. Consult at least four dictionaries for the meaning and etymology of *hippie*. Record variations in spelling and comments on social status. Consult the same dictionaries for *beatnik*. Summarize your findings in an essay.
5. If the *OED* is available to you, study the history of one of the following words: *asylum, butcher, board, candidate, dean, deer, enormity, girl, good-bye, fair* (adj.), *fast* (adv.), *monstrous, pester, quick, radical, rapid, trivial, very, zest.*
6. The raw data for lexicographers are quoted passages collected from many sources and illustrating the actual use of a word. These quotations are filed on citation slips for study by the dictionary editor. Be a word watcher for several weeks, recording on cards the uses of a word in context as you hear it or read it. Record also the age of the user and the social environment. Choose a relatively new word, such as *hard rock*, or an older word which seems to be undergoing semantic change, such as *environmental*. Check your data against several dictionary listings and summarize your material.
7. Dictionary users rarely read the editor's preface, which explains the theory of lexicography behind the dictionary. Read the prefaces to

Webster's Third, the *Random House Dictionary*, and the *American Heritage Dictionary*. How do these statements differ? Summarize your discoveries in an essay of comparison.

8. Dictionaries use various restrictive labels, which are explained in the introductory portions. Some labels specify social status (*substandard, nonstandard*); some, stylistic levels (*slang, colloquial*); some, time (*archaic, obsolete*); some, regional usage (*dialect* or the name of the region or country where the usage is common). Check one of the items below in several dictionaries and record the usage label or comment, if one appears. If there is no restrictive label, the lexicographer considers the item in general standard use.

gift (as a transitive verb: "He gifted the school with a painting.")

fault (as a transitive verb: "He faulted the new musical.")

schlemiel (an unlucky bungler)

cruller (an unraised doughnut)

mammy

nary

pop art

22
ETYMOLOGY AND MEANING
Simeon Potter

What does a word mean? There are people who insist that certain words, at least, have one true meaning—usually the original one. But meaning is elusive; it does not stay put. A word is a conventional symbol and means only what those using it generally accept it to mean. Word meanings not only change, but they change in certain predictable directions, as Hungerford suggests in "Change in Language." New meanings may replace old meanings or be added to them in a process of radiation.

In this essay six categories of change are discussed by Simeon Potter, emeritus professor of English at Liverpool University.

Few words have fixed significations like the pure numbers of mathematics or the technical formulas of chemistry. The mathematical sign π denotes a constant, namely, the ratio of the circumference of a circle to its diameter, or 3.14159.... The chemical formula NaCl denotes a substance, sodium chloride, or salt, and it always means that substance and nothing else. These symbols π and NaCl cannot vary with time or circumstance, nor do they ever change with their contexts. Few expressions in daily use have such simple and direct denotations as these. Even words like *mother* and *father*, *sun* and *horse*, denoting primary human relationships or natural objects and creatures, are not quite so definite. All four words occur in Old English and their meanings have not changed in twelve centuries. But in such sayings as 'Westminster is the mother of Parliaments', 'The child is father of the man', 'He seeks a place in the sun', and 'He rides the high horse', the primary meanings of these words are manifestly transcended.

What is the *sun*? According to *The Oxford English Dictionary* it is 'the brightest (as seen from the earth) of the heavenly bodies, the luminary or orb of day; the central body of the solar system, around which the earth and other planets revolve, being kept in their orbits by its attraction and supplied

---

Source: *Our Language*, rev. ed. (London: Penguin, 1950, 1967), chapter 9. Copyright 1950 by Simeon Potter. Reprinted by permission of the publisher and the author.

with light and heat by its radiation'. And what is the *horse*? It is 'a solid-hoofed perissodactyl quadruped (*Equus caballus*), having a flowing mane and tail, whose voice is a neigh'. Now are these so-called 'dictionary definitions' really definitions, or are they not descriptions? As long ago as 1891, when he was writing his magistral *Essai de Sémantique*, Michel Bréal demonstrated that the cause of shifting meaning in so many words lay in the impossibility of complete definition and in the varying complexity of the word-thing relationship. 'Language', he wrote, 'designates things in an incomplete and inaccurate manner: *incomplete*, since we have not exhausted all that can be said of the sun when we have declared it to be shining, or of the horse when we say that it trots: *inaccurate*, since we cannot say of the sun that it shines when it has set, or of the horse that it trots when it is at rest, or when it is wounded or dead.'

Could the word or symbol *sun* ever alter its reference and come to mean 'moon', or 'star', or something else? That, surely, is inconceivable. *Sun* is an ancient word, indicating the same 'heavenly body' as its ancestral equivalent in Indo-European five thousand and more years ago. Day by day during those five thousand years, man has observed it 'coming forth as a bridegroom out of his chamber, and rejoicing as a giant to run his course'. Nevertheless, it has happened that ūλ, the etymological equivalent of *sun* in Albanian (with *l*—instead of *n*—formative), has come to mean 'star'; whereas *súil*, its counterpart in Irish, has come to mean 'eye'. At some period in the history of each of these two languages that apparently simple and rigid relationship between word and thing, between *symbol* and *referend*, has been deflected and distorted. The meaning, we say, has been changed. The seemingly impossible has occurred and any notions that we may have entertained concerning the indissolubility of the links connecting *etymology* and *meaning* have been rudely dispelled. The shock is, to say the least, disconcerting. We should so much prefer to regard a 'speech-form as a relatively permanent object to which the meaning is attached as a kind of changeable satelite' (Leonard Bloomfield, *Language* (H. H. Rinehart & Winston: 1933), p. 426). The study of language would be so much easier for us if we could be assured that the etymology of a word is not only something *real* and *true* (as, indeed, the Greek *etymon* implies) but also that it is something permanent; and that the basic form or *root* of a word has some inherent connexion with the thing, quality or action denoted. Primitive peoples still believe that word has power over thing, that somehow the word participates of the nature of the thing. The word, in fact, is the symbol and it has no direct or immediate relation with the referend except through the image in the mind of the speaker. As Henri Delacroix once said (in *Le Langage et la pensée*), 'All thought is symbolic. Thought first constructs symbols which it substitutes for things.' The symbol *sun* has no connexion with the celestial luminary other than through the thoughts or images in the mind of the speaker and the hearer. Unless these two images are identical, there can be no complete understanding.

Latin grammarians sometimes taught wrong etymologies long ago and more recent writers, who should have known better, have occasionally had recourse to fictitious etymologies in order to buttress a theory or to point a moral. Carlyle liked to define *king* as 'he who can', associating the word with German *können* 'to be capable, to know how to'; and Ruskin found pleasure in reminding the married women in his audience that since *wife* meant 'she who weaves', their place was in the home. On the other hand, a speaker may knowingly or unwittingly ignore an etymology. He may refer to a 'dilapidated wooden shed', although *dilapidated* is strictly applicable only to a building of stone (Latin *lapis, lapidis*). He may say that 'the battalion was well equipped', although *to equip* (French *équiper*, from Old Norse *skipa*) means historically 'to fit out a ship'. He may say that 'the life-boat was manned by Wrens', 'the ocean liner sailed', and 'the cattle were shepherded into their stables'. A rediscovered etymology may be highly informative and may give pleasure. Those two attractive birds, the nuthatch and the redstart, have most interesting names. The nuthatch is that little creeping bird that breaks or *hacks* the nuts in order to feed on the kernel. For the alternation between final plosive and affricate in *hack* and *hatch*, you may like to compare *bake* and *batch*, *dike* and *ditch*, *lyke*wake and *lich*gate, *mickle* and *much*, *wake* and *watch*. The redstart is still called the fire-tail in some dialects and *start* 'tail' survives in *Start* Point 'tail-shaped promontory' and *stark*-naked, older *start*-naked. It is interesting to recall that a *governor* is etymologically a 'steersman', a *marshal* a 'horse-servant', and a *constable* a 'companion of the stable'. A *companion* is 'one who eats bread' with another, a *fellow* is 'one who lays down money', a *comrade* a 'chamber-fellow', and a *friend* 'one who loves'.

If the meanings of words are not fixed, if they are liable to flux and change, is there any way of predicting in which direction they are most likely to change? Do changes in meaning admit of empirical generalizations? It is the aim of students of *semantics* or *semasiology* to find the answers to these questions. So far there has been little coordination of semantic research and investigators have fallen into two groups according to their preoccupation with mental processes (Bronislaw Malinowski, C. K. Ogden, and I. A. Richards) or with mathematical symbols (Ludwig Wittgenstein, A. N. Whitehead, Bertrand Russell, and Rudolf Carnap). At present these two groups—the linguistic psychologists and the mathematical logicians—seem to be moving on different planes. The student of language sees many parallels, and he is able to distinguish certain semantic categories, but he inclines to the view that generalizations are dangerous and unprofitable.

The most obvious semantic category is that involving specialization or narrowing. When a speech-form is applied to a group of objects or ideas which resemble one another in some respect, it may naturally become restricted to just one object or idea, and if this particular restriction gains currency in a speech community, a specialized meaning prevails. *Meat*, as in *sweetmeat* and as in the archaic phrase 'meat and drink', meant any kind of food. It now means 'edible flesh', a sense formerly expressed by *flesh* and *flesh meat*. *Deer*, like Dutch *dier* and German *Tier*, used to mean 'animal' in general, as in Shakespeare's 'mice and rats and such small deer'. Latin *animal* and French *beast* have taken its place as the general words and *deer* now means 'wild ruminant of a particular (antlered) species'. *Fowl*, like Dutch and German *Vogel*, denoted 'birds in general' as in Chaucer's 'Parlement of Foules' and biblical 'fowls of the air' and as in modern names of larger kinds of birds used with a qualifying adjective, such as *sea fowl*, *water fowl*, and *wild fowl*. Otherwise, of course, *fowl* normally means a domestic cock or hen, especially when full grown. *Hound* formerly meant a dog of any breed and not, as now, a hunting-dog in particular. *Disease* was still conceived in Chaucer's day as being dis-ease 'absence of ease'. It might point to any kind of temporary discomfort and not, as now, to 'a morbid physical condition'. To *starve*, like Dutch *sterven* and German *sterben*, meant 'to die', not necessarily from lack of food. In modern Yorkshire dialect a body can still 'starve of cold'. A *wed* was a pledge of any kind. In conjunction with the suffix *-lock* forming nouns of action, it has come to be restricted to 'the marriage vow or obligation'. To the Elizabethans an *affection* was a feeling of any kind and both *lectures* and *lessons* were 'readings' of any kind. *Doctrine* was still teaching in general and *science* was still knowledge in general.

Sometimes a word has become restricted in use because a qualifier has been omitted. *Undertaker*, like French *entrepreneur* and German *Unternehmer*, used to mean 'contractor, one who *undertakes* to do a particular piece of work'. It is now used exclusively in the sense of *funeral undertaker*, although *mortician* has already superseded it in the cities and towns of America. In daily conversation *doctor* 'teacher' means 'medical doctor' and normally refers to a 'general practitioner'. Many words have both wider and narrower senses in the living language and many others have varying senses according to the persons addressed. *Pipe*, for example, evokes different images in the mind of the smoker, the plumber, the civil engineer, the geologist, the organist, and the boatswain. The *line* means a clothes-line to the laundry-woman, a fishing line to the fisherman, the equator to the seaman (as in Joseph Conrad's *Crossing the Line*), a communication wire to the telephonist, a succession of descent to the genealogist, and a particular kind of article to the man of business. To the geographer *cataract* means a cascade or waterfall, to the engineer a hydraulic controller, but a disease of the crystalline lens to the oculist.

The process of specialization and extension of meaning may take place in a language side by side. For instance, as we have just seen, *hound* has been restricted in the course of a thousand years from a dog in general to a hunting-dog in particular; contrariwise, *dog*, which [was an] eleventh-century *ex nihilo* word . . . , has been extended from 'a dog of ancient breed' to include any sort of dog, ranging from a formidable Alsatian to a puny and insignificant lap-dog. *Bird* meant 'young birdling', just as *pigeon* meant 'young dove' and *pig* 'young swine'. *Place* has had a remarkable history in

English, where it has largely superseded the older words *stead* and *stow*. It derives from the feminine form of the Greek adjective meaning 'broad', as in *plateîa hodós* 'broad way'. In one of its senses it still means 'a group of houses in a town or city, now or formerly possessing some of the characters (positive or negative) of a square', like its well-known cognate in French, as in *Place de la Concorde*, or like Italian *piazza*, Spanish *plaza*, and German *Platz*. Now, however, it is also used in a hundred ways: 'Keep him in his place', 'It is not my place to inquire into that', 'The meeting will not take place', 'There is a place for everything', 'I have lost the place (in reading)', 'That remark was quite out of place (inappropriate, improper)', 'In the first, second place (first, secondly)'.

If we assume that the central meaning of *place* is still 'square' and that these other diverse uses *radiate* from that centre, we might equally well put it into our third semantic category: radiation, polysemia, or multiplication. Another excellent example is the word *paper*. It is the same as *papyrus*, the paper-reed of the Nile from the thin strips of which writing-sheets were first made as a substitute for parchment. The name was naturally transferred to paper made of cotton and thence to paper of linen and other fibres. Today a paper may mean a document of any kind, for instance, a Government White Paper; an essay, dissertation or article on some particular topic, especially a communication read or sent to a learned society; a set of questions in an examination; a journal or a daily newspaper. *Power* 'ability to do, state of being able' may hold radiating meanings as diverse as 'capacity for mental or bodily action' (power of intellect, power of movement); 'mechanical or natural energy' (horse-power, candle-power, electric power-station); 'political or national strength' (the balance of power); 'possession of control or command over others, dominion, sway' (the power of the Cabinet); 'a political state' (the four great powers); and 'a mathematical conception' (5^4 or five to the fourth power). Because the *head* is that part of the human body containing the brain, it may be the top of anything, literally or metaphorically, whether it resembles the head in shape (the head of a nail, screw, pin, hammer, walking-stick, flower, or cabbage) or in position (the head of the page, the list, the bed, the table or the stairs); or it may signify the person who is the chief or leader (the head of the school, the business, the family, the house, the State, the Church). It may denote the head of a coin (that side of a coin bearing the sovereign's head); a headland or promontory (St Bees Head, Great Ormes Head, or Beachy Head, from tautologous Beau Chef Head); a single person or beast (lunch at five shillings a head, fifty head of cattle); or one of the main points or logical divisions of a subject or discourse (dealing with a theme under several heads). These and other senses do not derive from one another. They radiate from a common centre and are therefore mutually independent. Some of these senses will be translated by German *Kopf*, by French *tête*, by Spanish *cabeza* or by the ordinary word for *head* in other languages, but many senses will not permit of such direct translation. Each sense must be considered separately and, in the process of translating, our linguistic knowledge may be severely put to the test. It is surprising that in ordinary conversation in English there is so little ambiguity.

It is surprising, too, that every day we use words in both literal and metaphorical senses and that there is little danger of being misapprehended. We may speak as we will of 'bright sunshine' 'or 'a bright boy'; 'a sharp knife', 'a sharp frost' or 'a sharp rebuke'; 'a cold morning' or 'the cold war'; 'the Black Country' or 'the black market'. A person who is slow-witted may be described metaphorically as 'dull', 'obtuse', or 'dim', the latter term being associated with the German *dumm* meaning 'stupid', although cognate with our *dumb*. 'Dumb' in German is now *stumm*, which is related etymologically to our *stammer*. Many words are themselves old metaphors: *dependent* 'hanging from' (Latin *dē-pendens*); *egregious* 'selected from the herd' (Latin *ē* for *ex* + *grex, gregis* 'herd'); *precocious* 'too early ripe' (Latin *praecox* from *prae* 'before' + *coquere* 'to cook, ripen').

Our next category of semantic changes may be labelled concretization. The naming of abstract qualities, such as *whiteness, beauty,* and *justice,* comes late in the evolution of a language because it results from conscious or unconscious comparison in the mind of man. Does *beauty* really exist apart from beautiful things? On this question the medieval schoolmen argued for centuries. No sooner are abstract nouns formed than men tend to think of each appearance of a quality or action in the abstract as a separate entity and so, by concretization, they make abstractions tangible and visible once more. *Youth,* 'youngness' in the abstract, becomes a 'young man'. In the form *geogoþ* this word occurs eleven times in *Beowulf,* five times with the abstract meaning 'youth', but six times with the concrete and collective meaning 'young men'. In much the same way Latin *multitūdo* 'manyness, the quality of being many' came to signify 'a crowd' and *congregātio* 'flocking together' came to mean 'a body of people assembled'. Barristers appointed counsel to the Crown are named *Queen's Counsel*. A judge is addressed as *Your Honour* and an archbishop as *Your Grace*. *Health* is the quality of being *hale* or *whole,* soundness of body and mind. Modern man seeks diligently to maintain physical, mental, and social health. It is Greek *hugíeia* (from the adjectival form of which comes our hygiene), Latin *salūs,* French *la santé,* and German *die Gesundheit*. Clearly these are all highly abstract forms. Nevertheless, even *health* becomes concrete in the sense of a toast drunk—'Here's a health unto His Majesty!' *Wealth* was primarily 'weal', 'welfare', or 'well-being', the state of being 'well'. In the old assonantal formula 'health and wealth' the two abstract substantives were practically synonymous. But side by side with this meaning of *wealth* the concretized sense of 'worldly goods, riches, affluence' also developed. The expression *wealth of nations,* denoting 'the collective riches of a people or country', was certainly current before it was adopted by Adam Smith in 1776 as the title of his epoch-making book. 'Money', wrote John Stuart Mill in 1848, 'being the instrument of an important public and private purpose, is rightly regarded as wealth'. 'Let us substitute welfare for wealth as our governing purpose', said Edward Hallett Carr in 1948, exhorting us, in fact, to restore to the word *wealth* its older meaning. *Kindness*, *mercy*, *opportunity*, and *propriety* are historically abstractions, but today we speak of *kindnesses* in the plural in the sense of 'deeds of kindness', *mercies* as 'instances or manifestations of mercy', *opportunities* as 'favourable chances or occasions', and *proprieties* as 'proper forms of conduct'. Similarly *provision* 'foreseeing, foresight' has come to be applied in the plural to 'stores of food'.

Sometimes words, like men, 'fall away from their better selves' and show deterioration or catachresis. *Silly* once meant 'happy, blissful, holy', as in the 'sely child' of Chaucer's *Prioress's Tale*. Later it signified 'helpless, defenceless', becoming a conventional epithet in the 'silly sheep' of Milton, Cowper, and Matthew Arnold. Then it descended yet lower and came to imply 'foolish, feeble-minded, imbecile'. *Crafty* 'strong' and *cunning* 'knowing' were once attributes of unmingled praise. A crafty workman was one skilled in a handicraft; a cunning workman was one who knew his trade. *To counterfeit* meant simply 'to copy, reproduce', conveying no suggestion of fraud. 'What finde I here?' asked Bassanio, as he opened the leaden casket, 'Faire Portias counterfeit.' (*The Merchant of Venice*, III, ii, 115.) It was, in fact, no counterfeit in the modern sense, but a true and lifelike delineation that came 'so near creation'. A *villain* once meant 'a slave serving in a country-house or *villa*', a man occupying a lowly station in life. Chaucer's *vileynye* already showed depreciation, for it connoted the opposite of *courteisye*, that comprehensive term for a noble and chivalrous way of life, implying high courtly elegance and politeness of manners. A *knave*, like German *ein Knabe*, was just 'a boy'; later, as in 'the kokes knave, thet wassheth the disshes' of the *Ancrene Riwle*, 'a boy or lad employed as a servant'; later still, 'a base and crafty rogue'. Like *rogue* and *rascal*, *knave* may still be used jocularly without seriously implying bad qualities. *Varlet*, a variant of *valet*, has shown an almost identical catachresis. *Nice* has become just a pleasant verbal counter: anything or everything may be nice. But *nescius*, its Latin antecedent, had the precise meaning 'ignorant, unaware', a meaning maintained in Chaucer side by side with that of 'foolish'. From 'foolish' it developed the sense 'foolishly particular about small things', and so 'fastidious, precise', as in 'nice in one's dress'. Later it was made to refer to actions or qualities, as in 'a nice discrimination' and 'a nice sense of honour'. Since then, as H. W. Fowler sagaciously observed in *A Dictionary of Modern English Usage*, 'it has been too great a favourite with the ladies, who have charmed out of it all its individuality and converted it into a mere diffuser of vague and mild agreeableness'. It is a pleasant, lazy word which careful speakers are bound to avoid using in serious contexts. *Propaganda*, which now implies an organized and vicious distortion of facts for a particular purpose, has suffered sad depreciation in recent years. In 1622 Pope Gregory XV founded a special Committee or Congregation of Cardinals for the Propagation of the Faith, in Latin *Congregātio dē propāgandā fide*. That marked the beginning of the history of this word, which, you see, is the ablative singular feminine form of the gerundive of *propāgāre* 'to fasten or peg down slips of plants for growth, to multiply plants by layering'. Most appropriately the Latin metaphor is agricultural and botanical. *Propaganda* should mean, in its extended sense, the dissemination of news of any kind. Unfortunately, since the year 1880 the meaning of the world has been poisoned. Propaganda and trustworthy news are dissociated in our minds. We even hear of propaganda and counter-propaganda!

Now all these semantic categories—specialization, extension, radiation, metaphor, concretization, and deterioration—are very interesting. Others too might be added to show in yet greater detail how inconstant are the relationships between symbol, image, and referend (word, thought, and thing). Men have sometimes associated speech-forms wrongly and the meanings of words have thus been modified capriciously and unpredictably. Let us admit that there have been losses and gains. When we blunder and are forced to offer abject apologies, we talk of eating *humble pie* and not *umble pie*, one made of umbles or entrails. Vaguely and hazily we may associate the epithet with *humble bee*, which is the old *hummle bee*, the bee that continuously *hums*. Hazily and lazily we may associate an *insurance policy* with the Government's *foreign policy*, not pausing to recollect that these two *policies* are etymologically quite different words. We associate *touchy* with *to touch*, forgetting that *touchy, techy,* or *tetchy* derives from *tetch* 'a fit of petulance or anger, a tantrum'. We say *restive* 'refusing to move or budge' when we are half thinking of *restless*. Pardonably, perhaps, we connect *uproar* with *roar* and *outrage* with *rage*.

Certain expressions, like *comity* and *fruition*, are frequently 'used loosely', and, since they are correspondingly in danger of being 'understood loosely' too, careful speakers are almost compelled to refrain from using them. *Comity* means 'courtesy, urbanity', not 'company, assembly'. The *comity of nations* is 'the obligation recognized by civilized nations to respect one another's laws and customs'. *Fruition* signifies 'enjoyment', not 'bearing of fruit'. If we live by hope', said Bishop Hugh Latimer, 'let us desire the end and fruition of our hope'. Like Archbishop Thomas Cranmer in the Epiphany College, Latimer was here using the word correctly. Today we frequently hear of plans and projects 'coming, or being brought, to fruition'. *Definitive* 'having the quality or character of finality' should not be used as a more imposing form of *definite* 'clear, precise, unmistakable'. Our conception of the Middle Ages may be given a rosy tinge by an over-optimistic misinterpretation of the phrase 'merry England', echoed by Sir Walter Scott in the opening sentence of *Ivanhoe*. King Charles II was 'the merry monarch' and fun-fairs have their 'merry-go-rounds', but 'merry England' implied a pleasant and delightful countryside rather than a gay and carefree people. It was in the Northern *Cursor Mundi* that this epithet was first applied specifically to England. Later medieval poets repeated it and Spenser gave it wide currency in the First Book of *The Faerie Queene* (Canto X, Stanza 61) when he identified the Red Cross Knight with 'Saint George of mery England'. But Spenser's 'mery England' in the sixteenth century meant much the same as Blake's 'England's green and pleasant land' in the early nineteenth.

When Francis Bacon referred to various people in the course of his *Essays* as *indifferent, obnoxious,* and *officious,* he was describing them as 'impartial', 'submissive', and 'ready to serve'. When King James II observed that the new St. Paul's Cathedral was *amusing, awful,* and *artificial,* he implied that Sir Christopher Wren's recent creation was 'pleasing, awe-inspiring, and skilfully achieved'. When Dr. Johnson averred that Milton's *Lycidas* was '*easy, vulgar,* and therefore *disgusting*', he intended to say that it was 'effortless, popular, and therefore not in good taste'.

Men frequently find themselves at cross-purposes with one another because they persist in using words in different senses. Their long arguments emit more heat than light because their conceptions of the point at issue, whether Marxism, democracy, capitalism, the good life, western civilization, culture, art, internationalism, freedom of the individual, equality of opportunity, redistribution of wealth, social security, progress, or what not, are by no means identical. From heedlessness, sloth, or sheer lack of intelligence men do not trouble to clarify their conceptions. Symbols or counters remain unchanged, but as the argument proceeds images and referends (thoughts and things) vary without end. By the way, what do *you* mean by *progress*? To define your terms at every step may seem an intolerable burden, but it is a sobering and salutary discipline. It is, indeed, the only effective way to sharpen up a blunted word and to restore its cutting edge.

QUESTIONS FOR STUDY AND DISCUSSION

1. People who insist that certain words be restricted to their etymological meaning cannot apply that principle consistently to all words. To which of the italicized words as they are used in these sentences would such individuals be likely to object? On what grounds? Could similar objections logically be made to the other italicized words? To secure evidence for your discussion, consult a recent standard dictionary for the earliest given meaning of each word, its present meanings, and possible status labels. Specify the change in meaning that each word has undergone.

   a. An agreement was made *between* the three boys.
   b. There was *quite* a large crowd at the game.
   c. Jean was in *quarantine* for twenty days.
   d. That was the most *unique* party I ever attended.

e. We roasted wieners over a *bonfire.*

f. The package will be delivered *soon*—within a week.

g. I'm *mighty* glad to see you.

h. That was an *awful* mistake.

i. This is a small *room.*

j. Carl always shows *pluck.*

k. Ned has a sense of *humor.*

2. Bring to class a list of words that you think are undergoing changes in meaning today through deterioration, elevation, generalization, or specialization, and be ready to specify the type of change. Consider such areas as politics, education, and social organizations.

3. When words are used in a metaphorical sense, they designate new meanings. In *Webster's Seventh New Collegiate Dictionary metaphor* is defined as "a figure of speech in which a word or phrase literally denoting one kind of object or idea is used in place of another to suggest a likeness or analogy between them (as in *the ship plows the sea*)." After a metaphor has been used frequently, people are no longer aware of the implied comparison and the metaphor is said to be *frozen,* or *faded,* as in *the foot of a hill.* Select the words in the following sentences that are used in a metaphorical sense. Explain. Is the metaphor frozen or active?

   a. Our plans didn't pan out.

   b. The water in this stream is clear.

   c. Her lie was transparent.

   d. The crowd streamed out of the station.

   e. Who will foot the bill?

   f. His voice has an oily quality.

   g. He is a peppery fellow.

   h. This window pane is translucent.

   i. Miss Williams is a brilliant conversationalist.

   j. Some metaphors are frozen.

   k. Tom flew into a rage.

   l. Phil just dodged the issue.

   m. She gave him a stinging rebuke.

   n. Carol falls in love every spring.

4. When an abstract noun is made concrete, it is often preceded by a determiner and also can be used in the plural. Construct sentences in which you change each abstract noun into a concrete noun.

Example: truth "We hold these truths to be self-evident . . ."

activity	charity	sacrifice	chance
danger	civilization	religion	change
food	time	thought	

5. The English vocabulary lacks a general term to cover all groups of animals. What terms are used for groups of sheep, cattle, wolves, bees, birds (quail, partridge)? Supply as many terms as you can for these and other animals. Then see *flock* in a standard college dictionary for other terms.

SUGGESTED ACTIVITIES

1. Some of the following words have undergone specialization, or narrowing, in meaning; others, generalization, or extension, in meaning. List the earliest meaning in English for each word and classify the change in meaning as specialization or generalization.

   | apparition | companion | manuscript | speed | try |
   | butcher | liquor | paraphernalia | stool | very |

2. Some of the following words have undergone deterioration in meaning; others, elevation in meaning. It is interesting to note that it seems to be easier for meanings to go down than up. (A kind of Gresham's law operates.) List the etymological meaning for each word and classify the change in meaning as deterioration or elevation.

charity	gossip	lady	mean	protest
curiosity	lace	lord	paradise	vulgar
fun				

3. Record the etymological meaning for each word and list the category of change as specialization, extension, deterioration, or elevation.

ambition	constable	lewd	smug	tease
boor	fame	minister	spill	voyage
candidate	hazard	person		

4. The following words illustrate folk etymology. Record the etymology and original meaning of each word.

   | belfry | hangnail | nickname | pickax | shamefaced |
   | catsup | hiccough | penthouse | sand-blind | Welsh rarebit |

5. Show how the meaning of a word radiates into many meanings by writing a short essay on one of the following words or on a word of your own choosing: *foot, hand, head, voice, beat, belt, pipe, lumber.* Begin with the etymological meaning. Do the radiated meanings seem to have any relationship to that meaning? Effective illustrations will help to make a readable paper.
6. A word does not have exactly the same meaning for everyone. Write a short essay in which you show the significance of one of these words or of a word of your own choice to several individuals: *ring, joint, fun, police, rules, school.*
7. Does the tendency of words to multiply meanings interfere with communication, or does the context convey the meaning? Write sentences containing these words: *fast, line, pool, board, run.* Try out the sentences on your classmates.
8. Place names are fascinating. Investigate the origins of some place names in your state and report to the class. You will find these books helpful: George R. Stewart, *American Place Names* (Oxford University Press, 1970) and Isaac Taylor, *Words and Places* (Dutton, 1911).
9. Write a short essay about your own first name. The following books will be helpful: Ernest Weekley, *Jack and Jill, a Study in Christian Names* (Dutton, 1940) and Elsdon C. Smith, *Treasury of Name Lore* (Harper & Row, 1967). If you prefer, write a short essay about your surname. W. O. Hassall's *History Through Surnames* (Pergamon Press, 1967) is interesting.
10. Select a short poem that contains metaphors, for example, *Fog* by Carl Sandburg, *Tears* by Lizette Woodworth Reese, or one of Emily Dickinson's poems. Write an analysis of the metaphors. Consider the similarities between the two things compared, the sensory impressions created by the metaphors, and the contributions of the metaphors to the unity of the poem.

23
SEXISM IN ENGLISH: A FEMINIST VIEW
Alleen Pace Nilsen

One of the several "revolutions" of the sixties that sent us into "future shock" has come to be known as women's liberation. In fact, it has given us a new word, *sexism*, meaning "predetermined bias against a person because of sex." Many publications—from Betty Friedan's *Feminine Mystique* in 1963 to *Ms.* Magazine in 1972—reveal the multipronged drive of the movement. Protest against sexism in the English language is only one of the prongs. It is, of course, difficult to determine whether a language is inherently sexist; for, as linguists and anthropologists insist, language and culture form a seamless cloth. Simeon Potter, in "Etymology and Meaning," showed that a word means only what it is generally accepted to mean and that meanings change. But feminists are quick to point out that cultural attitudes are reinforced by language, since we tend to accept as true those ideas already given conceptual form in the words of a language.

In this essay Alleen Pace Nilsen develops the premise that not only does English reveal a cultural bias against women but also that this bias is reinforced by lexicographers. Mrs. Nilsen is the review editor of "Books for Young Adults" for the *English Journal*.

Does culture shape language? Or does language shape culture? This is as difficult a question as the old puzzler of which came first, the chicken or the egg, because there's no clear separation between language and culture.

A well-accepted linguistic principle is that as culture changes so will the language. The reverse of this—as a language changes so will the culture—

Source: Nancy Hoffman, Cynthia Secor, and Adrian Tinsley, *Female Studies VI: Closer to the Ground* (Old Westbury, N.Y.: The Feminist Press, 1972): 102–9. Copyright © 1972 by Nancy Hoffman, Cynthia Secor, and Adrian Tinsley. Reprinted by permission of The Feminist Press and the author.

is not so readily accepted. This is why some linguists smile (or even scoff) at feminist attempts to replace *Mrs.* and *Miss* with *Ms.* and to find replacements for those all-inclusive words which specify masculinity, e.g., *chairman, mankind, brotherhood, freshman,* etc.

Perhaps they are amused for the same reason that it is the doctor at a cocktail party who laughs the loudest at the joke about the man who couldn't afford an operation so he offered the doctor a little something to touch up the X-ray. A person working constantly with language is likely to be more aware of how really deep-seated sexism is in our communication system.

Last winter I took a standard desk dictionary and gave it a place of honor on my night table. Every night that I didn't have anything more interesting to do, I read myself to sleep making a card for each entry that seemed to tell something about male and female. By spring I had a rather dog-eared dictionary, but I also had a collection of note cards filling two shoe boxes. The cards tell some rather interesting things about American English.

First, in our culture it is a woman's body which is considered important while it is a man's mind or his activities which are valued. A woman is sexy. A man is successful.

I made a card for all the words which came into modern English from somebody's name. I have a two-and-one-half inch stack of cards which are men's names now used as everyday words. The women's stack is less than a half inch high and most of them came from Greek mythology. Words coming from the names of famous American men include *lynch, sousaphone, sideburns, Pullman, rickettsia, Schick test, Winchester rifle, Franklin stove, Bartlett pear, teddy bear,* and *boysenberry.* The only really common words coming from the names of American women are *bloomers* (after Amelia Jenks Bloomer) and *Mae West jacket.* Both of these words are related in some way to a woman's physical anatomy, while the male words (except for *sideburns* after General Burnsides) have nothing to do with the namesake's body.

This reminded me of an earlier observation that my husband and I made about geographical names. A few years ago we became interested in what we called "Topless Topography" when we learned that the Grand Tetons used to be simply called *The Tetons* by French explorers and *The Teats* by American frontiersmen. We wrote letters to several map makers and found the following listings: *Nippletop* and *Little Nipple Top* near Mt. Marcy in the Adirondacks, *Nipple Mountain* in Archuleta County, Colorado, *Nipple Peak* in Coke County, Texas, *Nipple Butte* in Pennington, South Dakota, *Squaw Peak* in Placer County, California (and many other places), *Maiden's Peak* and *Squaw Tit* (they're the same mountain) in the Cascade Range in Oregon, *Jane Russell Peaks* near Stark, New Hampshire, and *Mary's Nipple* near Salt Lake City, Utah.

We might compare these names to Jackson Hole, Wyoming, or Pikes Peak, Colorado. I'm sure we would get all kinds of protests from the Jackson and Pike descendants if we tried to say that these topographical features were named because they in some way resembled the bodies of Jackson and Pike, respectively.

This preoccupation with women's breasts is neither new nor strictly American. I was amused to read the derivation of the word *Amazon*. According to Greek folk etymology, the *a* means "without" as in *atypical* or *amoral* while *mazon* comes from *mazōs* meaning "breast." According to the legend, these women cut off one breast so that they could better shoot their bows. Perhaps the feeling was that the women had to trade in part of their femininity in exchange for their active or masculine role.

There are certain pairs of words which illustrate the way in which sexual connotations are given to feminine words while the masculine words retain a serious, businesslike aura. For example, being a *callboy* is perfectly respectable. It simply refers to a person who calls actors when it is time for them to go on stage, but being a *call girl* is being a prostitute.

Also we might compare *sir* and *madam*. *Sir* is a term of respect while *madam* has acquired the meaning of a brothel manager. The same thing has happened to the formerly cognate terms, *master* and *mistress*. Because of its acquired sexual connotations, *mistress* is now carefully avoided in certain contexts. For example, the Boy Scouts have *scoutmasters* but certainly not *scoutmistresses*. And in a dog show the female owner of a dog is never referred to as the *dog's mistress*, but rather as the *dog's master*.

Master appears in such terms as *master plan, concert master, schoolmaster, mixmaster, master charge, master craftsman*, etc. But *mistress* appears in very few compounds. This is the way it is with dozens of words which have male and female counterparts. I found two hundred such terms, e.g., *usher–usherette, heir–heiress, hero–heroine*, etc. In nearly all cases it is the masculine word which is the base with a feminine suffix being added for the alternate version. The masculine word also travels into compounds while the feminine word is a dead end; e.g., from *king–queen* comes *kingdom* but not *queendom*, from *sportsman–sportslady* comes *sportsmanship* but not *sportsladyship*, etc. There is one—and only one—semantic area in which the masculine word is not the base or more powerful word. This is in the area dealing with sex and marriage. Here it is the feminine word which is dominant. *Prostitute* is the base word with *male prostitute* being the derived term. *Bride* appears in *bridal shower, bridal gown, bridal attendant, bridesmaid*, and even in *bridegroom*, while *groom* in the sense of *bridegroom* does not appear in any compounds, not even to name the groom's attendants or his prenuptial party.

At the end of a marriage, this same emphasis is on the female. If it ends in divorce, the woman gets the title of *divorcée* while the man is usually described with a statement, such as, "He's divorced." When the marriage ends in death, the woman is a *widow* and the *-er* suffix which seems to connote masculine (probably because it is an agentive or actor type suffix) is added to make *widower*. *Widower* doesn't appear in any compounds (except for *grass widower*, which is another companion term), but *widow* appears in several compounds and in addition has some acquired meanings, such as the extra hand dealt to the table in certain card games and an undesirable leftover line of type in printing.

If I were an anthropological linguist making observations about a strange and primitive tribe, I would duly note on my tape recorder that I had found linguistic evidence to show that in the area of sex and marriage the female appears to be more important than the male, but in all other areas of the culture, it seems that the reverse is true.

But since I am not an anthropological linguist, I will simply go on to my second observation, which is that women are expected to play a passive role while men play an active one.

One indication of women's passive role is the fact that they are often identified as something to eat. What's more passive than a plate of food? Last spring I saw an announcement advertising the Indiana University English Department picnic. It read "Good Food! Delicious Women!" The publicity committee was probably jumped on by local feminists, but it's nothing new to look on women as "delectable morsels." Even women compliment each other with "You look good enough to eat," or "You have a peaches and cream complexion." Modern slang constantly comes up with new terms, but some of the old standbys for women are: *cute tomato*, *dish*, *peach*, *sharp cookie*, *cheese cake*, *honey*, *sugar*, and *sweetie-pie*. A man may occasionally be addressed as *honey* or described as *a hunk of meat*, but certainly men are not laid out on a buffet and labeled as women are.

Women's passivity is also shown in the comparisons made to plants. For example, to *deflower* a woman is to take away her virginity. A girl can be described as a *clinging vine*, a *shrinking violet*, or a *wall flower*. On the other hand, men are too active to be thought of as plants. The only time we make the comparison is when insulting a man we say he is like a woman by calling him a *pansy*.

We also see the active-passive contrast in the animal terms used with males and females. Men are referred to as *studs*, *bucks*, and *wolves*, and they go *tomcatting around*. These are all aggressive roles, but women have such pet names as *kitten*, *bunny*, *beaver*, *bird*, *chick*, *lamb*, and *fox*. The idea of being a pet seems much more closely related to females than to males. For instance, little girls grow up wearing *pigtails* and *ponytails* and they dress in *halters* and *dog collars*.

The active-passive contrast is also seen in the proper names given to boy babies and girl babies. Girls are much more likely to be given names like *Ivy*, *Rose*, *Ruby*, *Jewel*, *Pearl*, *Flora*, *Joy*, etc., while boys are given names describing active roles such as *Martin* (warlike), *Leo* (lion), *William* (protector), *Ernest* (resolute fighter), and so on.

Another way that women play a passive role is that they are defined in relationship to someone else. This is what feminists are protesting when they ask to be identified as *Ms.* rather than as *Mrs.* or *Miss*. It is a constant source of irritation to women's organizations that when they turn in items to newspapers under their own names, that is, Susan Glascoe, Jeanette

Jones, and so forth, the editors consistently rewrite the item so that the names read Mrs. John Glascoe, Mrs. Robert E. Jones.

In the dictionary I found what appears to be an attitude on the part of editors that it is almost indecent to let a respectable woman's name march unaccompanied across the pages of a dictionary. A woman's name must somehow be escorted by a male's name regardless of whether or not the male contributed to the woman's reason for being in the dictionary, or in his own right, was as famous as the woman. For example, Charlotte Brontë is identified as Mrs. Arthur B. Nicholls, Amelia Earhart is identified as Mrs. George Palmer Putnam, Helen Hayes is identified as Mrs. Charles MacArthur, Zona Gale is identified as Mrs. William Llwelyn Breese, and Jenny Lind is identified as Mme. Otto Goldschmidt.

Although most of the women are identified as Mrs. ——— or as the wife of ———, other women are listed with brothers, fathers, or lovers. Cornelia Otis Skinner is identified as the daughter of Otis, Harriet Beecher Stowe is identified as the sister of Henry Ward Beecher, Edith Sitwell is identified as the sister of Osbert and Sacheverell, Nell Gwyn is identified as the mistress of Charles II, and Madame Pompadour is identified as the mistress of Louis XV.

The women who did get into the dictionary without the benefit of a masculine escort are a group sort of on the fringes of respectability. They are the rebels and the crusaders: temperance leaders Frances Elizabeth Caroline Willard and Carry Nation, women's rights leaders Carrie Chapman Catt and Elizabeth Cady Stanton, birth control educator Margaret Sanger, religious leader Mary Baker Eddy, and slaves Harriet Tubman and Phillis Wheatley.

I would estimate that far more than fifty percent of the women listed in the dictionary were identified as someone's wife. But of all the men—and there are probably ten times as many men as women—only one was identified as "the husband of . . . ." This was the unusual case of Frederic Joliot who took the last name of Joliot-Curie and was identified as "husband of Irene." Apparently Irene, the daughter of Pierre and Marie Curie, did not want to give up her maiden name when she married and so the couple took the hyphenated last name.

There are several pairs of words which also illustrate the more powerful role of the male and the relational role of the female. For example a *count* is a high political officer with a *countess* being simply the wife of a count. The same is true for a *duke* and a *duchess* and a *king* and a *queen*. The fact that a king is usually more powerful than a queen might be the reason that Queen Elizabeth's husband is given the title of *prince* rather than *king*. Since *king* is a stronger word than *queen*, it is reserved for a true heir to the throne because if it were given to someone coming into the royal family by marriage, then the subjects might forget where the true power lies. With the weaker word of *queen*, this would not be a problem; so a woman marrying a ruling monarch is given the title without question.

My third observation is that there are many positive connotations connected with the concept of masculine, while there are either trivial or negative connotations connected with the corresponding feminine concept.

Conditioning toward the superiority of the masculine role starts very early in life. Child psychologists point out that the only area in which a girl has more freedom than a boy is in experimenting with an appropriate sex role. She is much freer to be a *tomboy* than is her brother to be a *sissy*. The proper names given to children reflect this same attitude. It's perfectly all right for a girl to have a boy's name, but not the other way around. As girls are given more and more of the boys' names, parents shy away from using boy names that might be mistaken for girl names, so the number of available masculine names is constantly shrinking. Fifty years ago *Hazel*, *Beverley*, *Marion*, *Frances*, and *Shirley* were all perfectly acceptable boys' names. Today few parents give these names to baby boys and adult men who are stuck with them self-consciously go by their initials or by abbreviated forms such as *Haze* or *Shirl*. But parents of little girls keep crowding the masculine set and currently popular girls' names include *Jo, Kelly, Teri, Cris, Pat, Shawn, Toni,* and *Sam*.

When the mother of one of these little girls tells her to *be a lady*, she means for her to sit with her knees together. But when the father of a little boy tells him to *be a man*, he means for him to be noble, strong, and virtuous. The whole concept of manliness has such positive connotations that it is a compliment to call a male a *he-man*, a *manly man*, or a *virile man* (*virile* comes from the Indo-European *vir*, meaning "man"). In each of these three terms, we are implying that someone is doubly good because he is doubly a man.

Compare *chef* with *cook*, *tailor* and *seamstress*, and *poet* with *poetess*. In each case, the masculine form carries with it an added degree of excellence. In comparing the masculine *governor* with the feminine *governess* and the masculine *major* with the feminine *majorette*, the added feature is power.

The difference between positive male and negative female connotations can be seen in several pairs of words which differ denotatively only in the matter of sex. For instance compare *bachelor* with the terms *spinster* and *old maid*. *Bachelor* has such positive connotations that modern girls have tried to borrow the feeling in the term *bachelor-girl*. *Bachelor* appears in glamorous terms such as *bachelor pad, bachelor party,* and *bachelor button*. But *old maid* has such strong negative feelings that it has been adopted into other areas, taking with it the feeling of undesirability. It has the metaphorical meaning of shriveled and unwanted kernels of pop corn, and it's the name of the last unwanted card in a popular game for children.

Patron and *matron* (Middle English for *father* and *mother*) are another set where women have tried to borrow the positive masculine connotations, this time through the word *patroness*, which literally means "female father." Such a peculiar term came about because of the high prestige attached to the word *patron* in such phrases as *"a patron of the arts"* or *"a patron saint."*

Matron is more apt to be used in talking about a woman who is in charge of a jail or a public restroom.

Even *lord* and *lady* have different levels of connotation. *Our Lord* is used as a title for deity, while the corresponding *Our Lady* is a relational title for Mary, the moral mother of Jesus. *Landlord* has more dignity than *landlady* probably because the landlord is more likely to be thought of as the owner while the landlady is the person who collects the rent and enforces the rules. *Lady* is used in many insignificant places where the corresponding *lord* would never be used, for example, *ladies room, ladies sizes, ladies aid society, ladybug,* etc.

This overuse of *lady* might be compared to the overuse of *queen* which is rapidly losing its prestige as compared to *king*. Hundreds of beauty queens are crowned each year and nearly every community in the United States has its *Dairy Queen* or its *Freezer Queen*, etc. Male homosexuals have adopted the term to identify the "feminine" partner. And advertisers who are constantly on the lookout for euphemisms to make unpleasant sounding products salable have recently dealt what might be a death blow to the prestige of the word *queen*. They have begun to use it as an indication of size. For example, *queen-size* panty hose are panty hose for fat women. The meaning comes through a comparison with *king-size*, meaning big. However, there's a subtle difference in that our culture considers it desirable for males to be big because size is an indication of power, but we prefer that females be small and petite. So using *king-size* as a term to indicate bigness partially enhances the prestige of *king*, but using *queen-size* to indicate bigness brings unpleasant associations to the word *queen*.

Another set that might be compared are *brave* and *squaw*. The word *brave* carries with it the connotations of youth, vigor, and courage, while *squaw* implies almost opposite characteristics. With the set *wizard* and *witch*, the main difference is that *wizard* implies skill and wisdom combined with magic, while *witch* implies evil intentions combined with magic. Part of the unattractiveness of both *squaw* and *witch* is that they suggest old age, which in women is particularly undesirable. When I lived in Afghanistan (1967–69), I was horrified to hear a proverb stating that when you see an old man you should sit down and take a lesson, but when you see an old woman you should throw a stone. I was equally startled when I went to compare the connotations of our two phrases *grandfatherly advice* and *old wives' tales*. Certainly it isn't expressed with the same force as in the Afghan proverb, but the implication is similar.

In some of the animal terms used for women the extreme undesirability of female old age is also seen. For instance consider the unattractiveness of *old nag* as compared to *filly*, of *old crow* or *old bat* as compared to *bird*, and of being *catty* as compared to being *kittenish*. The chicken metaphor tells the whole story of a girl's life. In her youth she is a *chick*, then she marries and begins feeling *cooped up*, so she goes to *hen parties* where she *cackles* with her friends. Then she has her *brood* and begins to *henpeck* her husband. Finally she turns into *an old biddy*.

QUESTIONS FOR STUDY AND DISCUSSION

1. Words derived from proper nouns are called eponyms. Mrs. Nilsen lists many formed from men's names but only a few from women's. How does she explain this imbalance? Do you agree? Can you think of words derived from women's names not mentioned by the author? (Consider *Melba toast, tawdry, Elizabethan, Victorian, maudlin.*) Eponyms have been collected in *Word People* by Nancy Caldwell Sorel (1971). If the book is available, it will help in your discussion.
2. Try to think of as many eponyms as you can to illustrate the following categories: food (*sandwich*); invention (*guillotine*), physical science (*fahrenheit*), botanical science (*poinsettia*), history (*quisling*). Count the ones derived from women's names.
3. Mrs. Nilsen says that words derived from women's names often come from Greek mythology. List examples from either Greek or Roman myths, such as *cereal, calliope, uranium, iris, fortune*.
4. Mrs. Nilsen's discussion of "topless topography" suggests explorers' preoccupation with feminine anatomy. Do place names in your state reinforce Mrs. Nilsen's thesis? Can you think of place names that recall a woman in other ways, such as Martha's Vineyard, Massachusetts, or Ladysmith, Wisconsin?
5. Words of address, such as *sir* and *madam*, may reveal cultural attitudes. One of the changes initiated by the women's movement has been the substitution of *Ms.* for *Miss* and *Mrs.*, both of which are abbreviated forms of *mistress*. What is the rationale behind the introduction of *Ms.*? Is it widely used, according to your observations? (The phonemic /miz/ is standard pronunciation in the South for *Mrs.*)
6. Linguists often point out that languages reveal what is important to a culture; for example, the many words for *snow*, in the Eskimo language, or for *kinship*, in the language of the Australian aborigines. What conclusion does Mrs. Nilsen draw about the importance of women in American culture after her study of an American dictionary?
7. Mrs. Nilsen sees significance in names traditionally given to boys and girls. Are the examples she lists fashionable among your friends? After the Norman conquest, Biblical names became popular, *Mary* and *John* being easily first. *John* is derived from Hebrew, meaning "Jehovah has been gracious," and occurs as *Ian, Sean, Evan, Hans, Jean, Juan, Jan,* and *Ivan,* to name only a few forms. Some sixty etymologies have been given for *Mary,* and its popularity continues, including such variants as *Maria, Marie,* and *Miriam.* Study the etymology and meaning of your

own name by consulting a dictionary or encyclopedia. Simeon Potter has a chapter, "Names of Persons and Places," in *Our Language*, as well as a helpful bibliography.
8. Novelists frequently give their characters names with symbolic significance. In *The Scarlet Letter* Hawthorne names two feminine characters Hester ("star") and Pearl. Is this significant? Two Daisys are important in more recent fiction, Henry James's *Daisy Miller* and Fitzgerald's Daisy Buchanan in *The Great Gatsby*. If you are familiar with these heroines in the novels or in motion pictures made from the novels, discuss the appropriateness of their name. Cite other examples of fictional names that have symbolic meaning. Do your examples reinforce Mrs. Nilsen's thesis?
9. Mrs. Nilsen discusses the redundancy in such a phrase as "manly man." Do we say "womanly woman"? What is the effect of the suffix *-ly*? Contrast this with the effect of *-ish* in *mannish, boyish, girlish*.
10. Mrs. Nilsen concludes her essay with a reference to animal metaphors for women, most of which are unflattering. What animal metaphors are commonly applied to men? Are they also unflattering?

SUGGESTED ACTIVITIES

1. Otto Jespersen, in his *Growth and Structure of the English Language*, writes: "It is, of course, impossible to characterize a language in one formula; languages, like men, are too composite to have their whole essence summed up in one short expression. Nevertheless, there is one expression that continually comes to mind whenever I think of the English language and compare it with others: it seems to me positively and expressly *masculine*, it is the language of a grown-up man and has very little childish or feminine about it" (p. 2). Jespersen then proceeds to develop this thesis. If the book is available, read and summarize his supporting statements. Do Jespersen's arguments support the contention that the English language is, indeed, sexist?
2. In the preceding quotation, Jespersen contrasts *masculine* with *childish* and *feminine*, as one might contrast *strong* and *weak*. Observe the unguarded speech of men and women of various ages and educational levels. Is there evidence that linguistic choices are made on the basis of sex differences? Summarize your findings in a short essay. (You may find suggestions for procedure from an article by Robin Lakoff, "Language and Woman's Place," in *Language and Society*, vol. 2, no. 1.)
3. The first issue of *Ms.* (Spring, 1972) suggested in "De-Sexing the English Language" that the use of *he* as common gender in a sentence such as "Each person must do as he thinks right" is discriminatory, since *he* in its various forms evokes images of *male*. What alternative does

English offer for the use of *he* in such a sentence? Why does the problem arise in English, which has natural gender, closely related to sex, and not in languages that have grammatical gender, such as Latin or German? (For example, in Latin *nauta*, "sailor," is feminine, for *gender* merely means "class" or "kind.")

4. Kate Miller and Casey Smith, authors of the article cited in number 3 above, suggest the introduction of a new pronoun in English to remove sexist bias. The paradigm would be as follows:

	Singular		Plural
	Distinct Gender	*Common Gender*	*Common Gender*
Nominative	he and she	tey	they
Possessive	his and her (or hers)	ter (or ters)	their (or theirs)
Objective	him and her	tem	them

Write a paragraph in which you use the *tey-ter-tem* system wherever appropriate. Do you find the substitution necessary and effective?

5. Feminists also argue that women tend to be invisible in the English language because *man*, meaning the species *homo sapiens*, or *mankind*, does not evoke images of women. (Latin, for example, has two words, *vir*, "a male," and *homo*, "a member of mankind.") For this reason *chairperson* is often substituted in convention programs for *chairman*. Consider the feminists' argument in the light of your own experience. Do you assume that, unless otherwise identified, people in general are male? Consider such nouns as *doctor, lawyer, merchant, chief, beggar, senator, alcoholic, professor, teacher*. Write an essay in which you analyze your responses to the words listed above and others you may wish to add.

6. What word could be substituted for *man* in these sentences?

   a. Man is a rational being.

   b. Man is created in the image of God.

   c. Man is by nature sinful and unclean.

7. Study the etymology of *woman* in the *OED*. Does it support the feminists' thesis that women's roles are in general defined in terms of their relationship to men? Summarize your data.

8. Men have traditionally referred to ships as *she*. Automobiles and hurricanes are also frequently feminine in gender. Write a short essay in which you illustrate and speculate upon this aspect of English.

9. Study the etymology of *lady* in the *OED*. What semantic shift has taken place? Make the same study of *lord*. Summarize your data and comment.

10. Other pairs of words that make interesting etymological studies are *sissy–buddy*; *shrewd–shrewish*; *cocky–coquette*; *chef–cook*. Choose a pair for study and reporting.
11. Feminists argue that there are over four hundred "sexist" words in American dictionaries for which male equivalents are rare. Some they consider patronizing, such as *flirt, doll,* or *babe*; but others are degrading, such as *crone, harpy, termagant*. Check the definitions of these words and others you may think of. Do you find a sexist bias in the definitions themselves? Summarize your data.

Part Eight

ENGLISH IN THE WORLD

24
ENGLISH SPOKEN: HERE, THERE, EVERYWHERE
William Benton

The title clearly indicates the subject of this essay. The growth of English around the world has been remarkable. In 1582 Richard Mulcaster wrote: "The English tongue is of small reach, stretching no further than this island of ours, nay not there over all." At that time English ranked fifth among European languages in the number of speakers, a position it continued to occupy until the middle of the nineteenth century, when it moved into first place, a position it has maintained ever since. Moreover, the growth of English as a worldwide language has been accelerating since World War II. Today English is spoken by more people than any other language except Chinese. Chinese, however, is not widespread throughout the world, and its many dialects are not all mutually intelligible.

Benton not only shows the global use of English but also analyzes the reasons for its rapid spread—reasons all external to the language itself and not reflecting any specific merits of the language. Perhaps a common language can help to break the barrier created by the estimated 3,000 languages in the world. At least Benton thinks that the spread of English is in the world's best interest.

William Benton is chairman of the board of *Encyclopaedia Britannica* Educational Corporation. At the time he wrote this article he was United States ambassador to UNESCO.

Except for our lexicographers and linguistic scholars, most Americans take little notice of the remarkable growth of our English language around the earth. For example, I have observed that in Paris, the home of the world language of recent centuries, about two-thirds of UNESCO's work is now

Source: *Think* 33 (January–February 1967): 19–22. Copyright © 1967 by William Benton. Reprinted by permission of *Think* Magazine, published by IBM, and of William Benton, publisher and chairman, *Encyclopaedia Britannica*.

conducted in English. Twenty years ago it was only a half. The late Edward Murrow, one of my successors in charge of the United States Information Agency, agreed with me that no objective of USIA over the next hundred years could be more important than the propagation of the English language. Mr. Murrow's and my agreement here was not chauvinism, though to some it will seem so. Nor were we verging into cultural imperialism. We felt this objective was in the world's interest, and not merely that of the English-speaking nations.

In our own time, English has supplanted French as the principal language of diplomacy and German as the language of science. English has even become the most useful language to the traveler in Europe and throughout most of the rest of the world.

The French are not enthusiastic about this. A couple of years ago, President de Gaulle instructed the members of the French Academy to write their communications in French, and a little later I was amused when Roger Seydoux, the French Ambassador to the U.N., wrote to me in French from his office in New York to congratulate me on my 65th birthday. He knows that I do not speak French and he speaks English as well as I do. France continues to promote its language and can point to the teaching of French in thousands of all-French schools throughout the world. In the case of Nicaragua alone, when I was Assistant Secretary of State 20 years ago, I recall there were seven weekly radio broadcasts of French lessons sponsored by the French Government.

Nevertheless, English has come to the front rapidly in the last century, largely as a result of the swift increase in the population of the United States and of the British dominions. English has also been stimulated by its role in commerce, communications, science and technology. In our country, because of an early commitment to universal education, we produced not merely a new population, but a population literate in English. Today the growth of English as a world-wide language is accelerating. Indeed, in the $21\frac{1}{2}$ years since World War II, English has advanced farther than in the entire preceding century. Inventions that make communications between nations easier have inevitably lent themselves to the spread of English: motion pictures, radio and television. Even though non-English subtitles may be used in the movies or TV, the voices carry impact and create the desire to understand.

Both World Wars took millions of Americans, Canadians, Australians and Britishers into places where they had never been before. Today airplane travel takes American tourists and businessmen almost everywhere. And wherever American tourists go, they carry the English language in their briefcases. And let us not overlook our own visitors from abroad; 90,000 foreign students are attending American colleges and universities at any one time and they carry home mastery of our language. It is estimated that some 70 percent of the world's mail is written in English and 60 percent of the world's broadcasts are in English. Even the embarrassing reluctance of Americans to learn foreign languages has helped promote our language.

The thrust behind the growth of English in our time has of course been further accelerated by the economic and military strength of the United States. The scientific and technological preeminence of the English-speaking peoples has created the need to master English in the new and underdeveloped countries. Many African countries, even when they try to emphasize indigenous languages, turn to English as a language of instruction. Scientists throughout the world increasingly use English, to name one example, in discussing atomic physics among themselves. They prefer to publish their findings in English to assure the widest possible international circulation.

In aviation, in shipping, in sports, English is already a near universal language. When a Russian pilot calls the control tower at Cairo, Egypt, for a landing, the conversation will be in English. When you fly to Israel, the stewardess announces your arrival in Hebrew, French, and English. Even in Israel, the flight operation and maintenance of the Israeli airline, El Al, is partially carried on in English. The code of the International Civil Aviation Organization provides that "in the absence of an 'international language' " pilots have the right to request guidance in English anywhere in the world.

There are 41,000 teachers of English in the Soviet Union. Is this not tacit recognition that English, not Russian, is becoming the auxiliary language of nation after nation? Every year the Soviet Union produces 100 million books for export in English, French, German and Spanish, and the major emphasis by far is on English. English is a requirement for admission to college in Japan, where there are 60,000 English teachers. It is compulsory in secondary schools in a growing number of countries.

For at least 270 millions in the world today, English is the primary language, the mother tongue. Of the three-quarters of the world's population who speak the 12 main existing languages, this constitutes only 11 percent. Twenty-five percent of them speak some form of Chinese, and 8.3 percent speak Russian. But in the last 400 years, the proportion of native speakers of English in the world has increased five-fold. In addition, another 270 million people, another 11 percent, now speak English as a second language —a total of more than half a billion who speak our language. This almost equals the number who speak the various dialects of Chinese.

The remaining quarter of the earth's population speaks nearly 3,000 so-called natural languages. Here is indeed a tower of Babel, and this figure dramatizes the need of mankind for a single tongue of universal intellectual discourse. Seven hundred languages, in total, have been invented to provide the single tongue, but none has taken hold. What is the choice before the world? Short of a world conquest by the Russians or the Chinese, it is a clear choice: English.

Should we deplore the tendency of newly independent nations to seek the development of an indigenous language, as a primary language, even if it is spoken by only a handful? Perhaps this desire is a temporary aspect of an ardent nationalism. Gaelic, for example, is required in the schools of Ireland, but it is not flourishing. Some observers believe an indigenous language is psychologically indispensable to the cohesion of new nations; there have been bloody riots on this issue in India and Ceylon. Some educators believe that the early years of school are best taught in the language the child hears at home. This may be true. Nevertheless, English is becoming indispensable at the higher levels of education. All of the readings in the more advanced courses at Hebrew University in Jerusalem are in English. There is a practical reason for this: nearly everything important is either written in English or translated into it. The books are available.

A READY-MADE TOOL

As one authority, describing his experiences in Southeast Asia, declares:

Amidst the contending nationalisms we can perceive an emerging world of community, a new mankind conscious of its common destiny. . . . Now, with no premeditated plan, English has become the language of much of this intercommunication. It was, paradoxically enough, the main language used in the Asian Relations Conference in New Delhi, the Afrasian Conference in Bandung, and the conference of Heads of African States in Addis Ababa. It would seem impracticable and unwise to refuse the aid of this ready-made tool of easy communication, no longer the King-Emperor's English but the self-chosen language of the free peoples.

Most people believe their native language excels all others. Certainly the French most passionately among all European nations believe this. They were the first nation in the modern world deliberately to promote their language as a cardinal aim of foreign policy. But in our time English, to the despair of the French, has even corrupted the linguistic purity of French—in France. *Anglais*, the French fret, is corrupting *français* into what is mockingly called "franglais." Parisians eat American-style quick lunches at "le snack bar," dance to "le jazz hot" at "le night club," and worry about "le parking" for "le shopping" at "le drugstore." The British and Americans, on the other hand, use French expressions constantly and with no feeling that they are betraying their own culture. English has no chauvinism. It is a product of many cultural streams and is constantly being enriched. It is not a national language and is not self-conscious about borrowing from others.

I suspect the French are going to have to resign themselves to more and more "franglais." Let those who object call the process an accident of history rather than the result of intrinsic merit in the English language. Nevertheless, English has become the language people are seeking to acquire.

QUESTIONS FOR STUDY AND DISCUSSION

1. Account for the rapid acceleration in the growth of English since World War II. Summarize and evaluate the reasons Benton lists and add any others you can think of.
2. Is English likely to continue to grow as a world language? Consider
    a. the fact that English was the primary language of 345 million people in 1974, according to *The World Almanac and Book of Facts*,
    b. the influences that have caused the growth of English as a world language and whether they seem likely to continue.
3. Name some American inventions that may have helped to spread the English language.
4. Myers, in "Development of the Language," lists several reasons for the ascendancy of the dialect of London in the fifteenth century. Do you see any similarity between those reasons and the reasons that have led to the ascendancy of the English language as a whole?
5. Discuss the advantages of the widespread use of a single language throughout the world. Are there any possible disadvantages?
6. Explain how the reluctance of Americans to learn foreign languages has helped to promote the spread of the English language. Do you agree with Benton that such reluctance is embarrassing? Explain.
7. Benton states that Chinese is the mother tongue of 25 percent of the people speaking one of the twelve main existing languages, and English the mother tongue of only 11 percent. Why, then, isn't Chinese, rather than English, becoming a world language?
8. No language in itself is more difficult than any other language. Would a native speaker of English as an adult, therefore, find it equally easy to learn either French or Japanese? Explain.
9. Some people have argued that an artificial language, such as Esperanto, has advantages over any natural language for international use. Esperanto has Latin as the chief base of its vocabulary, a grammatical system that is much simpler than the grammars of most European languages, and a phonetic spelling system. What arguments can you advance for or against the use of Esperanto instead of English as an international language?
10. According to Albert H. Marckwardt, in his *American English*, p. 171, "It is . . . in its development as a second language that the real opportunities for the future development of English seem to lie." Evaluate Marckwardt's assertion. Consider the areas of the world and the populations where English is likely to be used increasingly as a second language.

SUGGESTED ACTIVITIES

1. If you know people who have traveled abroad, ask them how widespread they have found the use of English. Many travelers report amusing incidents of making inquiries in halting, imperfect Spanish, French, or German, only to be answered in fluent English.
2. Interview any exchange students in your school about the status of English in their countries: its place in the schools, in business, and so on. Are English language newspapers published in the country? Are books, periodicals, and newspapers in English readily available? (In Japan the three largest newspapers all publish English-language editions.)
3. Conduct similar interviews with American exchange students who have studied abroad.
4. Write a feature story on one of these interviews.
5. In a single week note the number of speakers you hear on television or radio whose native language is not English. What is the native country of each one? How well does each speaker use the language? You may be able to detect whether he learned American English or British English.
6. List the twelve main existing languages of the world and the number of speakers of each. Consult the most recent edition of *The World Book Encyclopedia*, *The World Almanac and Book of Facts*, or *Information Please Almanac*.
7. If you are reading French, make a list of English words that you come upon. If you have access to a current French periodical, you will be more likely to find English words. Do English words in French look more or less strange than French words in English?
8. English is "not a national language and is not self-conscious about borrowing from others," Benton states. The three languages that have contributed most to the English word stock are Greek, Latin, and French. (Greek words have often entered the language through Latin and Latin words through French.) Borrowings from these languages and from Scandinavian were introduced in the unit on the history of the language. Italian and Spanish have also made large contributions to the English vocabulary. In addition, words from nearly every language in the world have become part of the English vocabulary. The following exercise is designed to show the range of borrowings:
    a. Select ten of the following words. Record the language from which each was borrowed and the original form and meaning of the word. If you do not know where a language is spoken, check a dictionary for that information. Use a recent standard dictionary, preferably a collegiate or an unabridged one.

Example: mahout from Hindi *mahāut:* a keeper and driver of an elephant.

Hindi: a literary and official language of Northern India.

(1) algebra	(16) kapok	(31) pecan
(2) alkali	(17) karate	(32) robot
(3) bungalow	(18) kayak	(33) samovar
(4) clan	(19) keen, v.	(34) schmaltz
(5) cockatoo	(20) kibitzer	(35) shampoo
(6) coleslaw	(21) kimono	(36) shawl
(7) colleen	(22) kindergarten	(37) shish kebab
(8) consommé	(23) kiwi	(38) smorgasbord
(9) garage	(24) kowtow	(39) steppe
(10) geyser	(25) kumquat	(40) taboo
(11) goulash	(26) loot	(41) tattoo
(12) guerrilla	(27) molasses	(42) tea
(13) hickory	(28) opera	(43) ukulele
(14) hoodoo	(29) pagoda	(44) umbrella
(15) jukebox	(30) pajamas	(45) yogi

b. Write a short essay on one of these words or some other borrowed word, tracing its origin and history in the language and discussing its present use. Consult dictionaries, encyclopedias, and books on word origins.

25
THE HOOTER'S THE HORN
Robert L. Coard

"The hooter's the horn, the dustman's the janitor, and the geyser's the water heater," Coard discovered, as he traveled through the British Isles. A common language, it was soon evident, did not guarantee common meanings for all words on both sides of the Atlantic.

Certain British pronunciations also sound strange to American ears. Two are most striking. The so-called broad *a* (*ä*) as in *father*, is much more widely used than in most parts of the United States. For example, *staff*, *class*, *laugh*, *path* are stäf, kläs, läf, päth. The vowel ă, as in *man*, used by most Americans in these words, also represents the sound in British English until the end of the eighteenth century, when ă began to give way to *ä*. In eastern New England the continued close ties with the mother country led to the British innovation as culturally preferable. The prevalence of ă is only one instance of an older form in the United States.

The absence of *r* before a consonant and after a vowel is also likely to be unfamiliar to an American unless he comes from New England or the South. To the average American, the British pronunciation of *dark* sounds much like *dock*; *sharp* like *shop*; *heart* like *hot*; *floor* like *flaw*; *lord* like *laud*, although the vowel sounds are not identical. The British also manage to get rid of a syllable in some words. *Secretary*, for example, is ′sek-rə-tre. But it is in intonation that the two main branches of the English language differ most. "Though they use the same words, the Englishman and the American do not speak the same tune," John Erskine wrote.

A few matters of syntax differentiate British English from American. Collective nouns are usually treated as plurals: *Parliament are, the government were*. An Englishman lives *in* a street, rather than *on* a street, and if he has something you would like to have, he may *give it you*. One thing is *different to* and not *different from* another.

Amusing as it is, however, to play up isolated differences between

---

Source: *The Minnesota Journal of Education* 45 (March 1967): 31–33. Copyright © 1967 by the Minnesota Education Association. Reprinted by permission of the publisher and the author.

British English and American English is misleading; for the English language, wherever it is spoken, has an essential unity that makes it possible for English-speaking people around the world to communicate with one another with little difficulty.

Robert L. Coard is professor of English at St. Cloud State College, St. Cloud, Minnesota.

"Here's the hooter."

"The what?"

"The hooter," the young Irishman from the car rental agency answered, apparently thinking that he hadn't been heard. He had been heard, but he hadn't been understood.

"Why, the hooter's the horn," suddenly said my fellow American, who had been receiving these driving instructions. "The hooter, the hooter," we Americans repeated, relishing the strange flavor of the word as used in this sense.

Through several weeks of driving in the Irish Republic and Great Britain, I found word adventures like the above kept popping up, not too often perhaps by actual count, but generally in ways that created surprise and amusement. I would like to set down here, in informal fashion, a number of these experiences in the hope that they might be of use to classes beginning a study of regional and national variations of English, which is always a lively topic.

Of course, we Americans are prepared for a good many British expressions like "petrol" and "bobby" and "lift" and "lorry." And with the popularity of the British comic strip *Andy of England* in our own country, we're getting used to a good many more. We're not puzzled, for example, when the rascally Andy borrows "ten bob" from his long-suffering wife, Flo, and heads, as usual, straight for the nearest "pub." Still, British expressions, like British driving, can be tricky. When the American is relaxed and the British road is straight, he'll drive smugly enough down the left-hand side of the road. But let him swirl and whirl awhile in city traffic on "High Street" (their "Main Street"), and habit will tell. The American is likely to switch to the right-hand side of the road to everybody's consternation. So too, when the American gets confused verbally, he grasps for his familiar word for an object, and lo, sometimes he discovers a stranger in its place.

BONNET, BOOT NOT WORN

I experienced a couple of these verbal shocks while stopping for petrol in Scotland. "Lift the bonnet," the station attendant said. My mind rang up a zero. Then I remembered one of those comparison tables of British-American expressions from a college freshman text of years back. Why, "bonnet" meant "hood." Another remark followed, "Put it in the boot." Again a zero, until an image of that list reappeared, and I remembered "boot" means "trunk."

Driving down the highways of the Irish Republic and Great Britain necessarily involved meeting a number of new words, or more usually perhaps, the old familiar words endowed with fresh and startling meanings. "Diversion," for example, is a garden variety word in the United States, but painted on a British highway sign, it caused a twinge, as would our equivalent "detour." "Caravan," another familiar word, has also suffered a sea change in meaning. To an American, "caravan" is likely to conjure up visions of swaying camels and picturesque Arabs, but on the British roadside "No Caravan Parking" is simply our "No Trailer Parking." "Gallon" would seem to be a dead ringer for our "gallon," but a long discussion in London convinced me (and any dictionary will verify it) that the British gallon is a larger measure than ours by about a quart. Here are a few more illustrations. "Circus" to an American retains associations of canvas tops and elephants, but in Great Britain it is likely to be just a square or circle where streets come together, as in St. Giles Circus or the much publicized Piccadilly Circus of neon lights and bars.

At other times, however, the British difference (and often that of the Irish Republic too) will be expressed in an unfamiliar word or at least in an unexpected combination of familiar words. In Northern Ireland, for example, "Slow" appeared just as we would place it, but where we would probably post "5 mph" their sign warned "Dead Slow." In a spot where we would admonish "Loose Gravel," theirs warned "Loose Chippings." I got so I would beam at the sign "Dual Carriageway Ahead," for I knew that on the coming four-lane we could pass—British "overtake"—the monster lorry and the lumbering caravan. During much of the journey from the Lake Country down to London we buzzed along on a limited access highway (in British phrasing a "motorway") and maintained a goodly speed because the "flyovers" (American "overpasses") eliminated traffic lights. Still, we didn't move very rapidly on the August Bank Holiday. Although it might differ in origin, the August Bank Holiday is amazingly like our Labor Day in creating traffic snarls and piling up a ghastly toll in injuries and deaths.

CHARITY OR ROBBERY?

When I write out British roadside words like "dual carriageway" and "flyover," I can still recall my pleasure on first meeting them. This is not so with the Irish meaning of "tinker." Even more than the August Bank Holiday with its long crawl of traffic, the Irish word "tinker" meaning "drifter" or "vagabond" or "gypsy," brings up a shudder of revulsion. Months later, I can reconstruct from memory, all too vividly, the forlorn little tents of the tinkers pitched on the cramped shoulder of the highway and see and hear the screeching women with their outthrust palms: "I have a sick baby, sir." "You gave her some money. Give me some. Give me some. Give me some." Under this assault out came those cart-wheel-sized British and Irish pennies, the odd-shaped three pence, the shiny little sixpence, the ever handy shilling, the two shilling piece, and the half crown or two shillings and sixpence. To this day I don't know whether I contributed to charity or was robbed.

Perhaps by now it's time to get off the British highway and visit a British town and continue this language tour up High Street. A sign with "City Centre" and an arrow will show the way. Incidentally, that spelling "centre" for "center" won't puzzle the American, but other British spellings like "gaol" for "jail" and "tyre" for automobile "tire" might. I recall an American student once reading "gaol" as our "goal," which it indeed resembles in spelling, though far apart in meaning.

In the business districts in various parts of the islands, I spotted several totally unfamiliar words for "butcher." In the Irish Republic I once noticed the sign "Victualler." Examining the contents of the shop window carefully, I could only conclude it was a butcher shop. Distrusting my memory, I consulted the great *Oxford English Dictionary* the other day and found this little note among the plethora of information: "Also *spec.* (in local Irish use), a butcher." In Scotland I was surprised by the word "flesher" for "butcher," a meaning again recorded in the *OED*.

To continue with these signs in the city centre. "Ironmonger" for "hardware dealer" I had anticipated, but I could never grow accustomed to it. Much more disturbing though, was the wayward manner in which British streets in large cities kept changing their names, one street in a few miles often acquiring four or five different names. Though I didn't find it as shocking as the street name turbulence, I still was surprised to learn that when a building directory in Great Britain said "first floor," you had to read in American "second floor." Our "first floor" is their "ground floor." Our "cigarette butts" turn into their "cigarette ends." Our "freight entrance" becomes their "goods entrance." The beginning of signs on the trash cans in Scotland very much resembled ours, except where ours will end with a plea to keep the city "clean," theirs will urge keeping the city "tidy." Again in Scotland I noticed our "alley" or "lane" became a "close." One such alley near the heart of old Edinburgh bore the picturesque appellation of "World's End Close." Some day I must go back and explore that dark and narrow close.

In Ireland I found with considerable frequency on offices the term "turf accountant," which certainly is a pretty fancy way of designating a "bookmaker" in betting. Also in Ireland, I particularly remember the numerous signs advertising "Player's Please," a cigarette, and "Guinness," a stout. Guinness has grown into something of a common noun. At least it receives an entry in the *Oxford English Dictionary Supplement*: "A brand of stout manufactured by the firm of Guinness of Dublin; a bottle or glass of this."

With a flower-pot-sized glass of Guinness, many an Irishman likes to set his troubles afloat. In appearance, Guinness is deep black with a crown of white foam. In taste, it suggests a combination of malt, hops, and shellac. The American, accustomed to the flamboyant colors and subtle psychologies of Madison Avenue, finds the advertising slogan of the firm naively appealing: "Guinness is good for you."

PINK STAMPS—NOT GREEN

On the streets of Ireland, Scotland, and England, I kept a sharp eye open for any traces of trading stamps or Dairy Queens, Dairy Maids, or Darie-Delites. Yes, the British do give trading stamps, pink stamps to match our green! But the quest for Dairy Queens proved far more elusive. Nevertheless, near the end of the trip, by the dread Tower of London, if I recall correctly, I spotted a stand. There they were, being offered for sale under the demure name of "soft ice cream."

In arranging the preceding British words into highway words and High Street words, I am conscious of a certain artificiality; for the words didn't sort themselves out that neatly, but instead came spattering and splattering against our consciousness. I remember in Scotland one of my friends exclaiming as he read a guide booklet, "What do they mean by 'standing outwith the door'?" "Outwith" as a preposition excited me too, but we guessed from the context it meant "outside"; and "outside" is listed as one of its meanings in the *OED*. In closing, I might mention a difference I seemed to detect in euphemisms. Our "restrooms" and overly coy "comfort stations" in Britain were usually "public conveniences" or "lavatories."

The other day in a public library I came across a copy of the *Illustrated London News* and couldn't resist examining the ads for British expressions. Oh yes, there was one I forgot: "guinea," a monetary unit used in price quotations by fancy shops. The word somehow made last summer live again. It would be good to be back in the seat of that little British car, to sound the hooter a couple of times from sheer exuberance, and to drive off in pursuit of landscapes and seascapes, museums and monuments, castle ruins and characters, and those surprising British and Irish words and meanings.

QUESTIONS FOR STUDY AND DISCUSSION

1. If you should travel in Great Britain, do you expect the differences between British and American English to create serious problems in communication? Why or why not?
2. Use five of the following words in sentences as the British might use them. Be prepared to read the sentences to the class.

(1) accumulator
(2) assurance
(3) biscuit
(4) blackleg
(5) bobby
(6) chapel
(7) chemist
(8) constable
(9) corn
(10) creek
(11) draper's shop
(12) draughts
(13) fly, n.
(14) form, n.
(15) guard, n.
(16) hire purchase
(17) hoarding, n.
(18) life, n.
(19) lorry
(20) milliard
(21) paraffin
(22) post, n.
(23) pram
(24) public house
(25) public school
(26) shivvy, n.
(27) sick
(28) spinney
(29) stall, n.
(30) stand, v.
(31) suspenders
(32) sweet, n.
(33) telly
(34) torch
(35) tramway
(36) treacle
(37) windscreen
(38) wireless

3. a. The following diacritical markings (used in the Merriam-Webster dictionaries) represent approximate British pronunciations. The stress mark precedes the stressed syllable. The symbol : represents a prolongation of the vowel. Try to pronounce the words as marked.

(1)	evolution	ˌēvə-'lü-shən	(14)	garden	'gä:d-ən
(2)	garage	'ga-räzh or 'gar-ij	(15)	water	'wȯ:t-ə
(3)	lieutenant	lef-'ten-ənt	(16)	four	fȯə
(4)	schedule	'shed-yül	(17)	bird	bə:d
(5)	tube	tyüb	(18)	example	ig-'zä:m-pəl
(6)	epoch	'ē-päk	(19)	laboratory	la-'bȯr-ə-trē
(7)	Magdalene	'möd-lin	(20)	immediate	im-'ē-jit
(8)	been	bē:n	(21)	library	'lī-brē
(9)	ask	ä:sk	(22)	dictionary	'dik-shən-rē
(10)	can't	kä:nt	(23)	necessary	'nes-ə-srē
(11)	vase	vä:z	(24)	fertile	'fər-tīl
(12)	here	hēə	(25)	futile	fyü-tīl
(13)	fair	feə	(26)	fragile	fraj-īl

b. Two patterns of British pronunciation, other than the absence of *r* and the use of *a*, are illustrated in these words. What are they? List some other words for each pattern.

SUGGESTED ACTIVITIES

1. If you know someone who has traveled in Great Britain, interview him to find out whether he had amusing or baffling experiences with British vocabulary, pronunciations, or syntactic structures. From this interview and the information you have acquired from this assignment, write a feature story, "So You're Going to Great Britain."
2. Listen to a British speaker on television, radio, or a record and note his intonation patterns. Record word usages and pronunciations that you think are British. Check some of the words in a recent standard dictionary. Write a brief report of your observations.
3. As you read an English novel, list words and expressions that you think are British; then check them in a recent standard dictionary. *Suggestions: The Prime of Miss Jean Brodie* by Muriel Spark, *Of Human Bondage* by Somerset Maugham, or a novel by Graham Greene, Aldous Huxley, John Galsworthy, Thomas Hardy, or Charles Dickens.